1-10

GLOBAL WARRING

GLOBAL WARRING

HOW ENVIRONMENTAL, ECONOMIC, AND POLITICAL CRISES WILL REDRAW THE WORLD MAP

CLEO PASKAL

GLOBAL WARRING
Copyright © Cleo Paskal, 2010.
All rights reserved.

First published in 2010 by PALGRAVE MACMILLAN® in the United States–a division of St. Martin's Press LLC, 175 Fifth Avenue, New York, NY 10010.

Where this book is distributed in the UK, Europe and the rest of the world, this is by Palgrave Macmillan, a division of Macmillan Publishers Limited, registered in England, company number 785998, of Houndmills, Basingstoke, Hampshire RG21 6XS.

Palgrave Macmillan is the global academic imprint of the above companies and has companies and representatives throughout the world.

Palgrave® and Macmillan® are registered trademarks in the United States, the United Kingdom, Europe and other countries.

ISBN-13: 978-0-230-62181-7

Paskal, Cleo.
   Global warring : how environmental, economic, and political crises will redraw the world map / Cleo Paskal.
      p.   cm.
   Includes bibliographical references and index.
   ISBN 0-230-62181-3 (alk. paper)
   1. Geopolitics—Environmental aspects.   2. World politics—21st century—Environmental aspects.   I. Title.
JC319.P325   2010
303.48'5—dc22

                                                                    2009039709

A catalogue record of the book is available from the British Library.

Design by Letra Libre, Inc.

First edition: January 2010
10   9   8   7   6   5   4   3   2   1
Printed in the United States of America.

For my father, the great thinker and writer Tom Paskal.
Without him, this book would not have been possible
(nor, coincidentally, would I).

CONTENTS

PART ONE
THE USS *SIEVE:*
HOW ENVIRONMENTAL CHANGE
IS DRILLING HOLES IN THE SHIP OF STATE

PART TWO
THE NEW GEOPOLITICAL ICEBERGS:
OR, HOW THE NORTH WAS LOST

PART THREE
PRECIPITATING CHANGE IN ASIA AND BEYOND:
HOW CHINA, INDIA, AND THE WEST ARE TRYING
TO MAKE FRIENDS IN INTERESTING TIMES

PART FOUR
THE TURBULENT PACIFIC:
HOW RISING SEA LEVELS COULD
WASH AWAY WHOLE COUNTRIES AND
SWAMP THE GLOBAL SHIP OF STATE

INTRODUCTION

BEEN THERE, DONE THAT, AND ALL I GOT WERE THESE LOUSY EXTINCTIONS

"I can gather all the news I need on the weather report."

—Paul Simon[1]

THE WEATHER REPORT

I am warm, dry, and, not coincidentally, inside. Outside, a thin sheet of shatterproof glass away, it is monsoon. Normally from this window I can see the graceful, glittering curve of Marine Drive, the elegant beachfront avenue where the residents of Mumbai go to remind themselves why they love their sprawling, crazy, overcrowded city. Today all I can see is a grayish-black wall of wet.

The monsoon rampages through Mumbai like a drunken mob, breaking storefronts, ripping up roads, raining blows and blowing rains on those too unlucky or too poor to be inside. It is terrifying. But it is also essential—Mumbai, and India, was built around the cyclical return of the rains at their most raw and violent.

This is a country that needs its monsoon. While India's modern cities are ravished by the downpour, out in the traditional countryside water and hydroelectric reservoirs are filling, tinder-dry forests are easing back from the brink of inferno, and waiting irrigation canals channel the rains toward parched, cracked farmland, making them moist and fertile.

There was a monsoon before there was an India. The country grew up with, and was shaped by, the periodic pounding of the slow-moving, heavy, life-giving and life-taking rains. The monsoon was a reliable climatic metronome that ticked away the years, telling people what season to plant, what season to harvest, what season to marry. Even today, in this increasingly high-tech country, the anticipated dates of the monsoon are announced in newspapers, and predictions about "good" or "bad" timing and amounts of rain throw the stock market into a tizzy. Somewhere at the core of this huge, intricate, and diversified economy is the knowledge that the monsoon still matters. A lot.

But recently the monsoons, and the climate in general, have been behaving oddly. They are less predictable, to the point of erratic. Precipitation distribution and temperatures are off kilter. There is rain when there should be snow, heat when there should be cold, floods in the desert, and drought in the wetlands. Overall, the rains in India have decreased by as much as 5 to 8 percent since the 1950s.[2] Meanwhile, flash floods are drowning whole districts.

Mumbai tried to conquer nature in a thoroughly modern way, with state-of-the-art buildings and city planning. Meanwhile the countryside tried to work with nature, largely through traditional irrigation techniques. Both are failing. Something has changed. Or, to be more accurate, something is changing faster than ever before.

To understand what it is that is changing, let's take a closer look at the weather on the other side of this window. As a system, the monsoon is complex and elegant—a melodic melding of diverse climatic notes into a cohesive symphony. There is the aggressive, persistent piccolo of the new rains on drought-hardened earth, the inexhaustible winds rustling the leaves, the bass boom of the thunder, the tinfoil crackle of the lightning. If you press your hand against the cold window, you can feel the vibrations, the sounds, the fury. It is Wagnerian.

The monsoon is also surprisingly sensitive. As with a powerful piece of music, a strong monsoon requires a vast number of elements to align perfectly. Winds, atmospheric pressure, water temperature, air quality, oceanic currents, and thousands of other factors both here and around the globe must work together before a single drop of rain can form and fall. A strong El Niño in the Pacific can devastate farmers in the Punjab. But, if you are sitting in the Punjab, waiting for the rain, it's hard to know if this is just a one-off bad year or if the good years are gone for a very, very long time. And that is the difference between weather and climate.

Weather is something that happens today, tomorrow, maybe next week. Climate is something that happens on a scale of years, decades, centuries, and millennia. In Manhattan, rain on a July 4 picnic is weather, something that is inconveniently unpredictable a month in advance. But the fact that someone's Independence Day is spoiled by rain, not snow, is climate—because the northeastern United States is, normally, above freezing in July. A sunny day is weather, summer is climate. Understanding that difference helps us guess what might come next, and guessing what might come next, and what to do about it, could mean the difference between a bumper crop and starvation.

It's getting harder to guess. It's not just the monsoon that is veering all over the map. At the start of every year, the UN's World Meteorological

Organization (WMO) puts out a summary of the previous year's climate conditions. The WMO assessment of the global climate in 2008 reported that:

- 2008 was one of the ten warmest years since modern records began in the 1850s;
- In one of Brazil's worst weather disasters in modern history, flooding affected 1.5 million people in the region;
- Tropical Storm Fay was the first storm to hit the same U.S. state four times;
- Portugal, Chile, Argentina, Paraguay, and Uruguay all experienced their worst droughts in decades. Some places in Australia have now had drought conditions for over a decade;
- Hurricane Ike was the third most destructive hurricane to hit the United States after Katrina (2005) and Andrew (1992);
- Arctic sea ice reached its second lowest extent on record. The lowest was in 2007;
- Tropical Cyclones Nargis was the worst cycle to hit Asia since 1991 and caused widespread devastation in Myanmar, reportedly killing over 140,000 people;
- Unusually heavy rains displaced approximately ten million people in India;
- In China over 78 million people were affected by the most severe winter weather in half a century.[3]

Is this just unusual weather or is the climate changing dramatically? The answer is so important to human security that people have been asking it in various forms ever since we first realized that spring follows winter. As a result, predicting the climate, and the weather, is one of the most crucial, one of the first, and one of the most studied sciences. It is also one of the hardest.

THE ALL-TOO-HUMAN HISTORY OF FORECASTING

Predicting the climate, and the weather, is a tricky business. Ever since their first attempts, scientific forecasters have come in for a lot of criticism, and now modern climate modelers are under near-constant assault. Too many people have watched the Friday evening news and gone to bed planning a sunny Saturday at the beach, only to spend the next morning watching the rain wash out their plans. The mistakes are visible and memorable, and they affect the way many of us think about climate change. "If they can't get tomorrow right," the thinking goes, "how can they predict what will happen in twenty years?" However, it turns out there is a big difference between predicting the weather and predicting the climate. We should know that by now—we've been trying to do both for millennia. Understanding how far we have come helps to dispel some of the concerns about the science that underpins the analysis in this book.

One of the hallmarks of modern life is a seeming immunity to the natural environment. This is especially true in the West. Most people in the West can go to work, eat, and spend time with their families regardless of the weather. This is a recent phenomenon. Throughout much of human history, and still in many places around the world, the weather is a daily matter of life and death.

Early hunter-gatherers followed flora and fauna that themselves followed climate cycles. One unusually cold summer could kill off the plant life that fed the bison that fed the humans. And we died. This was not a great long-term plan, and eventually we tried to get more control over our food supplies by rearing and growing it ourselves. Once we settled into agricultural societies, understanding weather and climate became even more critical. We invested everything in our small, static plots of land and watched desperately as they were tormented by rains, snows, droughts, and floods. Some of our earliest scientists focused on agrarian innovations, like irrigation, to make us less vulnerable to caprices of weather. Other early scientists concentrated on astronomical observation and created calendars, defined seasons, and gave some sense of climate in general.

Yet the unexpected still happened. Rains failed, crops withered, reservoirs ran dry, and again we died. There was ever more focus on predicting, and trying to control, the immediate impact of weather through everything from prayer to human sacrifice. Most major religions had a weather god. They are scattered throughout theology, from the Babylonian-Assyrian storm god Adad to the Greek's Zeus and his lightning bolts. Vikings worshipped Thor and his thunder, Polynesians pray that Apu-Hau will not send the storms, and Hindus have Indra, rider of the four-tusked albino elephant, tellingly a god not only of weather, but also of war. It's not the only time war and weather are linked, as we'll see.

Our quest and need to understand our weather and climate led to discoveries in the sciences and permeated popular culture. Predictive folk sayings started to appear, like "red sky at night, sailors delight. Red sky in the morning, sailors take warning." They gave a small feeling of confidence when figuring out crop cycles and auspicious dates for setting out to sea.

Generally, though, forecasts were so important and mysterious that ultimate control stayed firmly under the rubric of religion. When gods couldn't save us from bad weather, it was often assumed that countervailing evil was involved. For example, in 1484, in the heart of Europe's crop-devastating Little Ice Age, Pope Innocent VIII issued a papal bull exhorting the clergy to hunt down the witches who he believed were causing the bad weather. As a result, thousands were tortured, and many petrified, broken women, men, and children confessed to everything from causing hail to summoning rain clouds.[4] As late as 1653, when advancing glaciers threatened towns in the French Alps, priests were sent to perform an exorcism on the frozen rivers by sprinkling the ice with holy water. It didn't work.[5] (In 2009, Swiss villagers living near the

Aletsch glacier petitioned the Vatican for permission to pray that the glacier would stop *retreating*.)[6]

Meanwhile, the early weather watchers kept up with their much-in-
demand, if not entirely scientific, research. In eighteenth-century England, trade had reduced reliance on domestic crops sufficiently so local
weather, while potentially annoying, was less essential for survival. What
remained crucial to the English at this time was the weather at sea. With
Britannia ruling the waves, it was critical to know wind direction, exactly
how big the waves were, and where the boat-smashing storms lurked.
For this imperial island nation, trade and the military, which were often
intertwined, were completely weather dependent, and holding forth on
the weather was almost an act of patriotism. This widespread interest in
predicting spawned a huge, unregulated forecasting industry, leaving the
religious establishment gasping to keep up. Particularly popular were as-
trologers who used celestial alignments to create weather horoscopes for
up to a year in advance. In 1768 just one of these almanacs, *Vox Stel-
larum*, sold 107,000 copies.[7]

By 1851, weather was so key to Britain's naval strength, and therefore the economic and military health of the empire, that the Board of
Trade took predictions out of the hands of the Church and the charlatans
and set up an office of weather statistics, Britain's first dedicated scientific weather forecasting unit. Its first head, Robert FitzRoy (former cap-
tain of *The Beagle*, the ship that took Charles Darwin on his voyage),
invented cheap barometers, established weather stations and, critically,
made use of the new technology of telegraphy to get near-instant up-to-
date weather information from outlying regions. These Victorian technological innovations permeated the empire, and, as colonial offices in
various parts of the world exchanged information and global weather was
averaged out, climate events started to resolve into decipherable patterns.
This was when it was discovered, for example, that the climate phenomenon we know as El Niño affected both Australia and India. This is also

one of the reasons most global modern climate records date to around the 1860s.[8]

The science was firming up and, by 1861, FitzRoy started writing the first daily weather forecasts, printed in *The Times*.[9] After FitzRoy died in 1865, the meteorological office was restructured to make data gathering even more scientific. In the United Kingdom, a chain of eight observatories was set up, stocked with self-recording equipment. Slowly, the weather statistics office built its reputation, and the reputation of forecasting.[10]

Today, that British government institution, now known as the Meteorological Office, is one of the most respected and scientifically advanced weather and climate research and forecasting centers in the world. Its data drives decision making in governments, stock markets, corporations, and nongovernmental organizations (NGOs) around the globe. The Met Office and its thousand or so scientists are headquartered on FitzRoy Road, on the outskirts of Exeter, in the English countryside. Their offices are located in a purpose-built, modern, soaring, glass building—a secular cathedral to science. Offices are open plan, and pure geek territory, with Dilbert cartoons in the copy room and Einstein posters on the walls. This is a place that takes weather and climate seriously. They've built almost half a dozen flood defenses into the land surrounding the building, including a mini-wetland, protective hill, and complex drainage system. They know what's coming.

The Met Office is already good at forecasting the weather, but what it's working on now is improving the reputation of forecasting the climate. Attacked by people and groups who aim to undermine the very concept of climate change, it has to be meticulous about the scientific credibility of its forecasts. The British government, with its long history of understanding the critical economic and strategic role of weather and climate, is acutely aware of the potential impact of climate change and, consequently, is giving it full backing, but insulating it from politics.

The Met Office, now under the Ministry of Defence (again reinforcing the strategic importance of weather and climate), has created a
dedicated department, the Hadley Centre, entirely devoted to climate
forecasting.[11] More than 120 scientists use two supercomputers and work
with colleagues around the world to generate reliable visions of future
climates. They don't just run models, they run models of models, aver-
aging out different scenarios to give an idea not only of outcomes, but of
likelihoods of different outcomes. They also do "hindcasting," in which
they set up parameters and use historical data to try to predict the current climate. That way they can test their models against today's reality
before applying them to the future.

The Hadley Centre just looks at the physical world: the glacial melting, the sea level rises, and the disruption to precipitation patterns. It
doesn't model the refugees, the famines, and the economic loss. But in
order to assess some of the geopolitical consequences of climate change,
as this book will show, you need a scientific and non-politicized understanding of climate change, and Hadley is one of the best places in the
world to deconstruct the numbers and reassemble the pieces into a picture of the future.

Many of the forecasts I use come from the Hadley Centre. I also use
interviews with scientists and those on the front lines of the change, as
well as some of the findings produced by the Nobel-winning Intergovernmental Panel on Climate Change (IPCC), a UN panel of around two
thousand scientists from approximately one hundred countries. The
IPCC was established by the World Meteorological Organization and
the United Nations Environment Programme to analyze and synthesize
the thousands of peer-reviewed studies related to climate change, and it
produces periodic reports on the general global scientific consensus.[12]
The reports are your granddaddy's car of climate science: big, solid,
slightly unwieldy, but reliable. To err on the side of caution, I use the
more moderate end of the impact assessments, eschewing the "Storm

Surge that Will Eat Manhattan" scenarios for the much more likely slow but persistent erosion of coastal infrastructure. The goal is not to be alarmist, but to offer a realistic appraisal of some of the potentially destabilizing factors we are already seeing (repeated large-scale crop failures affecting global supply, coastal flooding, retreat of glaciers, etc.), and that we will continue to see.

While there may be disagreement over the cause, pretty much everyone, including almost all the skeptics, agree that the climate is changing; skeptics largely just disagree over the cause. While some places might get colder, and some years global temperatures might dip below "normal," the overall trend is a definite planetary warming. At this point, no matter what we do, some amount of climate change is inevitable.[13] And we will all feel it, in part because our environment is the foundation upon which we graft all other infrastructure. Our transportation systems, cities, defensive capabilities, agriculture, power generation, water supply, and more are all designed for the specific parameters of our physical environment and climate—or, more often, the physical environment and climate of the Victorian or post–World War II periods in which they were originally built. This is why unexpected environmental change, such as shifts in precipitation patterns, almost always has a negative effect. We literally aren't designed for it. It's like building a sandcastle on the beach a yard above the high-tide mark and thinking it is safe, only to find that the tide now varies by several extra yards a day.

In its own way, each country is as dependent on a stable environment as India is on the monsoon. We built infrastructure to fit a certain set of parameters that we thought were constants. Turns out they are not. So it's not surprising that changes to the environment and climate can result in crop failure, flooding, drought, and damaged infrastructure, which in turn can trigger economic, political, social, and security changes. At this point, while some focus on the causes of climate change, others must use the best science available to understand the implications of the inevitable in order to minimize the geopolitical, economic, and security fallout. That is what this book is about.

In military circles, the importance of weather and climate is well known. In the classic Chinese text *The Art of War,* Sun Tzu writes that there are five factors that must be considered before any military action: weather, terrain, discipline (including supply lines), politics, and leadership.[14] Climate change can directly affect: weather, terrain and supply lines, discipline, and politics. First, climate change can result in more unpredictable, extreme, and destructive one-off weather events, such as unseasonal storms washing out equipment and camps. Long-term climate change can dramatically alter terrain and, as a result, supply lines can be affected; for example, roads built on permafrost might thaw and become boggy sludge, rivers could move and flood, and erosion could undermine previously passable areas. The disruption can affect discipline and isn't restricted to the battlefield. At the same time the civilian population could be confronting damage to cities, water supply, agriculture, and so on, which has the potential to lead to political upheaval.

This scenario is not simply theoretical. Scattered throughout history there are myriad examples of the environment affecting war and politics. The link was brought home for me over tea with Professor W. M. S. Russell, author of the textbook study on humans and environmental change, *Man, Nature and History.*[15] We were at his home in Reading, England. It was early spring, but the weather was unusually warm and the summer flowers outside his window were already in bloom. Professor Russell started talking about the twelfth century, when the climate in England was warm enough to grow grapes. "We used to produce quite good English wine. But then the Little Ice Age came and froze the vines. Luckily, the cold temperatures were also particularly good for strengthening the best weapon of the time: yew bows. And with those yew bows, we took possession of a wine growing area of France." There it was: climate change directly altering a careful balance and leading to conflict. Now it is getting warm enough in the UK for the vines to grow again.[16] The question is, who will wield the yew bows of the future?

The effects of climate and weather on geopolitics can be dramatic. In the past, erratic weather and poor forecasting have changed history. Strong winds alone have been the deciding factor in several major historical turning points. In the late thirteenth century, Kublai Khan sent an invasion fleet to Japan. A typhoon sunk more than 200 of the 700 Mongol ships and drowned around 13,000 of the 28,000 troops. The rest retreated. The Japanese called this the Divine Wind, the *kamikaze*.[17] In 1588, storm winds finished off the remnants of the Spanish Armada sent to conquer England. In acknowledgment, the English struck the famous medal that read "God blew with His winds and they were scattered."[18] The British weren't so lucky during the American Revolution, when high winds kept them from landing during the Battle of Long Island. Had they been able to get ashore, they could have surrounded George Washington and his troops.[19] The United States was lucky again in 1991, during the Persian Gulf War, when heavy winds stopped Saddam Hussein from launching his Scud missiles.[20] And, in March 2003, the invasion of Iraq was held up for three days due to sand storms.[21] The weather matters. And climate change makes weather just that much more extreme and unpredictable.

Military planners are aware of the dangers. During World War II, meteorology saw major advances coming out of the United States Army Air Corps weather forecasters. And during the Cold War, when long-range bombing became an increasingly important tactic, being able to predict the weather at various altitudes a continent away became critical. While contemporary internal assessments of the role of weather on the battlefield are difficult to find, for obvious reasons, older reports can be telling. For example, a U.S. Army study on the military implications of

El Niño for security in the Korean peninsula noted that the North Korean leadership considered weather data a "strategic weapon" and that they would summarily execute any captured South Korean meteorologists. The report found that:

> With this type of extreme behavior [. . .] North Korean military planners will be strongly inclined to use their knowledge of local weather patterns to help negate any US military advantages [. . .] if they think the US is preoccupied with other world events, it becomes easier to believe that strategically we are not ready. It is, therefore, only a short step to "victory" to use a strong typhoon to cover their initial advance into South Korea. In the midst of winds, heavy rains, mud, and floods, chaos will rule. For their goals, the more chaos the better.[22]

In the case of Korea, the U.S. Army strategists were looking at the impact of a single extreme weather event, where it acts almost like a third army on the battlefield. The situation becomes more complex when the persistent and pervasive effects of climate change add to the general volatility of a region. Concern over the potential chaos caused by climate change led a group of almost a dozen retired U.S. admirals and generals to publish a report in 2007 titled *National Security and the Threat of Climate Change* that concluded, among other things, that "climate change acts as a threat multiplier for instability in some of the most volatile regions of the world."[23] The authors of the report foresaw environmental stressors pushing tense situations over the edge into serious conflict. They didn't think the United States would be spared. They concluded: "projected climate change poses a serious threat to America's national security."[24] It now seems inevitable that climate change will have a major effect on global economics, politics, and security. And it gets worse.

To understand the threats to global security and the challenge to policy makers, it is not enough just to look at climate change. Climate change is only one component, albeit a major one, of the larger problem of environmental change.

As a species, we humans regularly make direct and major alterations to the physical environment. Sometimes it is for the better. Thousands of years ago, irrigation (which substantially changes regional environments) made possible the early civilizations of Mesopotamia and the Indus Valley. More often, however, the effects of altering the physical environment are not as beneficial. Recently, for example, massive population and consumption increases have had a dramatic effect on global sustainability. At the turn of the twentieth century, there were around 1.65 billion people on the planet. At the turn of the twenty-first, there were around 6 billion.[25] At the end of 2008, the population was closing in on 7 billion. That scale of population growth has resulted in major environmental change such as groundwater depletion, deforestation, exhausted farmland, stress on urban infrastructure, overfishing, and developments in marginal areas such as floods plains. To understand the complex challenges to global stability, these other aspects of environmental change must be factored in as well.

As humans test the carrying capacity of the planet by, for example, increasing population and consumption while decreasing arable land, there is less margin for error, and a smaller degree of environmental variation has larger implications. In many areas we had already weakened our resilience before the climate even started to change. These changes may significantly exacerbate existing problems, however, if there were no climate change, those problems would still exist.

The textbook example of this is the political, social, economic, and security crises created in the United States in the summer of 2005 by a series of hurricanes, and in particular by Hurricane Katrina. The Katrina strike was well within expected parameters. When Katrina hit the New Orleans region, it was only a category 3 hurricane, in a known hurricane zone. However, the naturally dynamic U.S. Gulf Coast was also going through a period of direct man-made environmental change—including large-scale subsidence—in one area of New Orleans by about three feet in three decades. The subsidence is caused, at least in part, by the draining of wetlands, the extraction of groundwater, and inappropriately designed waterways.[26] This weakness was worsened by faulty levee design and implementation on the part of the U.S. Army Corps of Engineers, poor town planning, a failure of emergency services, and a breakdown in the chain of command of governance, security, and rescue services.[27]

Katrina can be used to show how poor regulations, planning, and emergency response can aggravate the crises that will almost certainly increase as a result of climate change, but one cannot say that the tragedy in New Orleans was caused by climate change alone. Curbing climate change without addressing the myriad ways we interact with our environment, including infrastructure planning, water management, and disaster response, will not stop other "Katrinas," although it may stop the frequency from increasing as climate change is predicted to result in more of this sort of extreme weather activity. By broadly labeling most environmental change–related security issues as being the result only of climate change, the military, governments, the UN, and others are inadvertently limiting the range of possible responses, and potentially adding further confusion to an already complex problem.

Essentially the implication is that cutting greenhouse gas emissions is the magic wand that will make most of our problems go away. Unfortunately, that is not the case. It is critical to accurately assess the specific causes of specific problems. That said, it *is* possible to parse out threats that are directly linked to climate change. Some challenges, such as rising sea levels, can only be mitigated by acknowledging, and trying to counter, if possible, the causes of climate change. But it is vital to remember that, even if somehow the climate miraculously stopped changing, there remains a whole other suite of dangers, such as those that caused the disaster on the Gulf Coast, that will need different solutions requiring a broader focus. And, to effectively counter these complex threats, we have to take into account the new political realities of the twenty-first century—which takes a whole other type of crystal ball.

Forecasting the climate is a cakewalk compared with forecasting global economic, political, and security issues. These are extraordinarily interesting times. In the same way that the climate is in a state of flux, and is likely to exhibit erratic behavior before settling into a new norm, since the thaw of the Cold War we have seen major shifts and realignments as nations try to figure out how to get comfortable in the new world order. We are also in an era in which energy supplies, which literally fuel modern society, are being re-evaluated due to concerns about greenhouse gas emissions, speculators, peak oil, the politicization of supply, and myriad other factors. Also, as the global population soars and, just as important, as consumption increases, many key commodities, including fresh water and agricultural land, are becoming scarce, creating economic, political, and security pressures. The period of flux isn't over yet, but some new, long-term geopolitical alliances, many driven by the need for resources and some due to ideology, geography, or history, seem to be solidifying.

For example, as we will see in greater depth later in the book, one of the big uncertainties is Russian foreign policy and how it will use its vast fossil fuel, commodity, and water reserves. After a brief flirtation with Europe following the Cold War, Russian nationalists suspected that the Europowers didn't want a strong Russian bear bursting in on their tea party. In their view, Russia was so vast and rich in resources that it made European giants like France and Germany look puny. As the people in the EU who would determine the nature of its relationship with Russia were the same ones who staffed the threatened power structures, Russia did not get the warm welcome-to-the-neighborhood reception it may have felt it deserved. Partially as a consequence, instead of looking West, Russian nationalists have increasingly started looking toward Asia, especially China, a country that takes Russia very seriously indeed. China returns the favor and values Russia highly as a geopolitical ally, a supplier of resources, and as a source of advanced weaponry. The leadership of the two countries also have many mutual goals, such as pushing U.S. influence out of Central Asia in the short term, and out of the entire region, including the Middle East, in the medium term. Russia is also rekindling old relationships in India for the sake of regional stability. These potential alliances have global implications.

Countries, like climates, operate on such a vast scale that there is a lot of inertia in their systems, making it difficult to change fundamentals such as economic and political systems.[28] The end of the Cold War shook many of the biggest nations to the core, but they are now settling into new (and sometimes old) patterns. By looking at their behavior, and national drivers, one can begin to identify constants that make it possible to guess at future actions. I used the same techniques for my geopolitical and climate analyses. I interviewed hundreds of experts from around the world—from military leaders and economists to city planners, politicians, and engineers—to identify strong geopolitical vectors that were unlikely to change in the next little while. I favored an analysis of systems and geographic imperatives over specific administrations. For example, regardless of who is in the White House, more than 50 percent of the U.S. population and much of its critical infrastructure are still located in coastal regions. Irrespective of elections in the UK, China and Russia will still be neighbors and will want to push U.S. influence out of Central Asia. Even if there is peace in the Middle East, the islands of the Pacific will still be essential staging areas for any war between Asia and the United States. The fact that environmental change increases the risk of U.S. coastal flooding and China's reliance on Russian resources, or that the geostrategic low-lying atolls of the Pacific might submerge with rising sea levels, doesn't necessarily change those trends but it does add a new element.

As with climate prediction, I use the most predictable geopolitical developments, such as the growing influence of Asia in world affairs and the West's attempts to maintain its current geopolitical position. By combining the clear trends in environmental change with the clear trends in geopolitics we start to see the broad brushstrokes of what may lie ahead. The new environment and the new global order both show definite directions. In some cases the two trends reinforce each other, as with China's need for food supplies pushing it closer toward Russia, already an increasing geopolitical ally. In other cases, the changing environmental situation could exacerbate the potential for conflict in areas where new geopolitical realities already chafe, as with China's desire to increase its influence with its Himalayan neighbors while at the same time appropriating shared water resources. This study is basic, but that's the goal: to create a solid base upon which we can start to build a sound analysis of what the future may bring. I hope very much that others will then take a more detailed look at the range of specific implications.

Throughout this book, I follow the ups and downs of the environment, as well as the waxing and waning of some major countries and empires. The goal is to find where environmental change (and in particular climate change) and major geopolitical vectors intersect, in order to see likely outcomes.

Global Warring is divided into four parts, with each using as its starting point a different conservative and scientifically sound prediction. While uncertainty exists concerning many aspects of environmental change, it is now accepted that the change is causing, among other things:

- rising sea levels,
- rising storm surges,
- melting glaciers, and
- changing precipitation patterns.

Those four simple scientific elements are irrefutable. They are already happening and show no signs of reversing.[29] This book offers an analysis of the potential repercussions for some of the major geopolitical powers.

The first section looks at how the West might be affected by environmental change, including rising sea levels and storm surges, and how the United States, the United Kingdom, and other seemingly strong nations are shockingly vulnerable, which demonstrate that this is not just an issue for the developing world. Some thought the devastation caused by Hurricane Katrina in 2005 was a one-time event, but in 2008, Hurricanes Ike and Gustav not only created massive on-shore damage, but they also shut down critical U.S. Gulf Coast oil production. We are more exposed than we think. For example, there are six ways London can flood: tidal surges can drive seawater up the Thames, swollen rivers can send swells down the Thames, heavy rains can overwhelm drainage systems, sewers can back up, dams or reservoir walls could give way, and groundwater can rise. The Thames Barrier, a flood control structure on the River Thames, is only designed to deal with tidal surges. As for the other five vulnerabilities, they form part of a picture of a very unstable future for the UK. The situation is no better in other major Western coastal cities—in fact many have not even gone so far as to construct any flood barriers at all. In order to remain a strong global force, the West will have to develop new ways to adapt to what are likely to be very costly and increasingly frequent environmental attacks on its infrastructure and society. The signs of effective response are so far, unfortunately, not promising.

The second section looks primarily at the importance of transportation routes and how climate change could alter those routes, disrupting some careful economic and geostrategic equations. Global trade relies on shipping, and shipping relies on safe sea-lanes. With climate change melting the Arctic ice, the Northwest Passage could become one of the most coveted trade routes in the world—with all the politics and military posturing that entails. These sorts of tussles over shipping lanes and chokepoints have made and broken empires in the past, as the UK painfully discovered with the Suez Canal in 1956. With Russia, and increasingly China, staking an Arctic claim, Canada, the United States, UK, and Europe will have to sort out their differences quickly or risk compromising North American and European security.

The third section explores changing precipitation patterns and how they could potentially create internal disruptions and affect geopolitical relationships, especially for India and China. Both countries are touted as major twenty-first-century powers, but both will face enormous challenges as a result of environmental change. The way they handle those challenges will determine their domestic and economic stability, and have implications for the balance of power in the Asia and beyond. Meanwhile, some Western powers are finding themselves increasingly marginalized as the rising powers forge new economic alliances among themselves and with Africa and South America. Environmental change could accelerate that marginalization.

The fourth section focuses in large part on how rising sea levels might affect access to resources and China's ability to project power, especially in the Pacific, a geostrategic buffer zone between Asia and the United States. Through China's relationships with Pacific nations we can see how China has been trying to make friends and influence countries all over the world in an effort to break Western hegemony in the developing world. It has had some success, but there are weaknesses in its approach that are leaving it vulnerable.

The conclusion of the book assesses various national adaptation programs, with a view to finding out which nations have the best chance of making it through the domestic and international flux relatively intact, what they can do to improve their positions, and what that could imply for global stability.

This book is designed primarily to demonstrate that environmental change is about to have enormous, and specific, geopolitical, economic, and security consequences for all of us. However, if we have an idea of what is coming, and we plan for it, maybe we can head off the worst of it. If not, we could find ourselves huddling under a broken umbrella when the monsoon comes.

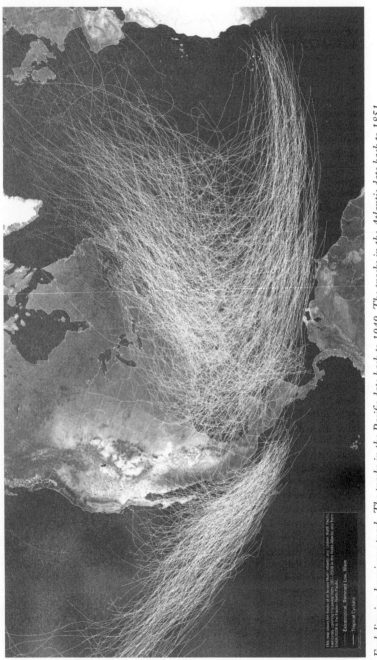

Each line is a hurricane track. The tracks in the Pacific date back to 1949. The tracks in the Atlantic date back to 1851.
Courtesy NOAA

1

THE COMING STORM

All I want for Christmas is my city back.

        —Handmade sign in a post-Katrina New Orleans window

L et me tell you how my civilization froze in its tracks. It was January 5, 1998. I was staying with my dad at his house in Montreal. The weather was oddly mild for mid-winter and so, instead of snowing, it started to rain.

As the rain landed, it froze drop by drop by drop wherever it found purchase. On and on it rained. Drop by drop by drop it froze. Soon there was a thick crystal shroud on everything: cars, roads, trees, roofs, phone and power lines. Electricity cables that didn't sag and break under the weight were soon knocked down by shattering branches and trees. Wood utility poles supporting the ice-heavy power lines eventually gave up and snapped like toothpicks. And finally, the steel pylons supporting now heavily weighted high-tension wires crumpled. The ice storm continued for four days. People started to lose electricity the night of day one. By night five, millions in eastern Canada and the northeastern United States were wrapped in the dark and cold. At the height of the crisis in Quebec, the worst affected region, three million people had no electricity. Quebec is a large hydroelectricity producer and the province encouraged industrial and domestic reliance on electricity, so for most no electricity also meant no heat.

With the temperature hovering around freezing, the situation was bad. But then the temperatures dropped to minus 31 degrees Fahrenheit and the situation became critical. Millions tried to stay warm any way they could, sleeping in running cars, making fires in long-ignored fireplaces, leaving gas-fired ovens on all night. Not surprisingly, by January 18, fifteen people had died, most from hypothermia, fires, and carbon monoxide poisoning. The city of Montreal declared a state of emergency.

Lack of power also meant, in many cases, no gas (the pumps at service stations ran on electricity), nowhere to buy food or get money (stores, banks, and bank machines closed), no postal deliveries (no paychecks for many), loss of TV and radio signals, and sometimes no phones (not only were telephone lines and transmission towers down, but many also just had electrically recharged handheld phones at home). Hospitals, full past capacity as people slipped on the ice and broke limbs, were running off generators, surgeries were canceled, and blood supplies were critically low. Panic started to set in on day six when one of the city's two water filtration plants shut down and tap water was declared unsafe to drink. We were instructed to boil water for five minutes to make it safe, a cruel irony for those with electric stoves. The Canadian Broadcasting Corporation radio station gave out survival information twenty-four hours a day, advising people to sleep in a tent pitched inside their house to conserve body heat. Thanks to the CBC, I now know how to cook off a car engine, burn nail polish remover for heat, and make a candle out of a potato.

Parts of the province looked like a war zone, with homes and cars crushed by falling trees and farm animals dying by the tens of thousands. Neighboring regions did their best to help. People from across Canada tried to send firewood, and the railways tried to use locomotive engines to generate power for frozen towns. The Rolling Stones canceled their concert, but the Montreal Symphony Orchestra played for free in shelters. And there were a lot of shelters.

In the largest peacetime mobilization in Canadian history, troops cleared away forests of dead trees, evacuated the seriously ill, set up field kitchens, rebuilt generators, and provided security. They were well prepared for the job as many had recently handled floods in Manitoba and then Quebec. The soldiers had the power to detain looters and compel people to leave their homes. Those without an alternative source of heat were evacuated to shelters set up all over the province in schools, community centers, army bases, even shopping malls. There were over a hundred shelters in Montreal alone.

My dad's area of Montreal is one of the most multicultural in Canada, with over half the residents born abroad. Many come from countries where a soldier knocking on your door and ordering you to leave home implies a destination far less benign than the local hockey rink turned shelter. Many residents left their homes reluctantly, and were distraught when they arrived at the overcrowded shelters. At my local shelter, at the height of the blackout, more than four hundred people were sleeping on mats on the floor of the community center.

My dad and brother, hardy veterans of summer camp, opted to stay at home and live off the Coleman stove. I slept at home and pitched in at the local shelter. My turf was two rooms, normally used for art classes and the like, that were now reserved for families with children. Most were mothers and kids. The fathers had stayed behind in cold apartments to ward off looters that, for the most part, never came. Everyone helped each other as best they could, but no one slept very well, apart from one mother of seven who took a Valium shortly before lights out. Smart woman.

The starkest moment came when I was detailed to another shelter, normally a school, that had taken in some men from a nearby home for the mentally ill. No one had seen "the boys" for a while, so I was sent to look for them and make sure all was well. I found them in the library, enjoying an afternoon of normally off-limit videos. Or, to be precise, one video: *A Clockwork Orange*. Some people were making the most of the chaos.

Two weeks after the first drops fell, large sections of downtown Montreal were still closed. Parts of the province didn't get power back for close to two months. The damage was estimated at around $5 billion.[1] For many, it was one of the most traumatic times of their lives. Yet, technically speaking, it wasn't even a major event. Largely it was just a matter of the power going out. But in a technologically advanced, and dependent, region, that was enough to stop society dead in its tracks. It is very likely to happen again. With increased winter precipitation, and milder temperatures, there is a likelihood that in currently cold areas, such as Canada and the northern United States, ice storms will become more common, and civilization will risk being unplugged more often.

Usually, the negative effects of environmental change on human society are thought of as mainly affecting countries with a low per capita income, the same way as malnutrition and infant mortality. Events such as the ice storm and the damage caused by Hurricanes Rita, Wilma, and Katrina in the summer of 2005 should have been wake-up calls, but still the West considers itself relatively insulated from the worst effects of environmental change, with the most common domestic fear being a wave of incoming refugees. That assessment sharply underestimates the actual threat and leaves some of the seemingly most powerful countries woefully unprotected. The reality is the West, including the United States, is potentially as vulnerable to costly and disruptive environmental change as the rest of the world.

The United States, United Kingdom, and the rest of the West will suffer from the same destructive effects of environmental change as the developing world, including problems with transportation infrastructure (especially along flooded and eroding coastlines), legal complexities (including lawsuits against emitters and between states over water supplies), threatened shifts in boundaries and territory, failing agriculture, increasing cost and decreasing availability of insurance, water scarcity (especially in the southern and western United States), spreading disease (including increased range of disease-bearing insects), mass movement of internal refugees (as seen with Katrina), floods, and droughts. Compared to developing nations, the United States, United Kingdom, and other Western nations have the added challenges of more expensive (and in many cases, pre–World War I era) infrastructure, relatively more expensive labor costs for shoring up that fragile infrastructure, and a population that is used to a high level of social services and quality of infrastructure, and that is reluctant to reduce either standard even for a short time.

Unless environmental change is accepted as a looming catastrophe and countered as such, when all—or even some—of the above factors combine, social instability and depletion of economic strength may become commonplace. On average, the United States has lost more than $20 billion a year to weather damage between 1995 and 2004,[2] with insured losses steadily increasing—and that count does not include the infrastructure destruction caused in 2005 by Hurricanes Katrina, Wilma, and Rita, which affected entire cities, transportation systems, and global economic engines, such as the petrochemical complexes off the U.S. Gulf Coast. This is not just a national problem. As the financial crisis of 2008–2009 has shown, a destabilized United States can be bad for the entire globe.

The challenges are many, complex, and widespread. As a result, it is difficult to decide where to prioritize investment in responses, as countries have widely varying vulnerabilities. Moreover, different regions within the same country face different threats and so need different countermeasures. The United States, for example, is suffering coastal erosion and destruction of infrastructure due to thawing permafrost in Alaska (potentially threatening the delivery of domestic oil supplies as pipelines are built on increasingly unstable ground), severe droughts in the western and southern agricultural areas, and flooding problems along its coastlines, which incidentally are home to many of its biggest cities and much of its national product. Clearly, the United States has many environment-related vulnerabilities, but for now we will concentrate on just two interrelated components: the effect of rising sea levels and coastal storm surges. Those two factors alone should be enough to give an idea of what's in store if we don't start planning now.

Over half the U.S. population lives near the coast, and large sections of the U.S. coastline, in particular much of the Atlantic and Gulf Coast, are vulnerable to flooding and erosion.[3] According to a major U.S. Department of Transport study, that means that, with a relative sea level rise (combining the effects of subsidence and sea level rise) along the Gulf Coast of 2 to 4 feet, "a vast portion of the Gulf Coast from Houston to Mobile may be inundated over the next 50 to 100 years."[4] That might seem like a long way off, but it falls within the expected lifespan of infrastructure and housing that are being put in place today through development, post-hurricane reconstruction, and stimulus spending. If those plans don't take the coming environmental change into account, those investments will be lost, and more people and businesses will be put in harm's way. I've been in a shelter. Valium or not, it's no fun. But, as bad as the ice storm was, as least we knew we would have homes to return to once the lights came back on. Flooding is much worse.

As for other vulnerable coastal regions, different geology has different risks. Florida, for example, presents a seemingly more stable environment, in large part because of its flat limestone base. This ensures that sea levels can continue to rise without a visible change in habitat. However, once the rise gets up to the threshold of, or above, that limestone base, then expansive losses of coastal areas will take place, a phenomenon being witnessed in at least one region of Florida even at the present level of sea water.

Across the country, the threat is real and imminent, and the United States is not prepared, as was evident in the summer of 2005.

Hurricane Katrina, which struck the Gulf Coast in the summer of 2005, made ice storm survivors look lucky. For several heart-rending weeks, people all over the planet watched as one of the great cities of the world, normally full of life, music, and history, became a fetid disaster zone. While most watched with despair, and a craving to help, national security organizations around the world studied it closely, making detailed analyses of the U.S. response to the devastation, in part because it showed the sort of cracks that could be expected, and ex-ploited, by hostiles attacking America.

One can't say that Hurricane Katrina was caused by climate change. Any single event is considered weather, not climate. But for the purposes of this section, the specific cause of Katrina is irrelevant. What is im-portant is what Katrina revealed about the United States' adaptive ca-pacity to the sort of environmental crises that are likely to become more common with environmental change. Katrina brought to global atten-tion several major, systemic U.S. vulnerabilities, and gave an indication of how the country may fare in the future when hit by a similar wide-ranging disaster. While extensive and excellent domestic studies and "lessons learned" have improved U.S. ability to respond to emergencies the next time around, more attention must be paid to the factors that make the nation more vulnerable in the first place. The best rescue in the world is still not as good as avoiding the crisis in the first place. Unfor-tunately, the vulnerabilities in the United States are many, varied, and have often been left unaddressed.

In the summer of 2005, the weaknesses were in place long before the first leaf was caught up in the gathering storm. Some of those problems were caused not by climate change but by a much more direct form of human-induced environmental change. According to Dr. Virginia Burkett of the U.S. Geological Survey, "In New Orleans we've got a real serious problem because a lot of the land is below sea level, and protected only by levees. The land wasn't below sea level when the city was first established. Even when the Native Americans lived there, they were right at sea level or slightly above. But as they built the levees, pumped out ground water, drained the soils and all that organic matter oxidized, the city accelerated its sinking relative to sea level. That's why it's below sea level right now."[5]

The result of those man-made interventions was a sinking city in a hurricane belt. Cities in hurricane belts get hit by hurricanes. Sinking cities flood. What happened in New Orleans shouldn't have been a surprise, but it was worse—it was a disaster.

When Katrina hit New Orleans, it was no stronger than a category 3 hurricane (out of a possible 5).[6] It caused some damage, but it was once the worst of the storm was over that the levees broke and water poured into the city, drowning entire neighborhoods, command stations, and escape routes. Evacuations were panicked and poorly coordinated. As an example, the New Orleans 911 emergency call center was quickly flooded and evacuated. The back-up plan was to transfer calls to the fire department, but that too had been abandoned. It took critical hours for some calls to find their way to unprepared operators in Baton Rouge, days for the answering system to stabilize and, in some cases, over a month for follow-up.[7]

As for the official response in general, rather than an overall plan into which component parts fit smoothly, there was an inchoate slew of separate sets of actions, several of which canceled each other out or exacerbated the problem. The situation had so deteriorated that, according to New Orleans police officer Thomas Redmann, "We didn't know

where the command structure of the police department was physically located, let alone how to communicate with them. [. . .] There were just
hundreds of people walking down Canal Street in broad daylight, tear-
ing the security gates off the front of stores, smashing out windows. They
were just stealing the city blind."[8] In most cases, there was no point in
making arrests as the prisons themselves were in chaos. According to two
reports, some prisoners, including juveniles, were left with little food or
water, some standing up to their chests in the fetid floodwater.[9] Many
city police officers did excellent work, but a large number did not. By
day three, around a third of the force had gone AWOL.[10]

After the National Guard arrived, on day four, Louisiana governor
Kathleen Blanco gave the Guard permission to "shoot to kill" if they
confronted violent offenders. As she put it, "They have M–16s, and
they're locked and loaded. These troops know how to shoot and kill, and
I expect they will."[11] Unsurprisingly, Operation Katrina resulted in some
questionable, and tragic, shootings.[12]

These things are inexcusable in civilian populations during times of
war—let alone in what had until then been a functional city. New Orleans, synonymous with life and romance, was allowed to become a combat zone, complete with armed troops trying to put down what in effect
were instant regional warlords. Putting "order" above relief resulted in
private security contractors such as Blackwater being inserted into New
Orleans before the Red Cross was allowed in.[13] By implicitly viewing the
bulk of the civilian population primarily as potential criminals rather
than victims needing rescue and relief, the response matrix to the crisis
developed in a way that potentially prolonged the torment. Blackwater,
for instance, appeared to focus less on rescue and relief than on securing
high-end private property from looting.[14]

The transition to anarchy took just four days. Various levels of government were paralyzed, the military was overstretched, and communication lines broke down. That brute force was seen as the "solution"

indicates an absence of a workable implementation of a response plan to a disaster that has always been on the "probable" list so far as New Orleans was concerned. The fallout is potentially far-reaching as the use of extreme force can have the effect of stun gun, at first terrifying citizens into compliance but then awakening within the affected population propensities for abandonment of the social compact. It is a bit like being bitten by your own guard dog. It is hard to trust it again. The wounds caused not only by the storm and its aftermath but by the catastrophic, and avoidable, administrative response to them still fester. Quick-fix solutions usually mean an intensification of problems the next time around, and what seems reasonably certain is that there will be a next time.

Post-hurricane policies were also marked by problems. Around a million people were evacuated, with families split up and hundreds of thousands relocated to emergency trailers set up for the purpose from Atlanta to San Antonio. The Federal Emergency Management Agency (FEMA) doled out billions of dollars, but the system failed in many areas. According to a report by the U.S. Government Accountability Office, between $600 million and $1.4 billion went to fraudulent claims.[15]

Hundreds of thousands of other evacuees received little follow-up, spreading the tensions into hitherto calm areas. The disruption caused by the environmental refugees was obvious in Houston, which took in 150,000 people. The city was not prepared. For example, within weeks of arriving in the local schools, fights broke out between teens relocated from New Orleans and local youths. By December, one riot at a Houston high school resulted in the arrest of 27 students, 15 of them from New Orleans.[16]

Almost a year after Katrina, the crime rate in Houston spiked, with a near 20 percent increase in homicides, and around one out of every five murders involving an evacuee as either a victim or a suspect.[17] Hospital emergency rooms were stretched to the point of neglect by Katrina victims with no health coverage; sexually transmitted diseases were up;

and disproportionate numbers of evacuees were on antidepressants. The city's budget was being burnt away. Mayor Bill White was clear that "there is still an emergency."[18] Steve Radack of the Harris County Commission agreed, saying, "This is going to create turmoil for many years to come."[19] Next time U.S. cities are asked to take in refugees, even domestic ones, they may not be as welcoming.

New Orleans itself continued to struggle. In June 2006, the worsening crime situation resulted in the governor asking for soldiers to come back to patrol the city.[20] A year after Katrina, the city had just half its pre-hurricane population, a mental health epidemic that had nearly tripled suicide rates, and parts of the city remained toxic.[21] Tragically, the social effects of Katrina are far from over. That hurt takes a long time to heal.

The human cost of Katrina and the subsequent floods was heartrending. And the extent of the physical destruction was staggering. Damages were estimated at more than $100 billion.[22] By comparison that same year, 2005, U.S. official military and diplomatic spending on the war in Iraq was $87.3 billion.[23] Katrina's impact was physically devastating. Louisiana alone lost an estimated 138,379 acres of land during the hurricane. Many barrier islands, already weakened by the draining of wetlands and the rechanneling of the Mississippi, were affected as well. The crucial Chandeleur Islands, which act as speed bumps for storms heading toward New Orleans, lost roughly 85 percent of their surface area.[24]

The central Gulf Coast region plays a critical economic and transport role in the American, and global, economy. Over a quarter of U.S. oil production and close to 15 percent of U.S. natural gas production comes from the Gulf of Mexico. As of August 2008, there were over 3,800 production platforms of various sizes operating in the Gulf. Additionally, this region refines around 30 percent of the U.S. oil supply and contains 26,421 miles of onshore pipelines. Hurricane Katrina destroyed

113 platforms, shut down what amounted to around 19 percent of U.S. refining capacity, and damaged 457 pipelines.[25] Oil and gas production dropped by more than half, causing a global spike in oil prices.

The region is also an important transportation hub. Around two-thirds of U.S. oil imports, half of the natural gas used in the United States, much of the nation's interior agricultural production, and approximately 40 percent of the country's water-borne tonnage transit through the area.[26] That infrastructure is part of a complex global system, and if one small part goes down, it can affect the entire network. Katrina knocked out much of the essential infrastructure, including airports, ports, rail lines, and highways. In one small but indicative example, Hurricanes Katrina and Rita combined that summer to overwhelm U.S. helicopter repair, servicing, and delivery industries. This meant foreign contracts languished. As a result, India's helicopter industry, which relied on American parts, was affected, with choppers grounded for months.[27] The lingering economic effect was widespread and has led some overseas partners to reconsider the reliability of the U.S. supply system, and rethink the value of a just-in-time approach versus a just-in-case safety net. Some of the business that was lost during that summer may never return.

After Katrina, the New Orleans area is slowly being rebuilt, but as planners often don't take environmental change into account, they are largely rebuilding in the same places, again leaving infrastructure vulnerable. In the summer of 2008, Hurricanes Gustav and Ike passed through the Gulf and destroyed 60 oil and gas platforms. Interestingly, even before the hurricanes arrived, the economic effect was felt. What amounted to almost 10 percent of U.S. refining capacity, as well as much of offshore Gulf production was shut down in preparation for the hurricanes. This shows that even just the threat of extreme weather can affect supply and price.

Climate change predictions imply that this sort of disruption is likely to become more common. The U.S. Department of Transportation re-

port found that just over 3 feet of sea level rise could permanently flood
24 percent of interstate highways along the Gulf Coast, as well as 72 percent of the area's ports, 9 percent of the rail lines, and 3 airports. A storm
surge of 18 feet (Katrina brought in a storm surge of 25 to 30 feet) would
flood 51 percent of interstate roads, 98 percent of ports, 43 percent of
freight facilities, 33 percent of rail miles, and 22 airports.[28] Nor are most
planners taking into account other environmental change factors; for example, increasing air temperature, subsidence, and erosion are also likely
to effect equipment and infrastructure, potentially leading to problems
like more buckling of railway lines and highways, and increased pressure
on bridge supports.[29]

Not long after Katrina, U.S. Treasury Secretary John Snow fore-
casted that Katrina could slow down U.S. growth, but he was optimistic
that the post-Katrina rebuilding would stimulate the 2006 economy.[30]
That failed to happen. In fact, a year later, with population levels down
and entire neighborhoods still in ruin, the United States as a whole was
entering a housing slump, triggered in part by the sub-prime lending crisis (at least some of those sub-prime borrowers were walking away from
uninsured properties destroyed by Rita, Wilma, and Katrina). With the
U.S. economy weakened, it will get increasingly difficult for badly ef-
fected areas to bounce back, rebuild, and put in reinforcements, leaving
some even more vulnerable the next time around.

It's not just the Gulf Coast that is at risk of more "Katrinas." Several
areas of the United States that are major population centers and global
economic drivers are also at risk.

FLORIDA

Katrina was America's first big environmental hit of the twenty-first century, but with more than 50 percent of the population living near the

coast, it's unlikely to be a one-off. South Florida, for example, is known to be at risk. A 2006 assessment done by scientists at the National Hurricane Center found that if a hurricane the size of Katrina hit southern Florida, six feet of floodwaters would drown the coastline, destroying infrastructure in Miami, knocking out power for months, and paralyzing the region. According to Max Mayfield, the center's director, "We know that it happened in southeast Florida before and there's no doubt in my mind that it will happen again. I can't tell people when, but I can guarantee that it will happen." Again poor development plans are putting increasing numbers of people at risk as more and more high-rises go up along the coast, and evacuation plans fall well short of what to do with hundreds of thousands, if not millions, of long-term refugees.[31]

Hurricanes aside, just rising sea levels and storm surges are predicted to put vast swaths of Southern Florida under water or at risk of persistent flooding by the end of the century, and that includes large sections of infrastructure, such as most of the state's airports, which tend to be built on the coast. Major installations have already had to be reexamined. Hurricane Andrew (1992) did so much damage to the regional economic driver, Homestead Air Force Base, that the base was permanently closed.

NEW YORK, NEW JERSEY, CONNECTICUT

Another area at risk is greater New York City, including coastal New York State, New Jersey, and Connecticut, an area with a combined population of around 20 million, and an economy of around $1 trillion, with approximately $2 trillion in built assets. The region had a small taste of what might be in store during a 1992 Nor'easter, when floodwaters poured into tunnels and subway entrances, cutting off sections of the city. The New York subway system shorted out (saltwater conducts electricity and corrodes wires), LaGuardia Airport closed down, the Battery Park Tunnel went under six feet of water, the sea level at the southern tip of Manhattan rose by close to nine feet, and the PATH link between New Jersey and Manhattan shut down for ten days.[32]

Much of Manhattan is only about 10 feet above sea level, with critical regional infrastructure, such as ports or tunnel entrances, even lower lying. A major climate vulnerability study on the region for the U.S. government's Global Change Research Program found that "By the end of this century, for two-thirds of [transportation infrastructure] facilities with elevations at or below 10 feet above sea level, flooding may occur at least once every decade."[33] The report goes on to note that the FDR Drive, LaGuardia Airport, the Holland Tunnel, and the entrances to over a dozen subway lines are all below 10 feet. The danger estimates may be conservative. In 2007–2008 alone, service at JFK Airport (11.7 feet above sea level) was disrupted several times because of storms. JFK is vulnerable not only because of elevation, but also due to its location at the western edge of Long Island Sound. A tropical storm headed west along the Sound could flood much of Queens, lower Manhattan, tunnel entrances, etc. JFK and the Hamptons would likely be hit hardest and first.

Apart from cataclysmic events, there are also concerns about freshwater supplies. Rising sea levels could push the salt front (where fresh river water turns to salty sea water) north up the Hudson River, possibly as far as the Chelsea Pump Station, thereby contaminating that supply. Saltwater may infiltrate the freshwater aquifers in certain areas, poisoning those as well. There are also concerns that the rising water levels could back up drainage systems, forcing raw sewage back up through manholes and toilets.[34] And that's not the worst of it.

There will likely be long-term health problems, as the average number of dangerously hot days in Manhattan is predicted to double between 1998 and 2020.[35] Heat waves can kill, contribute to crime, crash power systems, and slow the economy. A heat wave in Manhattan in the summer of 2006 prompted the city to set up 383 "cooling centers" for the public; to try to stave off a collapse of the energy grid, lights on the

Brooklyn Bridge and Empire State Building were dimmed and elevator use in city-administered buildings was rationed.

The above outlines just two regional examples of how environmental change could affect the United States. There are multiple areas at risk of a range of impacts. For example, the same summer the heat wave affected Manhatten, one in California killed 136 people and resulted in widespread power cuts affecting security and the economy.[36] The challenges are many. And many of those challenges are exacerbated by inappropriate national policy.

Katrina was devastating for those in the region, but the United States as a whole was able to absorb the impact without national-level instability. The problem comes with persistent and varied environmental crises that result in large-scale disruptions in many areas across the country. Major environmental change, like any protracted crisis, highlights and exacerbates existing problems in a society, economy, and political system. It's like stepping onto a frozen lake. If there are already cracks in the ice sheet, and weight is added, the cracks will get bigger. The United States has many present and potential cracks—institutional, regulatory, political, and social—that weaken the country's ability to absorb the stress of repeated, costly, and traumatic crises. The quick survey below of some of the most obvious national-level U.S. weak points includes: the way the U.S. Army Corps of Engineers is deployed; the irrationality of the National Flood Insurance Program; the exhausted and ill-prepared military; the lack of political will and public education; the nation's social structure and frayed civil order. There are others, but this should be more than enough to give an indication of the depth of the challenge.

U.S. ARMY CORPS OF ENGINEERS

The U.S. Army Corps of Engineers is a section of the military charged with providing "vital public engineering services in peace and war to strengthen our Nation's security, energize the economy, and reduce risks from disasters."[37] It employs approximately 35,000 people (both civilian and military) and is one of the largest public engineering agencies in the world. It was the job of the U.S. Army Corps of Engineers to plan, build, and maintain the flood defenses for New Orleans and the surrounding region. However, according to a 6,113-page post-Katrina report issued by the Corps, "The hurricane protection system in New Orleans and southeast Louisiana was a system in name only."[38] The problems included design flaws, walls that were built without taking into account subsidence, and safety checks that weren't done. The full list of failures is long—several thousand pages long.

Apart from technical issues, there are also questions about how the Corps is used by politicians. Reporter Michael Grunwald researched and wrote an exhaustive series on the Corps for the *Washington Post* and concluded: "[T]he Corps is an addiction for members of Congress, who use its water projects to steer jobs and money to their constituents and contributors [. . .] The Corps is allowed to endorse projects whenever it calculates that the economic benefits to private interests—even one private interest—would exceed the costs to taxpayers. And without executive-branch oversight, the Corps has traditionally inflated benefits, low-balled costs, and otherwise justified projects that keep its employees busy and its congressional patrons happy."[39] For example, the Corps's pre-construction estimates for its Tennessee-Tombigbee Waterway project were a cost of about $300 million and traffic of 28 million tons of cargo in its first year. It ended up being a cost of $2 billion and traffic of only 1.4 million tons.[40]

This way of functioning is particularly problematic in a time of environmental change, especially as the private interests the Corps is made to serve often involve development in environmentally unstable places. As Grunwald explained, in the area around New Orleans: "The Corps put most of its levees around undeveloped and highly vulnerable floodplains instead of focusing on protection for existing developments—

partly because Corps cost-benefit analyses did not consider the cost of human life or environmental degradation, and partly because powerful developers owned swampland in those vulnerable floodplains. Katrina destroyed many of the houses built on those former swamplands."[41] The cost is not just personal but has larger economic implications as well as, in some cases, businesses and homeowners walk away from destroyed, mortgaged properties, leaving lenders to pick up the loss.

These sorts of tragic boondoggles are being repeated all over the United States. Each one is a potential regional economic, social, political, and security disaster. The combined effect undermines U.S. stability. As the first line of structural defense, the Corps of Engineers is a part of the Pentagon. However, its mandate to increase national security and stability, including economic stability, has been sabotaged by short-term economic and political considerations. This is particularly troublesome as the skill and expertise of the Corps could potentially be an important part of the defense against environmental change. Its misuse is tragic and dangerous.

NATIONAL FLOOD INSURANCE PROGRAM

Right now, in the West, private insurers are absorbing some of the economic cost of environmental change, but this is unsustainable and insurance companies are already in massive retreat from vulnerable areas. According to Thomas Loster, a georisks expert with Munich Re, one of the world's largest reinsurers, "[2004] was the costliest year ever in terms of economic losses and insured losses. And this year [2005] will be a world record year. Historically, mankind never paid as much as it paid this year. The economic losses will be around 200 billion U.S. dollars and the insured losses around 70 billion. So if we look at these tremendous losses and these major storms, droughts and floods, we see that this situation will be aggravated in the future and climate change is dangerous already. And it has just started. So I foresee tremendous losses for mankind and for the insurance sector."[42] Munich Re is looking at ways to work with organizations like the World Bank in order to be able to afford to keep offering insurance in marginal areas. The company is also advocating that government policy makers consult more with industry to see if their development plans are insurable.

Rather than taking the hint from insurance professionals, the U.S. government has opened itself to significant additional problems, again apparently for short-term political considerations, by insuring the uninsurable through the government's National Flood Insurance Program (NFIP). The way the program works is that, when private insurers deem areas too risky to be eligible for coverage, the NFIP can step in. Policyholders buy the insurance through private companies and the government backs it through the NFIP.[43] This essentially subsidizes development in flood zones. The political rationale is that many of the flood zones are along the coast or rivers, and beachfront and riverview properties tend to have a high value, and so are attractive to politically influential developers. Also, local governments rely on property value–based tax revenue; as a result, they lobby federal-level representatives to continue the NFIP so that those expensive houses can be built, generating an increased local tax base.

The upshot is that in some places, such as Dauphin Island, Alabama, which has been hit by hurricanes multiple times since 1979, homes have been rebuilt after each strike, in part with cash infusions from the NFIP. More than two-thirds of all flood payments the town received went to properties that had been repeatedly damaged. The 1979 hurricane even knocked out the bridge to the island. It was reconstructed with millions in government money.[44]

Not surprisingly, the NFIP is a major money loser that needs to be regularly bailed out by the federal Treasury.[45] Larry Larson, executive director of the Association of State Floodplain Managers, summed up the situation when he said, "It may be time for Congress and states to say maybe there are areas of coastal land where we simply shouldn't build."[46]

So far, it doesn't look likely that the government's short-term-gain/mid- and long-term-loss approach to planning and regulations will change. As of 2008, there were discussions about creating a federal NFIP-style program for hurricane insurance, making it easier for people to afford to live in hurricane pathways as well as in flood zones.[47] These policies need to be revised, otherwise the federal government is making it easier to put increasing numbers of people and economic assets in harm's way.

A MILITARY ILL-PREPARED FOR "ENVIRONMENTAL DISOBEDIENCE"

The catastrophic response to Katrina forced the security establishment to rethink some of its policies on environmental change. Up to that point, most of the published security analysis about climate change largely revolved around concerns over absorbing waves of refugees coming into the United States, and the assumption that were would be an increased demand for U.S. military humanitarian intervention in affected regions abroad. After Katrina however, in 2007, the military coordinated a massive training exercise in which the United States would be hit by a hurricane, terrorist attack, and nuclear strike simultaneously. Major General R. Martin Umbarger, adjutant general of the Indiana National Guard, told the *Washington Post:* "We are all realizing that what we just went through is very probable for the nation."[48]

The 2007 disaster simulation found that the National Guard had only 38 percent of trucks, 27 percent of helicopters and other aircraft, and 46 percent of the communications equipment they needed to respond to a domestic crisis.[49] As of 2009, the U.S. military in Iraq was being supplemented by thousands of mercenaries, in the form of contractors, and still there was widespread unease that the nation's badly depleted and exhausted military was leaving the United States exposed domestically.

As early as 2004, Richard Clarke, the U.S. government's first National Coordinator for Security, Infrastructure Protection, and Counterterrorism, wrote, "Producing the 150,000 U.S. forces in the Iraqi theater has badly stretched the Army. Most of the maneuver brigades in the Army are deployed overseas. Those left in the U.S. are too few to maintain the contingency reserve or the training base necessary."[50] Senate Armed Services Committee member Senator Jack Reed summed up the problem: "How do you maintain overseas deployment of significant numbers and still maintain a Guard force in the United States capable of responding to disasters?"[51] However, just having the numbers may not solve the problem—the rescuers also need to be qualified to handle the crisis. There are dangers in putting war-zone-hardened troops, just back from a tour of duty, into a civilian rescue situation for which they may not have been adequately trained.

All in all, the U.S. military, as it now stands, is simply not ready to manage repeated major domestic environmental disasters. While currently the National Guard is supposed to be trained for this task, as was seen with Katrina, currently the Guard alone cannot deliver. One solution would be to augment and properly equip the National Guard, and ensure staffing by guaranteeing that National Guard reservists would not be deployed overseas (one of the main reasons for dropping enrollment in the National Guard is fear of being sent to war abroad). Also, as has been done in India, entire units of the regular military could be trained for, and tasked exclusively with, handling natural disasters at home and abroad. As the training required for dealing with civilians in crisis is different from what is needed to make troops combat ready, it is best if at least some these units are kept off the battlefield. Implementing these recommendations would, however, take political will.

LACK OF POLITICAL WILL AND PUBLIC EDUCATION

Due to rising sea levels, subsidence, and possibly more intense storm activity, sections of New Orleans will be uninhabitable unless substantial investments are made to create coastal defenses and to shore up the city's foundations. As more and more coastal towns in the United States are similarly affected, it will be impossible to offer that amount of spending to every location that needs it. It is worth remembering that the economic and social disruption that is still reverberating along the Gulf Coast was triggered by the inundation of an area with only a median population level. Before Katrina, the population of New Orleans and its surrounding area was around 1.5 million.[52] What would happen if Miami, Manhattan, and Houston all needed assistance within a short period of time?

In the future it may be a tragic necessity to perform "urban triage," in which sections—or the entirety—of severely threatened cities or regions are abandoned, and limited resources are concentrated on safer locations.

Such thinking bumps against the fact that U.S. elected officials have to focus on keeping voters (some of whom will live in the affected areas) happy in two-year election cycles. However, getting it wrong carries huge political costs. In some regions, President George W. Bush's lackluster response to Katrina had a bigger effect on U.S. politics than the Iraq war. According to an interview published in 2009 with Matthew Dowd, President Bush's chief strategist for the 2004 presidential campaign, "Katrina to me was the tipping point. The president broke his bond with the public. Once that bond was broken, he no longer had the capacity to talk to the American public. State of the Union addresses? It didn't matter. Legislative initiatives? It didn't matter. P.R.? It didn't matter. Travel? It didn't matter. I knew when Katrina—I was like, man, you know, this is it, man. We're done."[53] Dan Bartlett, White House communications director, was even more succinct about its impact on the Bush presidency, "Politically, it was the final nail in the coffin."

Long-term planning involving politically difficult decision making can be done in democracies, but it requires an electorate accurately informed about the dangers as well as feasible solutions. As public debate on the severity of environmental change has largely been focused on issues related to greenhouse gas emissions, most voters are not aware of some of the already unavoidable impacts of environmental change. Without such information few would willingly move out of their homes, preferring instead to vote the proposers out of office. This is exacerbated by the fact that voters who have seen the writing on the wall (or the floodline on the levee), and can afford it, have likely left the affected areas of their own accord, leaving behind mainly those with few other options or who are determined to continue living in vulnerable areas. Consequently, unless there is a concerted public education campaign combined with a viable resettlement plan, doomed cities will likely be band-aided and not abandoned. That means even more money being poured into the whirlpool that some areas around New Orleans and other vulnerable regions are likely to become, as well as more politicians breaking their bonds with the public as crisis response becomes overwhelmed. Even as a short-term policy, it doesn't seem to make much sense, especially at a time when many in the United States are already having an increasingly difficult time getting by.

SOCIAL STRUCTURE

The United States has the largest gap between rich and poor of any developed country, and that gap is widening.[54] According to a 2006 study done by *The Economist*, those at the very top, the taxpayers that make up the highest 0.01 percent, saw their share of aggregate income increase from 0.65 percent in 1980 to 2.87 percent in 2004.[55] Meanwhile, the middle class was being squeezed down the ladder and poverty rates climbed. In 2007, 37.3 million Americans officially lived below the poverty line.

The same year, the number of people with no health insurance reached 45.7 million.[56] And in 2005, America's largest network of food banks fed 25.35 million people, many of them the working poor. That's 18 percent more than in 1997.[57] Revised statistics that take into account the effect of the financial crisis have yet to be published, though as of May 2009 a record 34.4 million Americans (or 1 in 9) received food stamps.[58]

The main thrust of *The Economist* study was to see if that growing disparity might lead to political instability. It concluded that "America's income distribution is likely to continue the trends of the recent past. [. . .] The political consequences will depend on the pace of change and the economy's general health."[59] And those factors may themselves be affected by environmental change. For example, in the United States, persistent poverty tends to be localized.[60] In the District of Columbia, Mississippi, and Louisiana approximately one out of every three children lives in poverty (the national average is around 18.5 percent). Unfortunately, those regions contain substantial vulnerable coastal areas and are likely to be severely hit (again) by catastrophic weather, erosion, and subsidence. This corrosive combination of poverty and environmental crisis can, as we have seen, have significant social, economic, security, and political effects and can undermine civil order.

CIVIL ORDER

The impact of Hurricane Katrina on New Orleans was not confined to changes in the physical environment and infrastructure of the city. Much like the failed levees, the severe breakdown of civil order that followed in the storm's wake revealed the fragility of the line holding back chaos.

Law enforcement was problematic, but another aggravating factor was the quick and extreme social breakdown that led to whole areas coming under the control of criminal gangs. One possible contributing factor to the sudden collapse of social order is that, as of 2004, the year before Katrina, Louisiana had the highest incarceration rate in the

United States, with 816 sentenced prisoners per 100,000 state residents.[61] And there has been a marked lack of success of the reform process within the penal system. It sometimes seems that, taken as a whole, the prison system in the United States has become a school for criminalization rather than a process of reform from criminal to lawful behavior. According to the U.S. Department of Justice, a 15-state study showed that 67.5 percent of prisoners released in 1994 were rearrested within 3 years. In 1983, the recidivism rate was 62.5 percent.

While the situation may have been particularly bad in Louisiana, this is a nationwide problem. The United States has the largest prison population in the world, both in absolute numbers and by percentage of the population. As of 2008, there were around 2.3 million people, or approximately 1 in 100 adult Americans, in jail at any given time.[62] One in ten American children had a parent who was in prison, on probation, or on parole.[63]

Another potential contributor to social breakdown is the positive correlation between sudden, extreme high temperatures and violent crime.[64] As the country sees more relative heat wave days, and weeks, it is statistically likely that crime will increase, leading to more incarcerations, leading to more people entering a system that is problematic at best. Additionally, the stress of an overcrowded and underfunded prison system can create psychological problems for some of the 750,000 or so people who work in U.S. prisons and jails, which can ripple throughout the community.[65] All this can encourage a weakening social fabric and is one more reason why planners in the world's largest economy need to give a much higher priority to environmental change, and the wide range of potential instabilities it can cause.

When the effects of poor engineering, ill-conceived government programs, localized poverty, an exhausted defense force, a lack of political will and public education, and a weakening social structure are combined with the desperation and displacement caused by extreme weather events, what can one expect but tragedy? And we've largely only looked at some of the possible vulnerabilities associated with coastal flooding. There are also concerns in the United States about a range of other impacts, including impending persistent regional drought, the stability of northern permafrost-based infrastructure, and the long-term viability of internal water-based transportations systems.

Disasters such as Katrina cost billions, exacerbate social divides, and further weaken vulnerable infrastructure, creating a national security risk. Unfortunately, in spite of all the "lessons learned" reports, it seems as though there have been few fundamental changes that would ensure that the next time it won't be as bad.

It is likely that the United States will face more Katrinas. It is also likely that America's allies are going to find it increasingly difficult to come to the nation's aid if needed because they will be facing their own problems. The situation may not be much better in another pole of the Western world: Europe.

Europe has its own set of problems. Very roughly, southern Europe is becoming hot and dry, while northern Europe is getting warm and wet. Across Europe, extreme events are increasing. Europe's version of Katrina-style cataclysmic weather was the heat wave of 2003. Temperatures reached more than 104 degrees Fahrenheit across the continent, and Britain crossed 100 degrees for the first time in recorded history. Germany, Spain, Britain, France, and Italy combined had a heat-related total death toll of more than 30,000. The chief scientific advisor to the UK government, Sir David King, called it "the biggest natural disaster in Europe on record."[66] The Hadley Centre predicts that, by 2040, heat waves like the one that seared Europe in 2003 will be a one-in-two-year event.[67]

In Europe, mountain areas will likely see more flooding in the winter and spring, and drier summers, thereby disrupting hydroelectric power generation, eroding infrastructure, and damaging valuable industries. Northern Europe may end up with a longer growing season, but it also is already seeing an increase in tick-born diseases (such as Lyme disease).[68] Also, no one is certain what will happen to marine biology in the Mediterranean, a biosphere weakened by overfishing and pollution. The summer of 2006 saw a plague of jellyfish swept in-shore by the changing conditions. More than 30,000 people were stung and beaches had to be closed, badly affecting that region's economic engine: tourism. Jellyfish can be surprisingly problematic. They can decimate fish stocks and, that same years in a similar sudden plague off the coast of Japan, they blocked the water intake system of a nuclear power plant, forcing an emergency powering down.[69]

The UK, obsessed as it is with weather, is far ahead of the global pack when it comes to assessing specific climate impacts. A major study done by the Greater London Authority called *Climate change and London's transportation systems* gives an idea of the sort of problems much of the West, and beyond, will be facing.[70] The study notes that due to the "heat island" effect, urban areas heat up more than the countryside, so, while all of the UK will warm, the center of London is already at times up to 10.8 degrees Fahrenheit hotter than the surrounding countryside. Also, over the last century, there has been an increase in precipitation of 11 percent in winter and a precipitation decrease of 10 percent in summer, when it's needed for crops. By 2050, winter rains are predicted to increase by 20 percent, while summer rains could decrease by 20 to 40 percent. However, when the rains do come, at any time of the year, they are more likely to be hard and heavy.

What does this mean for infrastructure? Between 1992 and 2003, sections of the London underground flooded more than 1,200 times, resulting in 200 station closings. About half of that was due to flash flooding. That is expected to become much more common.[71] The increased heat affects train tracks and train safety, and is already causing more slowdowns and buckled rails. That will also become more usual. Roads are expected to experience more embankment subsidence, concrete deterioration, problems with expansion joints, and reduction in skid resistance. Temperature-related increases in the shrinkage and expansion of the clays in London's earth could affect the water pipes, which could then burst, causing a whole new set of problems.[72]

Then there is the threat of a full-on flood of London. According to *The London climate change adaptation strategy*, a 2008 report written for the mayor of London, "a significant proportion of London's critical infrastructure is at risk of flooding, including emergency services and utilities that London would be reliant upon in case of a flood."[73] London is on the Thames, a tidal river that is currently being tamed by the Thames Barrier, close to 186 miles of floodwalls, 35 major gates, and over 400 minor gates. The idea for the Thames Barrier gained credence following a 1953 London flood that drowned more than 300 people and made the politicians, in their riverside parliament, decide that perhaps something should be done.[74] The massive movable barrier became operational in 1982 and is designed to protect London until 2030. It has built in an 0.3-inch annual river level rise, just enough to compensate for the current 0.26-inch-a-year rise. The Barrier works hard. Around 1987, it was closed to prevent flooding on average once every two years. As of 2006 it was closed about four times a year.[75] It has not been decided what to do post-2030, but the UK government, echoing American-style short-term policies, is considering building 200,000 new homes in the Thames Gateway region by 2016.[76]

The Thames Barrier only protects London from one type of flooding—tidal. That still leaves five other ways the city could flood: heavy rainfall, river swells, an overwhelmed sewer system, rising groundwater, and a burst reservoir or dam.[77] Overall, when studying the dangers of flooding in the UK, the outlook is decidedly soggy. The UK government's *Flood and Coastal Defense* report came to two main conclusions:

"Firstly, if we continue with existing policies, in virtually every scenario considered, the risks grow very substantially. Secondly, the risks need to be tackled across a broad front."[78] So far, however, that isn't being done. As London is a key component of the global economic infrastructure, this should be a concern for us all.

F ood supply is another issue that the West, with its well-stocked su- permarkets and abundant cheap food, hoped it had sorted out long ago. Unfortunately, a range of environmental and economic factors is creating a potentially protracted crisis in agriculture. The reasons are complex and incorporate a constellation of some of the issues we've al- ready covered, as well as some new factors. They include: global popu- lation increases; increases and changes in consumption patterns; speculation in the marketplace; currently productive soils degrading, flooding, or drying out; crop pests and diseases moving into new areas or becoming more virulent in old areas; the large-scale switch to fuel crops; the spread of urban and industrial development into farmlands; the ris- ing cost of fuel, transport, and fertilizers; and increasing extreme climate events, such as the 2003 European heat wave, which alone resulted in a 30 percent drop in crops yields[79] and agricultural losses totaling $15 bil- lion.[80] That scale of sudden, unexpected loss is becoming more common. In 2006, climate conditions and beetles wrecked crops in Australia, Ukraine, Argentina, Canada, and the United States, driving wheat prices to a ten-year high.[81]

The "food crisis" has led to global unrest and a flurry of reports out of Washington, London, and Brussels. One finding is that the West will have increasing difficulty farming the way it is used to and, unless it ad- justs quickly, the competition over land, water, and crops in a time of en- vironmental change risks leading to more stress between states. For example, central and southern European agriculture will not only be af- fected by increasing summer heat, but also by less water and the attendant risks of fires. In the summer of 2005, a drought in Spain and Portugal caused an estimated $1 billion in losses, including nearly half of the cereal crop in central and southern Spain, and led Portugal to threaten to sue Spain for allegedly stealing its water.[82]

Even the world's breadbaskets are having trouble. Canada produces about 20 percent of internationally traded wheat. But the prairies are seeing dramatic weather extremes, going from severe drought from 2001 to 2003 to unprecedented floods in 2005.[83] These extremes might require new ways of thinking about agriculture. According to Dr. Henry Venema, a specialist in the Canadian prairies at the International Institute for Sustainable Development: "There's been a lot of pressure on the farmers in the prairies to get big and buy large equipment to farm very large farms. We had an interesting case in 2004 where it was so wet for so long the farmers couldn't move their big equipment onto the land and sow their crops, but smaller farmers with less land to sow and smaller equipment were more flexible and could get their lands sown in the short window of opportunity when the land was dry enough to seed."[84]

As the environment changes, a lot of assumptions will have to be reexamined if there is to be anything approaching stability in Western agricultural production. For example, a commonly held notion is that colder countries like Russia and Canada will benefit because, if it gets warmer, agriculture can spread farther north. Unfortunately that is not the case. Russian agricultural outputs are predicted to decline in large part due to an increase in extreme events,[85] and Canadian agriculture is currently limited as much by the northern limit of good soils as it is by climate.[86]

The West's agricultural production faces challenges that will take good science, cooperation, and leadership to overcome. Meanwhile, crops in the developing world are being kept home to feed the domestic market, or traded as part of basket deals with nations like China. The West may not be as immune from food scarcity, or at least sharply rising food prices, as it would like to think.

Another core area that may well face new challenges is energy security. The disruptions in the U.S. Gulf Coast are just one part of the problem. Energy generation, extraction, refining, processing, and distribution requires a complex, interlinked, expensive, and, sometimes, global infrastructure. However, much of that infrastructure lies in areas that may become increasingly physically unstable due to changes in the environment. There are two separate, but often interlinked, challenges. One is inherited, one is new. Both stem from the fact that energy infrastructure tends to have a long lifespan. The Hoover Dam in the western United States was completed in 1935 and is still an important hydroelectric generator. China's Three Gorges Dam has an expected lifespan of at least 50 years. Nuclear power stations, from design through decommissioning, may be on the same site for a hundred years. Additionally, constructions such as nuclear plants, refineries, coal power plants, and high voltage transmission lines can be perceived as undesirable to a community. As a result, when it comes time to build new installations, they are often erected in the same locations as the previous ones, as the local population is already accustomed to the infrastructure. This means that sites chosen in the 1980s may still be in operation in 2080 and beyond.

The lifespan of existing energy infrastructure is well within the time frame predicted for potentially disruptive environmental change. When much of it was installed, the degree of change was not understood and so was not factored in to its design. This is an inherited challenge.

The new challenge involves upcoming investments. A substantial segment of energy infrastructure in North America and Europe is scheduled to be decommissioned in the coming decades due to revised environmental standards and general age-related retiring. Combined with stimulus packages in the United States and other countries, and development in China, India, Africa, and elsewhere, it is likely that we are entering an era of large-scale investments in new infrastructure. In some cases, there is now the necessary science to anticipate at least the minimum amount of environmental change that can be expected over the next century (well within the lifespan of most new investments). However, in too many cases, proposed new builds still do not incorporate likely effects of environmental change.

When planners talk about performing "environmental impact assessments," almost invariably what is being assessed is how the construction would change the existing environment, not how a changing environment might affect the construction. While engineers and planners may perform a site inspection before designing an installation, they normally consider the parameters of that site a constant, not a variable. The general assumption is the coast won't move, river levels will remain the same, the ground won't subside, and precipitation will stay predictable. Most planners are not accustomed to, and often not trained for, incorporating environmental change–induced site variations into designs. Many hydroelectricity plants, for example, depend primarily on predictable seasonal precipitation. Some are already finding it increasingly difficult to manage. In 2008–09, hydroelectricity generation in India declined by 8.42 percent relative to the previous year. The loss was blamed on inadequate rainfall.[87]

Nuclear power generation may also face challenges in ensuring output and site security. Reactors usually require a large amount of water for cooling. As a result, they are generally situated in areas that are susceptible to environmental change. They are normally either on the coast, making them increasingly vulnerable to sea level rise, extreme weather, and storm surges, or they are on rivers, lakes, or reservoirs and are dependent on increasingly valuable, and variable, freshwater supplies.

Some installations have already been tested. There has been a degree of flooding at nuclear power plants in the United States, France, and India.[88] In the UK, many of the existing coastal power stations are just a few feet above sea level. Additionally, while sea level rise and storm surges may be increasingly well understood, other disruptive factors, such as the possibility that changes in wave action could liquefy coastal sands, are not.[89]

Riverside plants have different problems. In some areas drought is reducing river, lake, and reservoir levels at the same time as air and water temperatures are increasing. Power generation takes a lot of water. In Europe, for example, cooling for electrical power generation (including both nuclear and fossil fuel plants) accounts for around one-third of all water used. During Europe's record-breaking heat wave of 2003, temperatures across the continent reached more than 104 degrees Fahrenheit. As a result, in France, 17 nuclear reactors had to power down or be shut off. The reduction in generation capacity forced state-owned Électricité de France to buy power on the open market at close to ten times the cost it was charging clients. The inability to generate its own power in a heat wave cost the utility an estimated $424 million.[90] The Hadley Centre predicts that, by 2040, heat waves such as the one of 2003 would be "commonplace."[91] The effect on any form of power generation requiring large amounts of water (including coal-powered plants) is likely to be substantial. Some French nuclear plants had to power down again in the hot summers of 2006 and 2009. Some installations in the United States have experienced similar problems.

The same heat conditions that make it difficult to deliver power due to water problems also create a peak in demand due to the desire for air conditioning. As a result, as average temperatures increase, it may take less of a temperature spike to affect system stability.

There are vulnerabilities in power distribution as well. Any extreme weather event, such as high winds, heavy rains/snows, and ice storms, can impair power delivery, and there are global predictions of an increase in these kinds of disasters. One UK government report, commissioned after the costly summer floods of 2007, has found that potentially hundreds of UK substations are at risk of flooding.[92] The

wake-up call came that summer when a switching station near Glouces-
ter, servicing around 500,000 homes and businesses, came within inches
of being flooded. Stronger storms can also bring down power lines, and
some areas, such as parts of the northern United States and southeastern Canada, may face more ice storms like the one that cut off the power
for millions, including my family, in the winter of 1998. Extreme events
of all sorts are likely to become more common, straining power delivery systems.

Also, many of the world's largest oil and gas facilities (including: Ras
Tanura, Saudi Arabia; Jamnagar, India; Jurong Island Refinery, Singapore; Rotterdam Refinery; and major installations in the Niger Delta)
are only slightly above sea level. This leaves them vulnerable to rising
sea levels, storm surges, increasing storm activity, subsidence, and
changes in ground composition. If even one of these regions is affected,
it could affect local security and global supply and markets.

As an added challenge, even some financial mechanisms make it
more difficult to integrate environmental change into planning. For example, Clean Development Mechanism (CDM) financing and the push
for low-carbon power generation generally is resulting in a new era of
dam building. Over a quarter of all CDM projects are for hydroelectricity, with 784 slated for China alone.[93] Some projects are well conceived;
others much less so.

As the effects of environmental change become even more apparent,
it may also cause a recalculation of the cost of energy production. For example, the above-mentioned disruptions (or even the possibility of disruption) may affect insurance costs, potentially endangering the
economic viability of certain investments. Other factors may change cal-
culations as well. For example, if predictions of increasing water scarcity
hold true, fresh, clean water may substantially increase in value. This
would force a re-evaluation of the real cost not only of hydro and fresh-
water-cooled nuclear installations, but also of fossil fuel extraction and

refining techniques that pollute water that could otherwise be used for drinking and irrigation.

Already China has abandoned or suspended the vast majority of its coal-to-liquid projects, in part as a result of concerns about water availability. Another potential area of concern is Canada's oil sands. The method of extraction used in the oil sands requires and contaminates large amounts of water. Currently Canada is perceived to have abundant freshwater; however, that is predicted to change in some regions as the climate shifts. Already there are concerns about water quality in some of the communities that share river systems with the oil sands. Apart from the domestic value of freshwater availability, ensuring a stable supply of freshwater for agriculture in Canada has wider implications. It is increasingly likely that, as other areas of the planet, such as Australia, become less fertile, Canadian agriculture's contribution to global supply will gain in relative importance.

It is also possible, though quite controversial, that an increasingly parched United States will look to Canada to supplement its water deficiencies. In some areas of the United States, such as the agricultural belts and water-scarce cities such as Las Vegas, water security might become more important than oil security. Other forms of energy may be found, but it is more difficult to find other forms of water. In such a case, U.S. energy security policy (which has been supporting the water-polluting Canadian oil sands) might come into conflict with U.S. water and food security policy (which would benefit by ensuring that a vast water supply to the north is not contaminated).

Another problem related to the politics of water that might affect energy supply could arise when dam building deprives one group, region, or country of its expected supply of freshwater. Attacks on the installations themselves are even conceivable, should some people become desperate enough as a result of increasing water scarcity—their goal being to destroy the dam in order to attain water supply.

All in all, there are concerns about both older installations not being designed for new conditions and new installations not integrating change into their planning. Either situation could result in marked decreases in energy output and risks to the installations themselves. That, in turn, could affect energy prices, economic growth, and regional and global security. Volatile energy prices have the potential to destabilize major economies.

Many of the challenges outlined above can be overcome with sufficient research, planning, engineering, and financing. In some cases, it may even be possible to integrate change into planning in such a way that energy output increases with changes rather than decreases. For example, hydro installations in regions that are expecting higher rainfall could be designed to eventually take advantage of that excess flow, rather than be overwhelmed by it.

However, the reinforcement of global energy infrastructure is unlikely to happen overnight. It will take an acknowledgment that the problems are real and wide-ranging; a will to counter them; appropriate investment in, and research on, potential impacts as well as engineering and design solutions; implementation; and continual re-evaluation in light of changing environmental conditions and predictions.

It is in the best interest of those concerned with energy security, such as national governments and the business community, especially the energy and insurance industries, to ensure that this happens as quickly as possible. Until it does, it is to be expected that there will be increasingly frequent disruptions to energy supply, potentially in multiple locations and sectors at the same time. The economic, social, and political costs are likely to be substantial.

Also, it may make sense to focus on building a more decentralized energy structure, preferably based on locally available renewable energy supplies situated in secure locations. A degree of energy self-sufficiency could provide a better defense against the sort of large-scale outages that result when centralized power systems are compromised. This sort of regional, network-based system might also prove more flexible and adaptive, and therefore more able to cope with the increasing variability and unpredictability caused by environmental change.

Energy infrastructure is often among the best funded, planned, and maintained constructions available. The challenges that even this well-supported sector will face are an indication of the vulnerability of other large sections of the critical infrastructure that support our economies, security, and lives.

The challenges facing the United States, UK, and other Western nations are complex and often interrelated. They are intensified by the consistent and systemic fixation on short-term political and economic gain—as exemplified by the way the U.S. Army Corps of Engineers, the National Flood Insurance Program, the prison system, and energy policy is used—at the cost of long- (or even medium-) term stability and growth. Taken on their own, each of the elements above can probably be managed. Combined, they are like a plague of rats nibbling away at the hull of the ship of state, causing it to list dangerously. Even without environmental change, the results would be costly; with that change, they risk becoming unsustainable. Given the existing vulnerabilities in the United States and other Western nations, it is not surprising that stability may soon hinge on the environment.

Environmental change constitutes a national assault, and if there are any cracks in a state's defensive walls, it breaks them wide open and rides in accompanied by its own four horsemen: economic, social, political, and security crises. The pain won't be limited to the developing world. In fact, human tragedy aside, while the geopolitical and geoeconomic impact may not be much if a tiny Pacific country is threatened, when global powers such as the United States and the European Union fall victim to the same phenomenon, the repercussions for them, their neighborhood, and the planet, can be severe. The personal pain may start in the shelters of Montreal or New Orleans, but the political and economic effects ripple out to Manila and New Delhi.

To complicate matters, the world is also going through major geopolitical and geoeconomic readjustments; yet, in the same way some Western leaders still encourage flood-zone housing developments, they also often implement foreign policies designed primarily for expediency. The same shortsighted, narrow policies that serve to undermine a home front threatened by environmental change are eroding the West's position in the global balance of power. One doesn't have to look far to see where short-term interests are creating potential vulnerabilities; one just has to look north, to the thawing Arctic, where the shimmering mirage of untold riches is leading to decisions that may dangerously undermine North American and European security.

PART TWO

THE NEW GEOPOLITICAL ICEBERGS

OR, HOW THE NORTH WAS LOST

There are strange things done in the midnight sun
By the men who moil for gold;
The Arctic trails have their secret tales
That would make your blood run cold.

—Robert Service, "The Cremation of Sam McGee"

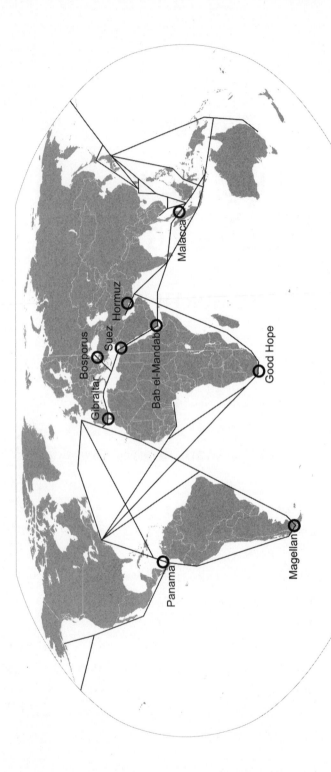

World's major maritime routes—and their choke points.
Map created by Justin Estrela-Reis.

2

LIFE ON THE NO LONGER PERMANENT PERMAFROST

It's not over until it's over.

—Louie Nigiyok, Inuvialuit nature guide

L ouie looks at me over his shoulder and says, "Time to stretch your legs." He gets off the four-wheeler, pulls out his bright yellow binoculars, and scans the horizon. Slowly, carefully, I pry my rigid fingers out from under the backseat rack I've been sitting on—and clutching for stability. My legs don't need stretching, but my fingers sure do. Clasping and unclasping my hands inside my double-thick mitts, I head over to see if Louie has spotted anything.

Today every ridge has been a disappointment for Louie, a local nature guide. He is looking for muskox, one of only two Arctic ungulates, along with the caribou, that survived the end of the last ice age. Once upon a time, the muskox roamed as far south as Kansas. But, as the ice retreated, so did they. Now you have to come up here to see them in the wild. We are in the high Arctic—about a three-hour flight north of the

Arctic Circle on Victoria Island in the Northwest Territories, outside the small Inuvialuit community of Ulukhaktok (population 400 or so). Even here the muskox are getting harder to find.

I've never seen country like this before. Every vista has two views—vast and subtle. When I look into the distance, I see miles and miles of treeless tundra, bordered by the slate gray of the Arctic Ocean. On land, the color is a uniform greenish brown, the hills muted and the valleys gentle. There is an overwhelming feeling of endless, empty space.

But then I look at details around my feet, and khaki colors resolve into the neon orange of lichen on jade-streaked rocks, little purple blooms, and tough, tiny, bright yellow flowers. The smooth stretches of featureless tundra refocus into a web of sodden ground, furrowed permafrost, and sudden drops. The beautiful, dehumanizing breadth of the infinite becomes the vibrant struggle for survival of the minute.

We've been on the trail of muskox for hours now, but the closest we've come are the droppings Louie has just found on the ridge. He is starting to worry. He is an excellent host and he wants to satisfy his guest. Sweeping the horizon, he mutters quietly, as much to himself as to me, "It's not over until it's over."

Louie's guiding partner, Roland Notiana, has been riding posse on his own four-wheeler. Roland, also Inuvialuit, is a Canadian Ranger, Canada's part-time reserve force of around 4,000 locals who patrol the north. The Rangers are Canada's first line of military defense in the vast Arctic. They are charged with protecting Canadian sovereignty, collecting strategic information, helping with search and rescue, and reporting unusual activity.[1] Roland also works check-in at the Ulukhaktok airport.

Louie and Roland look for specks of muskox in the distance. Nothing.

And so it's back on the four-wheelers as we head for another ridge and a new vantage point. Bumping along, I get lost inside my head. My hands aren't cold. My legs aren't stiff. The Arctic is so vast, it makes you feel very small, it pulls you into yourself and makes you think. And think.

Undistracted by cell phones and small talk, surrounded by a landscape at once brutal and delicate, in a world where small changes in ice or wind need to be felt to survive, with a long way to go and no fixed destination, you think. This land of vicious beauty has given birth to great artists. Holman (the old name for Ulukhaktok) prints are world famous for their vibrant colors and striking supernatural imagery. Louie himself is not only a naturalist, but also a superb artist.

We come to another ridge. Up ahead is a wall of fog. Again Louie stops and scans the horizon. Nothing. I shrug. Louie says we should probably turn back. Fine. He tries another "It's not over until it's over," but neither of us is convinced. The north that Louie learned from his parents, and that they learned from theirs, is melting away. The animals aren't where they should be. The land doesn't feel familiar. And so we head back. At least I know how to be comfortable now. I am floating on the caribou skin bungee-corded to the four-wheeler's rack, lost in my own thoughts.

"There's one!" Louie shouts as Roland pulls alongside. In the distance I can see what looks like yet another boulder. Then it moves. Slightly.

The two ATVs stop for a planning session. Roland gets out his Northern Ranger–issue gun (it is rutting season) and I pull out my camera. Louie directs Roland like a general. What route, how far away, how fast. Then we are off. Suddenly all the physical detachment I cultivated disappears with a wallop. I am here now. All of me. Holding on by the tips of my fingers, my legs flailing as we ford streams and jump mini-chasms. The animal is running, and we are traveling in its smelly wake (they don't call 'em *musk*ox for nothing). It looks like a rastabison—a buffalo covered in dreadlocks. Then, suddenly, it stops. Breathing puffs of white, wet steam, it stands still and looks at us. I take out my camera but I don't want to look through the viewfinder. The real sight is too mesmerizingly peculiar. It looks incredibly odd. Prehistoric. Perplexed and perplexing. A thing of myths and legends. A Holman print come to life.

After the longest minute of the day, the muskox shakes itself and starts to amble off. Within seconds, it's gone. Louie looks at me over his shoulder and says, with the first smile he's had for hours, "It's not over until it's over."

It's not over in the Arctic yet, but it's getting harder. Louie, the Rangers, the print makers, Ulukhaktok, the entire Arctic lifestyle are all under threat. Tragically, the muskox may have a better chance of surviving intact, albeit in zoos down south.

One of the reasons is that planetary warming will not have a uniform effect over the entire globe. For example, broadly speaking, the changes in temperature will be relatively small over the bulk of the oceans, as oceans themselves can absorb a lot of heat. Also, ocean and wind currents redistribute heat building up around the equator, pushing it toward the icy poles where it can cool, with the Arctic acting like a global air conditioner. As a result, in a climate where the global mean temperature increases by around, say, 5.4 degrees Fahrenheit, there will perhaps be roughly a 1.8- or 3.6-degree Fahrenheit increase over most oceans, while the Arctic temperatures might rise 12.8 to 14.4 degrees Fahrenheit.[2] Areas of the Arctic are already visibly changing, and that change will continue. According to the Arctic Climate Impact Assessment, a major study done by scientists from the United States, Norway, Iceland, Canada, Sweden, the UK, Finland, and Russia: "The Arctic is now experiencing some of the most rapid and severe climate change on earth. Over the next 100 years, climate change is expected to accelerate, contributing to major physical, ecological, social, and economic changes, many of which have already begun."[3]

There is regional variability across the Arctic. Some areas are hardly affected at all, but, since the mid-1950s, winter temperatures in western Canada and Alaska have risen by as much as 5.4 to 7.2 degrees Fahrenheit. The Assessment forecasts that by the end of the century, under a "moderate" scenario, average winter temperature over land could increase by 7.2 to 12.8 degrees Fahrenheit. Already the warming has had a dramatic effect on sea ice formation. Arctic sea ice normally covers an area about the size of Australia. In the past 30 years, the average annual reach of sea ice has retreated by around 8 percent, meaning it has lost an area larger than continental Norway, Sweden, and Demark combined. The late-summer extent alone declined by about 15 to 18 percent.

In 2005 the ice was 18.2 percent below the long-term average.[4] In the summer of 2007 the sea ice shrunk to its smallest cover in millennia, with the September ice extent 23 percent smaller than the previous record set in 2005.[5] In 2005, even before the recent dramatic shrinkage, Walt Meier of the U.S. National Snow and Ice Data Center at Colorado University said, "Having four years in a row with such low ice extents has never been seen before in the satellite record. It clearly indicates a downward trend, not just a short-term anomaly."[6] His colleague Dr. Mark Serreze has said, "The changes we've seen in the Arctic over the past few decades are nothing short of remarkable. [. . .] The feeling is we are reaching a tipping point or threshold beyond which sea ice will not recover."[7] Studies now forecast that, by 2050, if not decades earlier,[8] the Arctic summertime ice cap could completely disappear, creating a blue polar sea nearly five times the size of the Mediterranean.[9]

The decrease in ice cover allows Arctic Ocean waves and storm surges to batter the shore harder and longer, eating away at the fragile coastline. In Alaska, erosion has meant that, just to give one example, the U.S. government has to relocate several waterfront villages further inland at an estimated cost of around $100 million per village.[10] North and northwest Alaska now have one of the highest erosion rates in the world, with erosion around Barrow between 1979 and 2000 ranging from

2.3 to 10 feet a year.[11] This is particularly problematic as, in the North, infrastructure is often clustered near the water's edge. The coast is made even more unstable by extreme events, such as ivus (also known as ice shoves or frozen tsunamis), in which older, thicker ice forces huge ridges of newer ice up onto the shore. In one 2006 case near Barrow, an ice wall around 20 feet by 100 feet pushed up onto a main coastal road, leaving it with only one lane. It stopped only 33 feet short of a pump station that handles Barrow's underground water and sewer system. A previous ivu in the region knocked down power lines along the beachfront.[12] There are also odd phenomena, like a lake of recently melted sea ice the size of Maryland sitting on another patch of ice in northern Alaska.[13]

This structural instability is made even worse by the thawing of the permafrost. Permafrost, essentially permanently frozen land, has acted as a concrete foundation for life in the north. It covers about 20 percent of the planet's landmass, including large swaths of Russia; parts of the Alps, Andes, and Himalayas; and almost half of Canada. It is what Louie and I bounced over as we trawled for muskox. It is what his house is built on. It is what supports Roland's airport runway. As temperatures rise, the permafrost thaws. The ice trapped inside the frozen ground liquefies, turning the earth into a soggy mess. If there is poor drainage, the water sits on the earth's surface, drowning vegetation and turning the area into something like mucky, unstable quicksand—or frigid wetlands. If there is good drainage, the water runs off, causing erosion and depleting groundwater. If the permafrost supports lakes, they can drain away as well, like water out of an unplugged bathtub.

This thawing can have a devastating effect on vegetation. Permafrost is covered by a thin "active layer" of earth that thaws in summer and re-freezes in winter. The active layer is where plants can settle in and grow. A fast thaw puts a layer of water between the constantly frozen per-mafrost and the active layer and, if it's on a slope, the whole active layer can just slide away, sometimes in slices hundreds of feet long and only 20 inches deep. The slide takes all the vegetation with it and exposes the deeper permafrost. Over time, a new active layer forms and slowly plants find it and try to grow again. But the layer can slide off once more, starting the whole process all over again. The end result is structural instability, less food for animals, and degrading soil.

Permafrost ice can also be found cementing a rocky mountainside together. When that ice melts, the rocks can fall apart. That is what happened during the European heat wave of 2003, when a chunk of rockface that had been welded to the Matterhorn with ice unexpectedly broke off, stranding climbers.[14]

One of the few groups that are happy with all this is archeologists. The thaw is affecting such deep layers that all sorts of exceptionally preserved ancient goodies are being exposed. The most famous was "Otzi," the body of a 5,300-year-old man that emerged from a Swiss mountainside. Less media-friendly was the 8-foot-high and 2,625-foot-long pile of Stone Age caribou droppings, found in an area of the Yukon where there haven't been caribou for a hundred years.[15]

Ultimately, permafrost zones will be less able to support existing life and critical infrastructure, from the muskox to the oil pipelines. While those living south of the Arctic circle will feel the impact, the ones on the front lines of the change are Louie and Roland. Inuit and Inuvialuit culture and society are intricately linked to the physical environment. The traditional Inuit calendar is divided into thirteen flexible "moons" called: Sun Is Possible, Sun Gets Higher, Premature Seal Pups, Seal Pup, Bearded Seal Pups, Caribou Calves, Eggs (nesting season), Caribou Hair Sheds, Caribou Hair Thickens, Velvet Pelts from Caribou Antlers, Winter Starts, Hearing News from Neighbors, and the Great Darkness.[16]

The sun and the darkness will stay the same, but the seals, caribou, birds, and neighbors are all trying to adjust to major changes. Rune Fjellheim, head of the Arctic and Environmental Unit of the Saami Council

representing around 100,000 Saami (the indigenous people of Northern
Norway, Sweden, Finland, and Russia), told me:

> We are traditionally quite good at adapting to things, but the kind of
> conditions we are experiencing now are unprecedented in history. It's
> warmer in the winter, and the snow comes later and leaves earlier. But
> the main problem is that it is so variable. It freezes and thaws, and
> freezes and thaws, and that causes tremendous problems for us. Tradi-
> tional weather signals and the ability to predict the weather are not
> working anymore. We were able to predict weather months ahead, pre-
> dict if this was going to be a strong winter or a warm winter. But what
> the elders are telling us now is that they can't say anymore because they
> don't know. They try to follow the traditional weather signals but it is
> simply not working.[17]

This is not to say the north is about to become a barren wasteland.
New species will move in, and forests will likely spread; however, this
leads to other complications. The extra heat is helping along forest fires
and diseases. The average area of North American boreal forests destroyed by fires has more than doubled since 1970. As for disease, in the
1990s, the Kenai Peninsula in Alaska was devastated by the largest known
outbreak of spruce bark beetles. More than 6,000 square miles of mature spruce forests were affected. In Canada, more than a thousand
square miles in the Yukon alone were hit.[18]

There are also other large-scale disruptions of the ecosystem. A
study released in 2006 and funded by the National Science Foundation
and the National Oceanic and Atmospheric Administration correlated
two decades of climate data with wildlife observations. It found that in
the region studied in the Bering Sea, sea ice was melting three weeks
earlier than in 1997. Pacific grey whales were moving north, looking
for the cooler currents they were used to. Pink salmon were filling the
areas the whales had abandoned. Species that lived on the sea floor and

didn't have the mobility to move to more comfortable climates were being wiped out. The bottom was covered in broken shells, the last local remnants of a species of clam that couldn't adapt. Seal breeding grounds were disrupted, walruses were starving, and, yes, polar bears were drowning.[19] The changes are making it difficult for wildlife, as well as for others that depend on consistency in the natural world, such as the fishing industries.

As with Indians and the monsoon, the main problem for people in the area is that their lives and infrastructure are not designed for the new conditions. The people of the North have worked out a complex economy based on traditionally accessible resources. The invasive species don't have an established value, and it would take a cultural and economic shift to know how to use them. Meanwhile, existing livelihoods are threatened. Rune explained what that is doing to the Saami, who are traditionally reindeer herders: "For the reindeer to cope on frozen ground is not easy because the grazing areas get 'locked' due to the variability in the weather. Another new concern is a new parasite that has come to our area. Last summer, one of my colleagues recorded that seventy to seventy-five of his reindeer died from a parasite that is not known to that area. After some investigation, we found that it is a kind of parasite that usually dies during the wintertime during the extreme cold period. But, as the winter is not as cold, they survived. That scares us because it is new."[20] This costly spread of deadly diseases into what had been colder climates is being seen around the world, with outbreaks of the cattle disease bluetongue being seen more regularly in places like the UK, requiring livestock slaughter and quarantines and potentially affecting future food security.[21]

There are a few reasons why the Arctic is taking such a big climatic thumping. One is that ice, being light colored, reflects up to 90 percent of the sunlight that hits it. Dark ocean water, on the other hand,

absorbs up to 90 percent of sunlight. The same is true on land. Snow-
and ice-covered land reflects, while dark, exposed ground absorbs. As
the ice and snow start to melt, more relatively dark water and ground is
exposed. Less ultraviolet light is reflected back into space and more solar
radiation remains at the surface.[22] It's why black car seats burn you in the
summer, and silver windshield protectors look lousy but can keep a
parked car cool.

The result is a positive feedback mechanism that accelerates warming. Other feedback mechanisms include: the warming of the water itself contributes to faster melting at the ice edge; and, in the same way
that a mountain tends to be cooler at the top than at the base, as the ice
pack melts it becomes shorter, exposing it to warmer air and encouraging an even faster melt. It's why snow-capped mountains only have snow
at the top.

An even more serious problem is that the permafrost thaw is starting to release carbon dioxide and methane that has been frozen in the
earth for millennia. Methane (CH_4) is a greenhouse gas much more potent than carbon dioxide (CO_2). As the summers lengthen and the active layer grows, the sequestered methane produced by decomposing
organic material releases faster. A 2006 *Nature* study on methane bub-
bling up from under expanding Siberian lakes found that annual
methane emissions from all northern Siberian lakes is now estimated to
be over 4 million tons, or as much as 63 percent more than previously
thought.[23] Around 550 billion tons of carbon is thought to be frozen in
northern Siberia's permafrost. If that was released as carbon dioxide, it
would equal around two-thirds the amount that is already in the atmosphere. According to one of the study's authors, Katey M. Walter
from the University of Alaska, the thawing of the Siberian permafrost
and the subsequent release of methane is "a time bomb waiting to go
off."[24] Greenhouse gases released as part of feedback mechanisms are
often not included in climate models and, according to two studies,

might mean that temperature rise estimates will have to be increased by up to 50 percent.[25]

The core of it is, once the Arctic thaw gains momentum, it is hard to do anything about the warming. One of the world's main air conditioners ends up being one of the world's heaters. And it *is* gaining momentum. There might be cooler periods and locations in the Arctic, but the clear trend is a sharp warming.

The Arctic has undergone massive transformations before, otherwise it wouldn't have the vast sequestered carbon, oil, and gas reserves that come from enormous amounts of decomposed plants and animals. There have been at least 20 glacier advances in the last two million years. Some changes were fast and dramatic, including temperature rises of several degrees in just a few decades. In one shift, around 55 million years ago, there was a massive warming. According to Appy Sluijs, a paleoecologist from Utrecht University, "This time period is associated with a very enhanced greenhouse effect. Basically it looks like the Earth released a gigantic fart of greenhouse gases into the atmosphere—and globally the Earth warmed by about 5C (9F)."[26] Another huge change happened around 50 million years ago when torrential rains and run-offs from the Canadian and Siberian rivers turned the Arctic Ocean from salty to fresh water. That resulted in a vast bloom of freshwater fern. The Arctic Ocean essentially turned into a plant-choked lake. Henk Brinkhuis, also from Utrecht University, described that "whopping great growth": "When you have so much of this plant in this giant sea, you have a mechanism to pump out carbon dioxide from the atmosphere. It is sort of an anti-greenhouse effect. We argue that this sits right on the break from the really warm hot house period into the time when the ice house begins."[27] Massive climate shifts have happened before and, even without help from man, it is only to be expected that they will happen again.

During the most recent major ice age, which reached its peak only around 20,000 years ago or so, the Arctic's glacial tendrils smothered most of Canada and stretched down into the continental United States as far south as Seattle, Chicago, and Boston. Manhattan was covered by ice. So much water was locked up in ice sheets that global sea levels dropped by as much as 500 feet, and the Bering Strait became a thousand-mile-wide grassy tundra, joining Asia and North America. The region was too dry for glaciers to form, making it an ideal corridor for animals looking for uncovered feeding grounds, and for the humans who hunted them. This land bridge allowed human settlement of the Americas and, within a hundred generations, we made it from Siberia to South America.[28] It was a clear example of climate changing geography changing history.

As a species we have adapted to major changes in the Arctic environment before, but in the past we had more room to maneuver and were more maneuverable. This time Louie and Roland can't just follow the caribou and fish across national boundaries. They can't pack up their airport, school, and health clinic on the back of their four-wheelers and move camp to a more stable environment. This time, their existing way of life, formed in the first place by a changing climate, may not last the century, and they have some heart-wrenching decisions to make.

Meanwhile, the changes in the Arctic aren't just a tragedy for the people trying to live there; they are increasingly being seen as an opportunity for resource extraction. Among the new species migrating up from the south are representatives of the oil and gas industries, miners, and military planners. As the oceans open up, potentially one of the industries with the most to gain in the long term is global shipping. The melting Arctic sea ice opens up a whole new transportation route, the fabled Northwest Passage that weaves through the islands of the Canadian Arctic. It can cut days off travel between the Atlantic and Pacific. The London-Tokyo route alone would be thousands of miles shorter than traveling via either the Panama or Suez Canals. That means huge savings for companies, and a big strategic advantage for those with access. Things worth fighting for.

So, while Louie desperately looks for muskox, some of the largest companies and countries in the world are gearing up to try to bag their own northern trophies. Brave and determined as they are, it's going to take more than Roland and his fellow Rangers to keep that invasion out of the north.

3

THE GLOBAL ECONOMY

WAITING FOR THE SHIP TO COME IN

I am interested in the Panama Canal because I started it. If I had followed traditional, conservative methods I would have submitted a dig-
nified State paper of probably 200 pages to Congress and the debates
on it would have been going on yet; but I took the Canal Zone and let
Congress debate; and while the debate goes on the canal does also.

—President Theodore Roosevelt, on his method
of securing the Panama Canal[1]

And so here we are, in the menswear department of a sprawling department store in a typical, American suburban mall. In
front of us is their version of formal wear: the reasonably
priced suit that can be worn to a first job interview, subsequent family
birthdays, weddings, and funerals—until the endless buffets force us up
a size. We take one of the jackets off the rack. It is well cut, simple and
solid. The tag reads "Made in Russia," but this jacket or, to be precise,
the components of this jacket, have traveled more than most people. The

wool was shorn from sheep in Australia before being shipped to north India, where it was spun into cloth. The lining was made in Korea, the shoulder pads in China, and the buttons in Canada. The pieces came together for the first time in Hamburg, from where they were trucked to Russia. Once in Russia, the pieces were cut and assembled to an Italian design before being shipped here, to this suburb.[2] Each facet of this jacket, from labor to lining, was sourced from the cheapest reliable location on the planet, the way water flows down into crevices and furrows. It is a triumph of globalization, and it is another reason why environmental change in general, and the new sea lanes opened up by the Arctic melt in particular, are going to have a widespread impact.

Shipping is the circulatory system of the global economy. Cheap, reliable shipping. Around 90 percent of world trade products are carried by sea at some point; from the gas in your car, to the car itself, to each individual component of the car, to the shoes you wear when you push the accelerator, to the cell phone you aren't supposed to use when you are stuck in the inevitable traffic surrounded by all the other cars.[3] Nowadays, almost everything comes from somewhere else, usually really, really far away.

Shipping trade is measured in tonne-miles, that is, the amount of tonnes (1 tonne equals just over 1.1 tons) carried, multiplied by the number of miles traveled. In the past 40 years, shipping is estimated to have more than quadrupled, from less than 6 trillion tonne-miles in the early 1960s to more than 33 trillion tonne-miles in 2006. One of the reasons for that jump is the growth of standardized containers, and ships specially built to carry them.[4] Containers were introduced in the 1950s, and by 2004, around 71 percent of general cargo was containerized, with that percentage rapidly increasing. This standardization has speeded up loading, off-loading, and onward shipping. An average ship of 4,000 containers needs the equivalent of 2,000 trucks and 10 trains carrying 200 containers each to unload.[5]

Shipping is big business—just on its own it's estimated to constitute about 5 percent of world trade.[6] Coal moves from North America, Australia, and Southern Africa to power stations in Europe and Asia. Grain goes from the Americas to storehouses in Asia and Africa. Iron ore moves from the Americas to plants in Europe and Asia. Oil goes from the Middle East, South America, and Africa to gas stations in the United States, India, China, and Europe. Consumer products move from Japan, China, Vietnam, and Korea to markets in Europe and the Americas. Only the most basic societies are self-sufficient anymore.

All this redistribution is done in a surprisingly cost-effective manner. The real cost of shipping has dropped by around 80 percent in 25 years because of containerization, bigger ships, and computer-assisted resource allocation.[7] Depending on fuel costs, shipping adds only about 2 percent to the cost of a TV, 1.2 percent for a two-pound bag of coffee, two cents for a gallon of gas, and about the price of a nice matching pocket handkerchief to our reasonably priced suit. As of 2008, moving a tonne of ore from Australia to Europe costs around $12, or the price of a movie ticket in London. Moving a 20-foot container weighing 20 tons from Asia to Europe is about the same price as an economy-class flight on the same route.[8] While shipping is far from perfect, and the technology can still be substantially cleaned up, it is the best way we currently have of moving products around the globe cheaply, quickly, and safely.

It is also a good way to compare markets and see what roles each country plays in the global economy and, as a result, what its geopolitical leverage might be. For example, a look at shipping routes shows how Asia is a key supplier to North America and Europe, with traffic on those trade lanes increasing annually by an estimated 10 to 14 percent and 13.5 to 16.5 percent, respectively, between 2004 and 2006. Meanwhile trade coming from North Europe to North America increased annually just 1.5 to 3.1 percent over the same period (and the United States is Europe's largest export market).[9] The comparison shows that Asia is vastly outstripping

North Europe when it comes to supplying North America, creating a dependence that could later be used to political advantage, but also creating a potential Asian vulnerability to protectionist sentiments or slowdowns in Western markets. This relationship became clear during the financial crisis that started in 2008, when the slowdown in the U.S. (and world) economy resulted in ships lying idle in Asian ports, waiting for orders to pick up again.

However, Asia isn't just exporting, it's also becoming a major factor in international shipping. In 2008, Chinese (including Hong Kong) parent companies controlled the third highest percentage of the world fleet (11.79 percent), after Greece (17.39 percent) and Japan (15.07 percent). By comparison, U.S.-based parent companies controlled 4.93 percent and UK companies controlled 2.73 percent.[10] China isn't just a producer—its exports are speeding along its expansion into the physical infrastructure of global trade. China's ships establish new routes, its government helps developing countries build new ports, and Chinese companies bid low to get port management contracts around the world. The People's Republic is building not only a trade network, but a geostrategic infrastructure. One key element of that infrastructure is control over chokepoints.

Global shipping tends to travel along tried-and-true routes, call in at the same large and efficient ports, and use the same easy-to-navigate and secure sea-lanes. With sea level rise and increasing storm surges, flooding and eroding coastlines will likely affect some of those ports, but most of them can be redesigned. A bigger problem is that the routes themselves have geographic chokepoints, areas that force the wide flow of traffic through narrow, geostrategic alleys. Chokepoints can be natural, such as the Strait of Hormuz, which leads to the oil fields of the Persian Gulf and through which passes around one-third of the world's daily oil supply, or man-made, such as the Panama Canal. These chokepoints are the sorts of thing empires go to war over. They are such important strategic sites that they often end up becoming military bases. Tussles over control of chokepoints and trade routes have escalated into wars and decided empires. And the melting Arctic sea ice and the opening of the Northwest Passage creates new chokepoints of global strategic importance. That is why it is inaccurate to write off the Northwest Passage as simply a "Canadian issue." It is about as much of a "Canadian issue" as the Suez Canal is simply an Egyptian issue.

If shipping starts going through the Northwest Passage, much of it will have to pass through the 53-mile-wide Bering Strait. If the Northeast Passage, along the Russuan Arctic Coast, and Northwest Passage, which passes mostly through the Canadian Arctic, become major routes for Arctic oil and gas to reach markets, the Bering Strait could become another Strait of Hormuz. As the natural western entrance point into the Arctic, it is the ideal location to verify that ships passing through are sound enough for the potentially rough voyage, to make sure that they are not a security threat, and even possibly to set up a toll to cover the increased costs of northern security, search-and-rescue, and clean-up efforts (an equivalent eastern entrance could be set up in the Faroe Islands, Iceland, Greenland, Scotland or Canada, and could double as a cargo transit hub). While the Northwest Passage primarily cuts through Canada, the country has no hold over the Bering Strait. On one side the strait belongs to the United States, on the other, to Russia. As it stands, Canada doesn't have much of a say over the future of the Bering Strait, but that could, and should, change. Otherwise, it's as if Canada has a front door to which only the United States and Russia have keys. The United States doesn't seem to think the door is worth keeping locked, preferring instead to invite one and all to wander through at will. Some have yet to fully realize that, being adjacent to Canada, its security is being compromised as well.

To understand the stakes, and the likely maneuvering in the Arctic as the Passage thaws, it helps to look at the recent history of two of the world's major chokepoints: the Suez and Panama Canals. Conveniently, though perhaps not coincidentally, an examination of who controlled these two chokepoints, and how that control ended, gives insight into the broad brushstrokes of global politics in the nineteenth and twentieth centuries, and helps to understand and set the stage for what might happen in the twenty-first. Both chokepoints helped to create, perpetuate, and possibly foreshadow the end of empires. This is not only about dominance over two trade routes and who gets to sell, metaphorically speaking, the cheaper suit, but it also is about having critical strategic advantage. By looking at Suez and Panama, we can see what the opening of the Northwest Passage might really mean for the global balance of power in the twenty-first century.

4

A SHORT HISTORY OF MODERN GEOPOLITICS, AS SEEN FROM THE DECK OF A SHIP

There was nothing but Suez, Suez, Suez, morning, noon and night in Number 10.

—Lady Eden, wife of British prime minister
Sir Anthony Eden, on the Suez Crisis of 1956[1]

The Suez Canal has long been a critical chokepoint on the supply routes between Europe and eastern Africa, the Middle East, and Asia. It is essentially a 101-mile-long man-made river, created to link the Mediterranean and the Red Sea, and was built with mostly French money and Egyptian forced labor. Opened to traffic in 1869, when European powers were fighting for global influence, the canal had an immediate impact on geopolitics and trade.[2]

Britain, the dominant naval power of the nineteenth century, used the Suez Canal to increase the speed with which it could get products and troops in and out of its restive colonies, and to boost trade with the home market. The effect of the shortcut was like giving the empire a turbo charge. By 1880, British traffic accounted for 80 percent of the tonnage on the canal.[3] Due to its obvious geostrategic importance to the British Empire, and in order to limit other European powers from having the same advantage, in 1882 Britain used local unrest as a pretext to occupy Egypt and take outright control of the canal. One can get a glimpse of the military advantage Britain derived from the canal. It used Indian troops that had already been transported to Portsmouth, England, via the canal, to quickly go to Egypt and help put down the rebellion.[4]

Other European nations wanted the same access to their colonies. In 1888, various powers assembled at the Convention of Constantinople and optimistically declared the canal should be open to all ships of all countries, both in times of peace and war. Not surprisingly, Britain didn't sign on. It continued to use access to the canal to tweak global politics to its advantage, aiding allies and hindering competitors. During the Spanish-American War (1898), Spanish ships were turned back. Meanwhile, Italians heading down to invade Ethiopia (1935–36) were let through, and Germany and its allies were blocked during both World Wars.[5]

After World War II, the canal became an engine of trade and, by 1955, two-thirds of Europe's oil passed through the Suez. But something had changed. The war had left the old European empires in states of ruin. In a period not dissimilar to the one we are going through now, the collapse of old structures created a state of flux and left openings for new power bases to emerge. Postwar anti-colonialism became a strong force, one by one colonies sought independence, and nationalist movements around the world gained momentum. A new, amorphous power center, that of nationalistic public opinion, had been created and was about to become a major force. That said, countries may have been striving for independence, but they still needed development money and access to international markets, leaving them vulnerable to international pressure. In 1956, the United States and the United Kingdom decided not to finance the Aswan Dam in order to put pressure on newly independent Egypt to cut ties with the Soviet Union. Instead of immediately buckling, Egyptian president Gamal Abdel Nasser announced he was going to nationalize the British- and French-controlled Suez Canal Company, pay shareholders market price for their holdings, then use the canal toll fees to pay for the dam.

The UK and France weren't amused. It wasn't just a matter of coming to terms with the fact that their empires were disintegrating; it was that suddenly, due to their reliance on the Suez chokepoint, *they* were now the vulnerable ones. British Prime Minister Anthony Eden, concerned about the flow of oil supplies, told colleagues that he would not allow Nasser to "have his thumb on our windpipe."[6] The French, already bitter about Nasser's support of the Algerian nationalist independence movement, were furious. The canal became a focal point for British and French concern over their reduced post-War influence, and they started drawing up military plans to get it back.

The United States urged a more multilateral approach. President Dwight D. Eisenhower argued for more international consensus before invading. In a letter to Prime Minister Eden, he made two things clear: first, that the age of overtly ignoring public opinion was waning; and second, that he well understood the importance of the Suez chokepoint and shipping route:

> We recognize the transcendent worth of the Canal to the free world and the possibility that eventually the use of force might become necessary in order to protect international rights. [. . .] [But, without showing every peaceful means of resolving the impasse had been exhausted], there would be a reaction that could very seriously affect our peoples' feeling toward our Western Allies. I do not want to exaggerate, but I assure you

that this could grow to such an intensity as to have the most far reaching consequences. [. . .] [Should negotiations fail] then world opinion would understand how earnestly all of us had attempted to be just, fair and considerate, but that we simply could not accept a situation that would in the long run prove disastrous to the prosperity and living standards of every nation whose economy depends directly or indirectly upon East-West shipping.[7]

Eden's reply was clear. He didn't feel he could trust Nasser and the Egyptian nationalists. He wanted control of the canal, and he wanted regime change. It was to be the last big throw of the dice for the go-it-alone, nineteenth-century-style European powers—and it was all over a shipping route.

British reservists were called up, and the Bank of England made plates for a currency to be used during the occupation. Eden wrote to Eisenhower, "The removal of Nasser and the installation in Egypt of a regime less hostile to the West, must [. . .] rank high among our objectives. You know us better than anyone, and so I need not tell you that our people here are neither excited nor eager to use force. They are, however, grimly determined that Nasser shall not get away with it this time because they are convinced that if he does their existence will be at his mercy. So am I."[8]

The UK and France found an ally in Israel, also partially for shipping route reasons. Israel was being blocked by Egypt from using the Straits of Tiran—a chokepoint for Israel, as it is the country's only access to the Red Sea.

The complex operation was launched on October 29, 1956, when Israel invaded Egypt to set up a pretext for subsequent European intervention. Israeli troops advanced quickly toward the canal, almost too quickly. They had to hold back or risk ruining the plan. As secretly arranged, the UK and France demanded that Israel and Egypt withdraw from the canal so that they could "save" it under the aegis of the UN. Within a week they had arrived to take control of the canal. But the world had changed. There was loud public opposition at home, from the UN, and from the Soviets. But the real problem for the UK was that there was a run on the pound, and the United States refused to back an International Monetary Fund loan to bail them out.

Under pressure, the UK and France completed their pull-out on December 22, 1956, tails firmly between their legs. Eden resigned in January 1957. The age of European powers overtly playing the Great Game on their own was over.[9] The loss was a huge shock, especially to the UK. It was now clear that advice from the U.S. president would have to be taken much, much more seriously. The Suez Crisis wasn't the cause, but it made the UK's and France's positions clear: They had literally lost their chokehold on world affairs.

The Suez Crisis forced a reexamination within Europe's security establishments. The British reacted, in part, by forging a stronger relationship with the United States, even if it meant not necessarily being the senior partner on all endeavors. The situation had so changed by 1961 that, when the UK felt its Hong Kong colony might be threatened by China, it asked the United States to show muscle on its behalf by "encouraging" China to believe the United States would defend the British possession with a nuclear strike.[10] Meanwhile, the French embedded themselves in Europe and worked toward developing a European Union that could have more leverage vis-à-vis the United States. Both the UK and France continued to try to apply international pressure for perceived national gain (which is their job as national governments), but in more quiet ways, and in areas that didn't risk U.S. reprobation.

Meanwhile, Nasser became the poster boy of Egyptian, and Arab, nationalism until Egypt's defeat by Israel in 1967. And the canal? Well, today around 7.5 percent of world trade passes through the Suez, including much of Europe's oil supply.[11] The United States followed through on its plan to keep the canal open and safe for the West through non-military means. As of 2004 Egypt was the third largest recipient of U.S. aid, after Iraq and Israel.[12] The Suez Crisis was a decisive turning point in twentieth-century geopolitics, and the importance of shipping routes and geostrategic chokepoints has only increased since then.

Europe may have dominated in the nineteenth century, but the United States was already gaining influence. Its reach first expanded regionally, in the Americas, and another massive man-made environmental change, the Panama Canal, was as critical for U.S. development as the Suez Canal was for Britain.

The Panama Canal is a 101-mile-long chokepoint in the middle of the Americas that connects the Atlantic and Pacific. Without it, ships traveling between the East and West Coast of the United States would have to route down across the tip of South America. The canal cuts the travel distance by over 9,300 miles. Depending on the route, the Northwest Passage could cut traveling distances between the Atlantic and Pacific by substantially more. If the Northwest Passage becomes easily navigable, the Panama Canal is the route it is most likely to replace, at least during the summers, when the Passage would be ice-free. Therefore it's worth reviewing the Panama Canal's value to the United States from economic and security perspectives. There are marked parallels with the relationship between the United States and Panama Canal, and Britain and the Suez Canal.

The Panama Canal was built by the United States between 1904 and 1914, in part so the United States could have easier control over its new territories in the Caribbean and Pacific. The canal's strategic importance made it almost inevitable that control over the chokepoint would spark conflict. In fact, the canal started a war even before it was built. Panama used to be part of Colombia but, when the Colombian senate refused to ratify a treaty that would give the United States sovereignty over a strip of its country across the Isthmus of Panama in order to build the canal, the United States encouraged friendly locals to "revolt" and demand independence, sending war ships to make the point even clearer. The new republic of Panama was formally declared in November 1903. Three days later, the new country signed a treaty with the United States granting it exclusive control of the Canal Zone, in perpetuity. The Canal Zone included not only the soon-to-be built canal itself, but approximately five miles on either side of it. Between 1903 and 1979 this colonial-style possession was directly administered by a governor appointed by the U.S. president, and the majority of the thousands of people who lived in the Zone were Americans.[13] It was U.S. territory, slicing through the heart of a foreign country.

By the 1960s, anti-colonial movements were springing up all over the world, and the U.S. control of the Canal Zone rankled many Panamanians, especially in light of Nasser's success over the Suez. It didn't take much to focus discontent. In January 1964 American students illegally and provocatively flew the U.S. flag at their Canal Zone high school. Riots broke out. But, unlike the French and British in the Suez, the United States was on the rise, and perfectly able to control the situation on its own. In this second fight over the canal, the American military was mobilized and, when it was over, more than 20 Panamanians were dead and the United States was in complete command of the Zone.[14] In a touch of geopolitical pantomime, Britain and France rushed to the front row of nations chastising U.S. heavy-handedness. They were ignored. But the new power of public opinion spurred the United States to make a quiet shift in policy.

In a 1970 interview, Dean Rusk, the U.S. secretary of state in both the Kennedy and Johnson administrations, explained the importance of the canal to the United States. His position foreshadows some of the current U.S. thinking over the Northwest Passage (a need to have both security and efficient access for commerce, in one politically palatable package): "We have only two basic interests in the Panama Canal—the one is its security and the other is its efficient operation—and our view was that so long as the security of the canal and its operational responsibility remained more or less in American hands that we could take almost any changes in the theory of our presence there that the Panamanians would insist upon."[15]

For Panama, the U.S. government's shift in policy toward a more media-friendly relationship (possibly because of the geopolitical fallout of the Vietnam War) meant that two new treaties were signed in 1977.[16] In one treaty, the United States agreed to hand over the canal to Panama in 2000. That's the "changes in the theory" part of Rusk's statement. The other contained a condition that: "[T]he US retains the permanent right to defend the canal from any threat that might interfere with its continued neutral service to ships of all nations [. . .] Panama and the US, acting alone or jointly, may defend the canal against any threat and defend the peaceful transit of vessels through it [and] both US and Panamanian warships entering the canal may go to the head of the line if necessary."[17] That's the "more or less in American hands" part of Rusk's statement.

This is likely the sort of arrangement some in the United States (and Canada) would like for the Northwest Passage—a secure and efficient route more or less under U.S. control but with a recognizable role for Canada.

By December 20, 1989, the U.S. militarily intervened in Panama for the third time. It's hard to know exactly why the United States moved in. It's possible that the timing of the invasion had something to do with the fact that leadership of the administration of the canal was due to shift to the Panamanians in 1990. The invasion was officially called Operation Just Cause, but some waggish Pentagon planners dubbed it Operation Just Because.[18] At least 200 Panamanian civilians and more than 20 U.S.

soldiers died. Panamanian leader General Manuel Noriega was taken into U.S. custody.[19]

If the invasion was meant to keep the canal under direct U.S. control, it didn't work. That may have been because soon direct control seemed unnecessary. By the time the United States eventually handed over the canal to Panama in 2000, the world had changed. The Cold War was over. To many Americans, it seemed as though the United States was the sole superpower, and likely to stay that way for the foreseeable future. If so, the need for direct oversight was lessened. There didn't seem to be anyone else who could take the canal from it, and by treaty the United States had the right to come back at any time.

The U.S. approach to the canal shifted away from security and veered toward commercial interests. This was part of a global sea change in which areas that had been the preserve of the security establishment were suddenly open for business. What were once strategic assets became just more commodities. Canadian researchers bought Soviet weaponry, U.S. corporations invested in oil and gas concessions in what only years before had been off-limits areas of the USSR, and China, well, China saw the world differently and started in on one of the most strategic buying sprees the world has ever seen.

If the United States wants direct control over the Panama Canal again, it will find the situation much more complicated than the one it encountered in 1989 during Operation Just Cause. That's because a new player, with its own style of creating and using power, is now on the global stage. Following the overt force of nineteenth-century Europe in the Suez, and the late-twentieth-century "you are independent in theory" U.S. treaties in Panama, one of the centers of twenty-first-century geopolitics, China, is using its own approach to projecting power. Its method, best described as nationalistic capitalism, can be seen in the way it got effective control of that still-important chokepoint, the Panama

Canal. The shift wasn't as dramatic as the Suez Crisis, but it was enlightening, and potentially as far reaching.

The needs of great powers are similar. It usually doesn't take long before the growing center outstrips locally available resources, resulting in a reliance on imported raw materials and commodities. Disruption in that supply can lead to vulnerabilities. Take, for example, crops. Products that the West considers commodities, such as grain, China (and others) considers strategic assets. For the sake of civil order, the Chinese Communist Party (CCP) needs to ensure food is affordable. It cannot allow the market to dictate access if doing so risks compromising domestic stability. If high food prices were a blip, China could probably ride it out, but a quick survey of the factors that have gone into the recent price increases, not the least of which are major environmental changes, show that this will likely be a protracted crisis.[20]

Between March 2007 and March 2008, the price of rice increased 74 percent, soya (a primary protein for many) rose 87 percent, and wheat went up 130 percent. It is often said that as crop production stagnates or declines, and populations increase, those in the developing world will be hardest hit. While this may be true to some degree, China, for one, is working toward creating a major geoeconomic shift that will help it secure a supply of various strategic essentials, including food.

Typically, countries have two parallel economic policies: domestic and international. For example, when it comes to its domestic market, the United States may tend toward subsidies, especially in areas like agriculture, but internationally it pushes for free markets.

Conversely, domestically China is a something of an economic Wild West (there is a lot of latitude as long as the CCP doesn't disapprove), but internationally most major Chinese-owned companies work with the Chinese government (sometimes at a loss) in order to advance China's national strategic interests. When it comes to international agreements, China practices capitalism, but it is a nationalistic capitalism.

Countries practicing nationalistic capitalism can sign nation-to-nation package deals that cut out the open market and overtly link much-needed resources to wide-ranging agreements on other goods and services, including military equipment. For example, while many in the West were trying to isolate the Sudanese government, China was taking advantage of the lack of competition to craft comprehensive trade deals with those in power. As of 2007, China was the biggest foreign investor in Sudan, buying much of its oil and, according to an Amnesty International report, supplying the government with weaponry, training, and infrastructure.[21] As a result, China secured Sudanese oil before it reached the market.

In an era of food supply scarcity, where authoritarian regimes in particular need to make sure their populations are fed for the sake of domestic stability (democracies have the safety valve of elections), crops are likely to be increasingly included in nation-to-nation package agreements. For example, one would expect China to start including food crops in its growing number of deals with African nations, which could explain part of China's long-standing support for Robert Mugabe in that potential breadbasket, Zimbabwe. Already in countries such as Laos, Indonesia, and Cambodia, Chinese companies are farming products destined to be shipped straight back to China. What that means is that large quantities of wheat, corn, rice, etc., will never make it to the open market, restricting supply and potentially making it even more expensive for those relying on the marketplace, such as many in the West, to feed themselves. Countries that simply rely on the market and regional partners for resources could find themselves suddenly caught short.

This sort of nationalistic capitalism seems to be spreading, with countries such as South Korea also trying to set up fully controlled food supplies farmed on foreign lands. South Korea's Daewoo Logistics made such a large-scale grab for land in Madagascar that the local population became enraged and it contributed to toppling the government there. China took the hint and has released several statements trying to distance itself from the idea that it is taking food out of the mouths of starving Africans.

In many ways, and in many sectors, nationalistic capitalism is changing the relationship between economics, politics, and security. Another one of those sectors is trade routes. In the colonial model, during the early Suez days, securing trade routes was often done by incorporating colonies and chokepoints to some degree or another into the body politic of the metropolitan power. Afterward, as was seen with the Panama Canal, control over the route was demonstrated more by treaty. Now, often, control is manifested through the marketplace. This gives an advantage to nationalist capitalist countries, which are willing to bid at a loss to secure a national benefit. If an asset is up for tender and is seen as being strategically important to a national capitalist country such as China, whether it be agricultural acreage or a chokepoint, government-linked companies will try to put in the best bid, even if winning the tender could mean the company will lose money. The result is that, when the West shifted certain sectors from strategic assets to commercial interests in the 1990s, it opened up whole new areas for national capitalist countries to gain a toehold. China's interests, for one, are now quietly advancing through the market system, rather than through potentially more contentious or overt routes.

A good example of this is what happened to the Panama Canal. When Panama regained control of the canal they put its management out for tender. A Chinese company, Hutchison Port Holdings (HPH), won the contract. In China, major companies have ties to the government. And HPH, which runs many of the most significant civilian maritime installations and is the largest port operator in the world, is definitely a major company. According to Hutchison's website, "Since 1994, HPH has expanded globally to strategic locations in twenty-one countries throughout Asia, the Middle East, Africa, Europe and the Americas."[22] HPH runs ports in Saudi Arabia, Egypt, Pakistan, Thailand, Myanmar, Indonesia, and Malaysia. It has Thamesport (just outside London), Felixstowe (the biggest port in the UK), and Harwich (well located for North Sea freight, something that could become more important with opening of the Northwest Passage). HPH also has contracts to run the largest inland port in the world (in Germany), a port in the Bahamas that is a major transshipment point for the eastern coast of the Americas, Grand Bahamas Airport (the largest privately owned airport in the world), and Ensenada, which, also according to Hutchison's website: "is strategically situated 110 kilometers [74 miles] south of the U.S.-Mexico border along the Pacific Ocean."[23]

From China's point of view, why risk Suez-style debacles, or become an unpopular occupier, when instead you can be *subsidized* to run some of the world's most strategic ports and chokepoints, including the Panama Canal? Tie that to China's enormous shipping fleet and the result is a global maritime reach and Chinese resupply depots scattered strategically all over the globe, including in the middle of the Americas. China could also quietly use its influence in Panama to close the canal, forcing U.S. military and supply ships heading from the Atlantic to the Pacific to detour through the rough seas off the tip of South America. One of the big concerns that the United States had during Just Cause was that the Panamanian Defense Force itself would sabotage the canal (it's easier to destroy a canal than to keep it open, which is another reason why, once the Northwest Passage becomes navigable, it becomes exceptionally valuable: It can't be blown up).[24] China's strategic investments are an intelligent policy and have raised concern among some U.S. strategists. In some countries it's gone beyond mere concern. India has no Hutchison-operated installations. HPH put in bids for ports in Mumbai and Chennai, but it was turned down because it "failed to get the security clearance from the Indian government."[25]

China's method of using its international investments to strategically shore up the home front extends to other fields as well. By and large,

China has been less interested in the sort of Western-oriented purchases that saw waves of Japanese, Russian, and Middle Eastern investments in prestige buys like Manhattan and London real estate, Western art, and high-end hotels, much of which lost value with the recent global financial crisis. While far from immune from the crash, China tended to focus on buying, managing, and building long-term strategic investments. Often, Chinese government–linked companies are investing overseas in essential commodities (food, mining, lumber, etc.), as well as transport infrastructure.

The energy sector, in particular oil and gas production, is an area where it is easy to see the spreading strength of nationalistic capitalism. Outside the West there is a growing movement toward effectively nationalizing fossil fuel resources, as seen in Russia, Venezuela, Bolivia, and elsewhere. In Saudi Arabia and other Middle East oil-producing states, the political elite have always controlled the taps. Oil and gas supplies are tremendously potent political tools, and nations practicing this sort of nationalistic capitalism are much more powerful on the world stage than they might be otherwise. No one would think much about Venezuela if its oil was simply being extracted by multinationals and sold on the open market, but when its leaders talk about using its oil to subsidize one country or cut off another, people pay attention. Even the government of Norway has kept close relations with Norway-based StatoilHydro and, through it, the major oil and gas developments in the north.

That sort of integration between political power and fuel also means that countries with a nationalistic capitalist approach can overtly link energy supplies to wide-ranging deals, including military alliances. One oil company executive told me that Western-based oil companies used to be the ones that brokered the deals, representing both suppliers and buyers. Increasingly, the deals are being done directly between governments, with the oil companies being reduced to running the infrastructure. The executive I spoke with was concerned about the future role of his company. That sort of shift toward nationalistic capitalism in the energy sector was clearly at play in Russia when, in 2006, the government forced Shell to sell it the majority share of the Sakhalin gas field. Michael Bradshaw, an expert on the energy project, was quoted as saying: "There's a new reality in Russia. Majority foreign-owned investment doesn't work anymore."[26] Neither do political power plays. Clifford Gaddy, a Brookings Institution scholar, described the new relationship with Russia as: "We [the United States] have zero leverage. The only leverage we ever had on the Russians was the financial dependence of Russia in the late 1980s and 1990s. With the current oil boom, that is gone."[27] While lower oil prices can lessen Russian domestic solvency and international influence, simply controlling the resource provides geopolitical benefits. Most countries import oil and/or gas and want to make friends with nations that can provide a secure supply.

The situation is very different for the United States and other countries where oil and other strategic industries are not beholden to the government. For example, while the United States talks about the need for domestic oil security, one report found that one company "had systematically jacked up West Coast oil prices by exporting Alaska crude to Asia."[28] In 2005, Senator Ron Wyden (Democrat-OR) tried to get an amendment to ban oil exports attached to the legislation allowing drilling in the Alaskan National Wildlife Refuge. It was rejected. Wyden summed it up: "Exporting Arctic oil overseas does not reduce our nation's dependence on foreign oil one drop. In failing to adopt this measure today, the Committee has missed an important opportunity to boost American energy security and head off price manipulations."[29]

Countries in which national security policy makers don't have control over energy supplies (which is globally acknowledged as a national security issue) are geopolitically more vulnerable than more economically and politically integrated nations. A Russian government that has the ability to cut off energy supplies to Europe is much more powerful than one that simply gets a drilling fee from transiting multinationals. It may not be desirable, but it's a geopolitical reality. For example, concern over energy supplies would have made it even more difficult for the EU to intervene in any substantive way in the Russia-Georgia war of 2008. Additionally, in an increasingly shifting world due to resource scarcity caused by environmental change, control over energy sources is a substantial negotiating advantage.

Governments that propound the market-is-always-right line find the new reality infuriating. Just before the 2006 G8 summit, Canadian prime minister Stephen Harper made his position clear by saying "[W]e believe in the free exchange of energy products based on competitive market principles, not self-serving monopolistic political strategies."[30] In May 2007, U.S. secretary of state Condoleezza Rice said: "I think everybody around the world, in Europe, in the United States, is very concerned, [. . .] the concentration of power in the Kremlin has been troubling."[31] However, many national governments don't see what's wrong with being self-serving, and more and more countries are going that route, including ones that are perceived as part of, or allies of, the West, such as Norway and South Korea. Those that don't are finding it harder to compete.

An interesting element of nationalistic capitalism is its implicit long-term perspective. Nationalistic capitalism is fundamentally about building alliances and creating domestic stability over the long run, rather than maneuvering for short-term advantage. That can be seen in the different approaches to negotiations. I've heard top-level negotiators from major developing nations say that they don't like dealing with the U.S. government because it adopts a "salami slicer" approach, promising one thing but then whittling it away to something substantially reduced. Sometimes the United States explains the change by claiming that without it, various interest groups would pressure Congress into not signing. Sometimes the changes happen even after the deal is agreed upon. Sometimes there are repeated court challenges, particularly with trade issues such as the U.S.-Canada softwood lumber dispute. This may lead to immediate payoffs for the United States, but it can also affect perceptions of the United States as a long-term partner.

Meanwhile, British and Indian business people say that they like dealing with China because it negotiates hard, its interests are clear (what is good for China), and it generally sticks to the deal and delivers what is promised. As former U.S. defense secretary William Cohen put it, "That's why it's so easy to do business in China. It has dictatorial powers and they can say, here's the agreement, let's sign it, let's do it."[32] But delivering on promises is not simply the difference between a dictatorship and a democracy. Some democracies, especially those that value multilateral ties and prioritize domestic security, make a deal and stick with it. Democratic India, for example, while not a signatory of the Non-Proliferation Treaty, never proliferated its nuclear weapons. In spite of its promises, Pakistan, a dictatorship, did. The difference is that India generally has a strong nationalist agenda and a long-term view. As a result, it is trying to build many, and varied, multilateral ties. That takes trust. And that means sticking to your word.

All in all, this means countries practicing nationalistic capitalism have an advantage when dealing with "free market" nations, and can also be perceived as better partners, especially in the developing world. China, for example, is trying to position itself as the leader of the developing world. In its dealings with Asian, African, and Latin American countries, China presents itself as a nation that was a fellow "victim of Western colonialism," and now just wants to help fellow developing nations to grow without the sort of political and economic interference that the West has tied to aid. True or not, it's been an appealing message, especially to some of the more repressive nations such as Sudan and Mugabe's Zimbabwe.

As for the deals themselves, China is largely interested in buying raw commodities, fossil fuels, and, increasingly, food supplies. Meanwhile, much of China's foreign aid, driven by nationalistic capitalism, seems to be directed toward building transport infrastructure, such as railways in Africa. As a country that has developed an enormous amount of internal infrastructure very quickly, China has ample quantities of the technical skills and trained workers needed for massive construction projects abroad. By building and managing critical infrastructure in developing nations, China not only shows a tangible interest in cooperation (which is strategically useful) but it also gains valuable on-the-ground political influence and speeds up access to vital resources destined for the Chinese market.

China's method of using aid and markets forces for strategic advantage can be effective. As a result, for the United States, taking on China over the Panama Canal (or elsewhere) would be much more costly than taking on Panama. It's not just nationalistic capitalism. While the Chinese economy used to orbit around the U.S. economy, the gravitational pull is shifting. In 2007, U.S. exports to China totaled $65.2 billion, while Chinese exports to the United States totaled $321.4 billion.[33] Those ships full of cheap Chinese goods sustained the American lifestyle. And, as the United States spent itself into unimaginable debt, China became the largest holder of U.S. Treasury securities. As of June 2009, China held $776.4 billion in Treasury securities, up from $535.1 billion just a year earlier.[34] The trend had been developing for a while. In 2005, *The Economist* wrote, "China is beginning to drive, in a new and pervasive way, economic trends that many countries assume to be domestically determined."[35] Others, like Ian Williams writing in the *Asia Times* in 2004, were even more blunt: "[I]f push came to shove [. . .] all Beijing has to do is to mention the possibility of a sell order going down the wires. It would devastate the US economy more than any nuclear strike the Chinese could manage at the moment."[36]

Through the intertwining of economies and China's strategic focus, power is imperceptibly shifting away from the United States. A conflict with China would mean U.S. businesses would suffer enormously, which, in the current American climate that still largely favors commerce over security, hamstrings U.S. national security policy makers. Of course, it would also have a huge economic effect on China—a potential mutually assured economic destruction. But China, being authoritarian and therefore not subject to government-changing votes, can likely absorb more disruption and is buttressed by its broad range of economic bilateral deals. It also may be willing to suffer more in the short term if it advances the long-term goals of the nation, as envisioned by the ruling elite of the Chinese Communist Party. And what are those goals? Well, the main one is for China to become a, if not *the*, dominant world power.

As we saw with the UK in Suez and the U.S. in Panama, control over, or at least unfettered access to, key maritime routes and chokepoints is extremely helpful for projecting both commercial and strategic power. With a new route through the Arctic still in the process of forming, those with a viable plan may have the advantage. The way China used market forces to position itself in the Panama Canal showed that its use of nationalistic capitalism as a strategic lever can be effective. China is still a long way from controlling shipping routes and resources the way the British Empire did in the nineteenth century and the United States did in the twentieth century (and still does to a large extent). But if the West continues to put short-term commercial interests above long-term security interests, it is leaving the door open for some dramatic geopolitical shifts. And the Arctic may play an important role in those shifts, given its chokepoints, valuable shipping routes, abundant resources, and fossil fuels. We are just starting to see who might benefit—or be harmed—by the opening up of the Northwest Passage. Right now, it is North America's to lose. And, as of now, it seems to be doing just that.

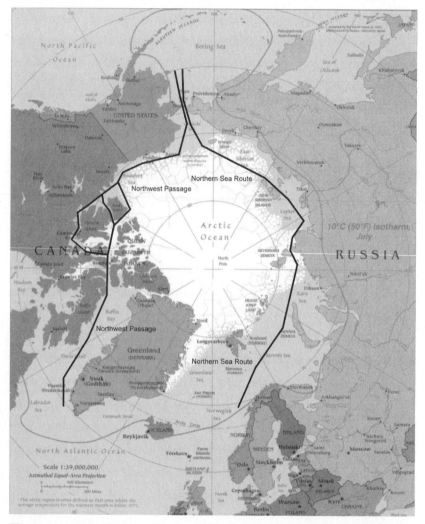

The Arctic, with the Northwest Passage and Northern Sea Route (Northeast Passage).
CREATED/PUBLISHED: Washington, D.C., Central Intelligence Agency, 2007.
Addition of Northwest Passage and Northern Sea Route by Justin Estrela-Reis.

THE GREAT COLD RUSH OF '08

I know your feelings on the present state of the world, and hope they will be cheered by the successful course of our war, and the addition of Canada to our confederacy.

—Letter from U.S. president Thomas Jefferson
to General Kosciusko, June 1812[1]

We cannot leave these northern treasures to a bunch of bilingual draft dodgers [Canada] and socialist herring fiends [Denmark]. We must claim this new frontier for America, plant our flag, suck out the fossil fuels, and convert the puffins to Christianity!

—Stephen Colbert, *The Colbert Report*, March 2007[2]

While European powers created the Suez Canal, and the United States created the Panama Canal, it is climate change that is opening up the Northwest Passage. Perhaps that's why many policy makers have been caught off guard. Over a century and a half after British explorer Sir John Franklin died for queen and country trying to find this geostrategic route from the Atlantic to the Pacific over the top of North America, it suddenly just appeared.

The Northwest Passage is a catch-all term for one of several sea routes between the Atlantic and Pacific that passes mostly through the Canadian Arctic. It was the Holy Grail of early explorers. For Europeans, it was a dreamt-of shortcut to the riches of Asia, and a way to get their navies there in order to secure those riches. Many died trying to find it. And some died trying to find the people who died trying to find it.[3] But given the ships of the day, and the climate, the passage didn't really exist then. It does now. As the ice melts, the route becomes more and more navigable. By 2050, and possibly decades earlier, it may well be completely free of summer ice.[4] In the summer of 2008, the first commercial ship traveled through the eastern part of the Passage to deliver supplies to remote Arctic communities in Northern Canada. A general manager of the shipping line said: "I didn't see one cube of ice" on the trip.[5] Russian ships are also testing the route.

Traveling between Asia and Europe through the Northwest Passage may prove days faster, and much cheaper, than current routes. For example, the distance from London to Tokyo via Panama is approximately 14,300 miles; through the Suez Canal it is approximately 13,000 miles; through northern Canada, it is approximately less than 10,000 miles.[6] And there are no locks or inspection sites. Major Asia-Europe military, illegal aliens, equipment, contraband, and other movement would prefer to pass through this hard-to-monitor area rather than the slow, regulated, and easy-to-cripple Panama Canal. As a result, deciding who, if anyone, controls the route becomes very important indeed. It is a shipping route that dreams, and empires, are made on. It is geography making history, writ large.

What that might mean for northern Canada is already being seen in northern Russia. The Russian Northeast Passage (also called the Northern Sea Route) runs along the north coast of Russia, linking ports in Europe and Asia.[7] It has been clearing a lot faster than the Canadian North-west Passage, in part because of the way the Arctic winds pack the float-ing ice into the Canadian coast. Also, while the Russian shoreline is more or less straightforward, the Canadian coast disintegrates into a mass of is-lands, creating ample nooks to snag and hold the ice.[8] The end result is that Russia has a head start—and is using it.

It's hard to overestimate how the thawing of the Russian route alone could affect political alliances. Just over a hundred years ago, in 1904, Russia sent its Baltic fleet to defend its possessions in China from Japan. At that point, the Northeast route was still impassible. The best option was a shortcut through the Suez Canal, but Britain controlled the canal and was an ally of Japan. Since Russia worried that Britain would use its chokepoint for geopolitical advantage and take the Russian fleet hostage in transit, only a few of the smaller vessels went through the canal. The rest made the nearly 18,000-mile detour from Russia, around the UK (where they almost started a war by firing on British fishing ships they thought were Japanese torpedo boats), down below the tip of Africa and India, until they finally reached Asia. They arrived about nine months later with barnacle-covered ships and exhausted crews. The Japanese de-stroyed them in hours.[9] Reinforcements weren't on the way.

With the melt, Russia and China (and the rest of Asia) will seem a lot closer to each other, and to North America and Europe. As the sea route opens, and land routes built on permafrost become unreliable, it is pos-sible that Asia-Europe shipping over the top of Russia, on Russian terms, will become more common. Russia and China are already coming to-gether more than ever for other geopolitical reasons, including a mutual desire to erode Western influence in Asia and beyond. The opening of the Northeast Passage just makes that process easier.

And it's not just the route itself that is garnering geopolitical at-tention. Important mineral and fossil-fuel resources might also become more accessible. While it is difficult to know for sure the size of the deposits, the U.S. Geological Survey estimates that the Arctic might contain up to a quarter of all undiscovered oil and gas reserves.[10] Other estimates put it at closer to 40 percent—Siberia alone could have as much oil as the Middle East.[11]

The melt is speeding up access to Russia's vast northern oil and gas reserves, thus increasing its geopolitical leverage. Russia's Shtokman field is potentially the largest offshore gas field in the world.[12] As a result, when oil prices are high, Russia's northern towns boom. Murmansk, on the Arctic coast, has an ice-free harbor, a population of 325,000, and is a major base for the Russian shipping and military fleets. It also has an important fishing fleet. As environmental change and chronic over-fishing stress the oceanic ecosystems, fish stocks will become even more valuable, and the Arctic might have a good portion of the dwindling global supply, especially as coldwater fish, like cod, move north.

That said, dreams of a big resources bonanza in the north with new ports and rail routes to the south are extremely premature. The northern environment is brutal and becoming unpredictable. Norway's northern Snohvit gas field ended up costing almost 50 percent more than the original budget, and, in the fall of 2006, North Sea storms sunk a 500-foot Swedish cargo ship and caused one oil rig to break away from its tow and be set adrift off the coast of Norway.[13] As one North Sea oil industry executive told me in 2008, "We've had our third 'once-in-a-hundred-year' storm so far this year."[14] Also, during the melt period, there will be more icebergs for offshore rigs to deal with, not less,[15] and, with warmer and wetter air freezing and thawing more often, ships, aircraft, and infrastructure icing will become more common.[16]

One of the biggest problems is that the thawing of the permafrost is going to devastate infrastructure in the North.[17] Already, pipelines, roads, ports, airports, and entire communities are at risk of imminent structural damage and possible permanent loss. An oil storage tank on unstable permafrost can do untold damage. In 2006, one of China's top permafrost experts who was involved in the multibillion-dollar Tibet railway, partly built on hundreds of miles of Himalayan permafrost, said, "Every day I think about whether the railway will have problems in the next ten to twenty years."[18] He was right to be worried. Not long after opening, sections of the foundation started sinking.[19] In cold climates, industrial equipment is often moved in the winter on iceroads (frozen lakes and rivers that can support the weight), and on the frozen tundra. In some parts of the Arctic, the number of drivable days on the tundra has halved since 1970.

Not only does environmental change create challenges for new resource extraction, but existing operations (such as diamond mines that rely on iceroads and pipelines laid over what is now permafrost but may soon be mudflats) also will likely need to be reassessed. In August 2006, the world got a small peek at a possible future when a BP pipeline in Alaska corroded and broke. While not a direct result of environmental change, the event gave an indication of the sort of vulnerabilities that may become more likely as the permafrost thaws under the pipelines. The line carried close to 2.6 percent of the U.S. daily supply, and the closure created an immediate spike in oil prices and futures. The government considered releasing emergency stockpiles and the Alaska government faced a financial crunch.[20]

With environmental change, infrastructure problems are likely to become more common. Pipelines, like railway lines and transmission wires, are only as good as their weakest point. If one section goes out, delivery is disrupted. It is going to take a major investment in permafrost and Arctic engineering research to determine if there is any way to rebuild Arctic infrastructure in a manner that is viable over the long term. If the engineering proves too costly, nations such as Russia might switch from pipelines to tankers, allowing them much more flexibility in delivery and subjecting the supply to even greater geopolitical maneuverings of the sort seen when Russia cut off gas supply to the Ukraine in 2006. That is another reason Arctic shipping routes will likely increase in importance.

Currently, in the West, the Arctic focus is mostly on resource extraction (oil, gas, and fish), but, once obtained, those resources need to be moved out, joining the potential flow of commercial and military traffic through the northern waters. In the end, the intrinsic long-term value of the thawing Arctic is more likely to be the new shipping routes than just the resources. Settling the issue of control over the Passage and, by extension, ensuring its security, is critical.

However, as was evident with the Panama Canal, the balance between commerce and security in the United States is presently tilting more toward commerce. The primarily commercial approach to the Arctic that the United States has taken is not only undermining American security, but it is also causing problems with longtime loyal allies.

Control over the north stirs up strong emotions for Canadians, resurrecting in some ways the never-quite-dead fear that the United States is still trying to complete its Manifest Destiny by absorbing Canada. The idea that America has a manifest destiny to spread its way of life was probably stored in the luggage of the Puritans when they landed at Plymouth Rock in 1620. Had the nascent United States not been expansionist, it would now consist in its entirety of, roughly, bits of Virginia.

Manifest destiny suffused U.S. political life from the very inception of the nation. The first U.S. president, George Washington, called the United States "a rising empire."[21] The second U.S. president, John Adams, wrote: "Canada must be ours; Quebec must be taken."[22] And the third, Thomas Jefferson, thought the United States was "the nest from which all America, North and South, is to be peopled."[23] Presidents tend to be a bit more diplomatic these days, but, as recently as 2006, Paul Cellucci, the former U.S. ambassador to Canada, said in a speech to the Canadian Defense and Foreign Affairs Institute: "Ten years from now, or maybe fifteen years from now, we're going to look back and we're going to have a union in everything but name."[24]

Much of the impetus for a U.S. union with Canada comes from commercial interests. From the start it seemed that in some U.S. business quarters there was a feeling that it was simply unfair that Canada had comparatively large resources and such a small population. An 1891 U.S. article titled "Can We Coerce Canada?"[25] summed up the argument (and foreshadowed the rationale behind the 1994 North American Free Trade Agreement as well as some elements of the "deep integration" currently being sought by the Task Force on the Future of North America[26]):

> A condition of commercial belligerency exists along the entire northern border of the United States. The extent of this border-line, four thousand miles in length, and the fact that beyond it lies the greater half of the continent, impart to this condition of hostility an importance which makes the question of its abatement second to nothing else now before the American public. Along this unequalled line of demarcation, which runs athwart the continent some degrees to the south of its centre, the vast commerce of the United States breaks like a huge wave, and rolls back upon itself. Beyond it lies a region larger, richer, and more susceptible of development for the good of mankind than any other region on the earth's surface. [. . .] The trade of the United States should yield just as good a return from Manitoba as from Minnesota; in Algoma as in Michigan. As much money should be made by Pennsylvania out of Ontario as out of Ohio indeed, out of Ohio, Illinois, and Indiana, the province of Ontario being larger and richer than all these three combined.[27]

Canadians were almost paranoid in their concerns over U.S. expansion, and one of the main drivers for the formation of Canada was a fear of U.S. annexation. As Thomas D'Arcy McGee, one of the Fathers of Canadian Confederation, put it: "The United States have frightful numbers of soldiers and guns. They wanted Florida and seized it. They wanted Louisiana and purchased it. They wanted Texas and stole it. Then they picked a quarrel with Mexico and got California. If we had not the strong arm of England over us, we too would be part of the states."[28]

Canada alone could not withstand U.S. expansionism; the country needed a stronger ally to back it up. It needed Britain. Several times the UK sent troops to defend Canada against U.S. incursions. But, after World War II, and especially after the Suez Crisis, the UK was no longer in a position to rile the United States, especially in its own backyard. Without that cover, the whole dynamic changed. Canada was orphaned. And the United States knew it. Out came the treaties.

As happened in Panama in the 1970s, the U.S. desire to have a strong voice on Canadian issues that effect it has taken on a new, and much less messy form—wrapped in agreements and acronyms. One area that has been affected is the independence of the Canadian military.

In a post-9/11 world, the United States sees itself as Fort Knox, and Canada as the flabby, shoulda-been-retired-in-the-eighties security guard with a broken flashlight stationed at the back door. In 2002, the *National Review* ran a cover photo of Mounties on horses with "Wimps!" stamped over them. The cover story, "Bomb Canada," stated: "Canada is, quite simply, not a serious country anymore [. . .] they are simply unarmed. If al-Qaeda launched a September 11–style attack from Canadian soil, we would have only two choices: ask Canada to take charge, or take charge ourselves. The predictable—and necessary—US action would spark outrage."[29] While that position was deliberately provocative, it does capture the prevailing view in the United States that Canada is a military marshmallow. Without a British cover, the country is seen as vulnerable. Geopolitics abhors a vacuum, or even just the appearance of a vacuum, so the United States is doing its best to step into the breech.

Since 9/11, there has been a strong push toward coordinating aspects of the Canadian military command structure with that of the United States. Primarily, it has been done through U.S. Northern

Command (USNORTHCOM), created in 2002 and based in Colorado. Part of USNORTHCOM's specific mission is to "Conduct operations to deter, prevent, and defeat threats and aggression aimed at the United States, its territories and interests within the assigned area of responsibility (AOR)." These areas of responsibility "include air, land and sea approaches and encompasses the continental United States, Alaska, Canada, Mexico and the surrounding water out to approximately 500 nautical miles."[30] Which means the Canadian Arctic falls under its prevue.

USNORTHCOM is putting in place a structure in which U.S. troops can be deployed anywhere in its AOR (including Canada) in case of "emergency" (though it isn't made clear who makes the decision on what is an emergency). This is not a trivial, administrative change. The U.S. secretary of defense at the time, Donald Rumsfeld, was quoted as saying that NORTHCOM—with all of North America as its geographic command—is part of the greatest transformation of the Unified Command Plan since its inception in 1946.[31]

The problem, from a Canadian or Mexican point of view, is while USNORTHCOM's motto is "Protecting our people, national power and freedom of action,"[32] it seems that the main people they are protecting are not New Brunswick fishermen or the latte-sipping Mexican business elite, but rather American citizens. To U.S. commanders Canada is often seen as a buffer zone. When they talk about a missile defense shield that will shoot down incoming warheads, a success would be to shoot them down over Canada before they can get to the United States. That mindset was clear during 9/11 when planes en route to the United States were diverted to Canada, with the implied logic that it was better if they blew up over Gander, Newfoundland, than Bangor, Maine.

The success of the integration of sections of the United States and Canadian military was shown on October 11, 2006, when, minutes after a small plane crashed into an apartment building in New York City, fighter jets were simultaneously scrambled over cities in the United States and Canada.[33] That degree of coordination, while not new, is growing, and desirable. But the problem is that, while Canada surely agreed, the order likely came from the United States, and it's questionable whether there would have been the same level of response had the plane flown into an apartment building in Toronto.

The de facto approach that Canada is a buffer as opposed to an integral part of the U.S. security perimeter is clear from U.S. policy in the Arctic. Legally, Canada claims the Northwest Passage as its internal waters, giving it the right to control entry and search and seize vessels it considers a danger. The United States claims it to be an international strait, meaning free access for all. This makes it legally difficult to stop, search, and seize suspect vessels, including submerged military submarines, ships full of illegal immigrants, and cargo vessels carrying weapons. Bearing in mind that no matter its designation, the Passage is well inside the northern perimeter of North America, and is supposed to be defended under USNORTHCOM, the current American position leaves a huge gap in the U.S.'s stated mission of securing North America's borders.

It is as though we have built Fortress North America, and then allowed an open highway to run right through the middle of it. There needs to be an understanding that Canada is not a buffer zone, but an integral part of North American security. All levers available should be used to secure the Arctic, including declaring the Northwest Passage internal waters so that it can be legally monitored by Canada and its allies.

The threats to Arctic security are real. According to *Naval Operations in an Iceless Arctic*, a U.S. Navy document, "Canada has recently experienced infringements on Canadian sovereignty. A Chinese vessel armed with a number of machine guns and a passport that could not be accounted for that arrived in an Inuvialuit community. An unknown foreign submarine was spotted in Cumberland Sound. An unannounced IL–76 [military transport plane] landed in Manitoba, picked up a helicopter, and returned to a site that intelligence sources say is a known Russian Mafia base."[34]

Given the obvious vulnerabilities being created, why are some in the United States pushing for a policy that would in effect open the waterway to military naval vessels, including those from countries that are hostile to U.S. interests? An alternative to the current U.S. position can be seen in what happened after the United States and Canada signed the 1988 Arctic Co-operation Agreement, which stated roughly that the United States would ask permission before sending ships through the Passage but that, when so asked, Canada would give permission.[35] This seemed like a good solution because it would give the United States unfettered passage while limiting access from competitors and foreign military. However, it didn't take long before the United States started sending through vessels without asking permission, and by 2005, it was reported that a U.S. military submarine passed through the region without asking permission on its way to a photo-op at the North Pole, where crewmembers played a quick game of football for the cameras.[36]

The problem was that the 1988 agreement didn't do anything to satisfy U.S. commercial interests. Most ships belonging to major American corporations aren't flagged in the United States; they are flagged in places like Panama and Liberia, and so weren't covered by the agreement (even the tanker Chevron named after Condoleezza Rice was flagged in the Bahamas).[37] These "flags of convenience" can be bought online for about $500. Regardless of the location of the parent company, once a ship is flagged in a given nation, it is subject to that nation's regulations. Countries that sell flags of convenience typically have more lax safety and labor laws, lower taxes, and cheaper registration procedures. The ship also operates under the (frequently almost non-existent) maritime environmental laws of the flagged nation. Some of the "open registry" nations, like Bolivia, are even landlocked. For many Western companies that would otherwise have to contend with stringent local laws, such flags are an obvious choice for registering their shipping fleets on the cheap.

So, while the 1988 Arctic Co-operation Agreement made sense from a national security point of view (and was negotiated during the Cold War, when security issues had more weight), it was a potential problem for the private sector, whose foreign-flagged ships were not covered by the deal. Once the Cold War ended, rather than trying to find a compromise, the United States, in keeping with its general 1990s approach of commerce over security, decided to push for free access for all in the Northwest Passage. Canada aside, other countries didn't object, as it could potentially give them unfettered access as well, and in Europe many were also focused on commerce over security (and still are).

The push for open access for all was a controversial position even within the United States. Not long after leaving office, the former U.S. ambassador to Canada Paul Cellucci said: "It is in the security interests of the United States that [the Northwest Passage] be under the control of Canada [. . .] If we thought there was a ship coming through there that had a weapon of mass destruction, there'd be much more authority to stop it and board it [. . .] I think it is in our national interests to look at this and to do what's in our security interests as opposed to what might be in our trade interests."[38]

Regardless, some in the United States continue in their attempt to poke holes in North America's northern border—its closest point to Russia—and erode ally Canada's position, even though the United States itself is not equipped to defend the Arctic should a problem arise. Nor are the combined forces of USNORTHCOM prepared. Just as the thaw of the Cold War created new alliances and approaches, so too is the physical thaw requiring a reassessment of military priorities and equipment. The United States has submarines and planes capable of monitoring the North, but they are not practical for day-to-day operations. That takes people on the ground, and ships. The entire U.S. fleet has four ice-capable ships; two are over 30 years old and spend most of their time being repaired, a third is fit for light ice only, and the fourth is at best "ice-strengthened."[39] The situation is so dire that the United States had to hire a Russian icebreaker to get to its research station in Antarctica.[40] Canada isn't much better off.

The U.S. military is aware that it is dangerously underequipped and poorly trained to secure the Arctic. A 2006 U.S. Congressional report concluded that the United States should immediately build two new polar icebreakers because "melting sea ice in the Arctic is opening new shipping routes and sparking economic activity, such as exploration for natural resources. This increased activity will raise demands for the United States to assert a more active and influential presence in the region, and adequate icebreaking capability is needed to do so. [. . .] The federal government has an obligation not only to protect the Alaskan citizens and US territory in the Arctic, but also to protect national interests. There are security, economic, and sovereignty interests to protect."[41] The United States wants to be in a position to dominate the North. It is a long way away from mission accomplished. While it has a potential command structure in place, with USNORTHCOM, a potential legal structure with the 1988 agreement, and a willing ally in Canada, the two major impediments are the promotion of short-term commercial gains offered by unfettered "freedom of the seas" over the longer-term security offered by Canadian administration of the Passage, and a lack of defensive ability.

A third major impediment is the perception that the United States wants its allies not only loyal, but also subservient. It seems to be looking for allegiances, not alliances. This perception is underscored by incidents such as the restricting of last-minute riders attached to the proposed U.S.-India nuclear deal and reported threats of trade reprisals for allies who didn't support the Iraq war.[42]

In the case of the Northwest Passage, it was made clear as early as 1970 that *because* Canada is an ally it is supposed to fall in line quickly and completely. An internal State Department memo summarizing the situation in the Canadian north for Secretary of State Henry Kissinger read: "[O]ur efforts to limit extensions of coastal state sovereignty over the high seas worldwide will be damaged when other nations see that a country—physically, politically and economically—as close to the United States as Canada, feels it can undertake such action in the face of United States opposition."[43] The irony is that by weakening close allies, the United States is weakening itself. This is especially true in the context of combined defenses, such as USNORTHCOM. By impeding Canada's ability to defend itself, either through restricting its access to technologies or through legal mechanisms (as with the Northwest Passage), it is undermining not only Canada's defenses but also the ability of Canada to buttress U.S. defenses.

The U.S. position makes it difficult for Canada to defend the Arctic, and, possibly as a result, Canada began toying with some unconventional options in the North. The Canadian department of Foreign Affairs proposed that, "Perhaps more than any other country, Canada is uniquely positioned to build a strategic partnership with Russia for development of the Arctic."[44] This position ignored the increasing divergence between Western and Russian security perceptions and interests, the increasing Russian posturing in the Arctic, and the emerging convergence between Moscow and Beijing. It is an example of how, by making lopsided and intransigent demands, the United States can inadvertently push even its closest allies to at least consider other options.

While a Canada-Russia strategic partnership in the Arctic is extremely unlikely, there are possibilities for increasing commercial ties between the two countries, and it is worth examining why. One reason for the appeal of Russia as some sort of a partner in the Arctic is that, unlike the United States, Russia has around 16 icebreakers,[45] many of them nuclear powered (the U.S. and Canada have no nuclear-powered icebreakers). Russia is already equipped to help Canada patrol the area (and indeed probably knows it better than Canada does due to its illicit activity in the region during the Cold War and more recently as it surveys the area to bolster its territorial claims). Russia is also interested in developing more shipping routes through the Canadian Arctic. Russia and Canada are considering cooperating in a range of fields, including a multibillion-dollar deal to move Russian natural gas via Canada into the U.S. markets.[46]

Another plan is to have a shipping route that leads from Russia to Canada through the Arctic, and from there by rail into the heart of North America. Russia has even offered to help keep the Canadian segment of the route open year-round with its icebreakers. The proposed Russian terminal is Murmansk. The proposed Canadian one is Churchill, Manitoba, on Hudson Bay. Churchill is the closest port to the great wheat fields of Canada, and shipping via Churchill, rather than by rail and boat though Montreal, cuts hundreds of miles off transit routes. As Russia expands its ability to load oil and gas tankers directly from offshore Arctic platforms, fossil fuels could also join the route.

Some in Canada are all for it. Russia announced plans to appoint an honorary consul to Churchill, and the ex-foreign affairs minister of Canada Lloyd Axworthy is involved with the Churchill Gateway Development Corp. According to Axworthy, it's only a matter of time before "Churchill really becomes crucial strategically."[47] But Churchill has a long way to go before becoming another Murmansk. So far, it only has a population of a little over 800, not including polar bears.[48] Also, the railway leading to Churchill suffers from deteriorating tracks and is built on thawing permafrost. There have already been derailments and at times in the summer the train can't travel faster than six miles an hour.

Another reason floated for why Canada should develop Arctic cooperation with Russia is that Russia controls half of the Bering Strait, the critical western chokepoint entry to the Northwest Passage. No matter how the legal claims over the North are resolved, traffic is going to increase in the Arctic and, eventually, the over-the-top route that goes more or less over the North Pole will open up and take ships completely out of Canada's control. That means that the only way to ensure that polluting or dangerous shipping isn't passing through or near North American waters is to monitor chokepoints. If the ships are coming from the east coast of Asia or the west coast of the Americas, they have to pass through the Strait.

The Bering Strait is about 53 miles at its narrowest, with small islands in the middle. It might be possible to set up a verification station, and a toll system to cover the cost of patrols and search-and-rescue teams. This sort of system, usually reserved for man-made canals, is not common for the open seas, but there is growing support for (as well as resistance to) the idea. It could also serve to lower insurance costs to shipping lines, allowing them to more than recoup the "toll" cost. Under such a setup Canada would need to partner with either the United States or Russia or both. Stringent requirements on ships passing through might decrease the Passage's use, but would likely cut costs in the long run as there would be less loss of valuable fisheries and other resources, and less need for expensive cleanups. The ideal situation would be for the United States to partner with Canada and the two nations to then work with Russia. However, the present U.S. position has made that option difficult.

From a Russian point of view the relationship with Canada is unlikely to remain simply commercial. Russia is becoming a nationalistic capitalist country with growing ties to China. It is no coincidence that China has increased its Arctic profile. It has an icebreaker, observer status at the Arctic Council, a research base in the Arctic (Svalbard), and two research bases in the Antarctic.[49] Consistent with its approach of nationalistic capitalism, China is also paying attention to Canadian resources and, not surprisingly, is keen to acquire Canadian companies in key industries. According to Saskatchewan premier Lorne Calvert, China "floated some ideas for the actual purchase of [oil field] properties that they would develop themselves."[50] And Saskatchewan's minister of industry and resources Eric Cline said: "[T]he meetings we're having are at a very high level. Certainly they're looking very seriously at Saskatchewan as a source of uranium. They would be a stable long-term customer for us, because they're going to have a lot of nuclear energy."[51]

China has also been actively courting Canadian aboriginal leaders. In the fall of 2008, over two dozen first nation chiefs and representatives were invited to China. According to delegation head Chief Calvin Helin, "Canadian aboriginals own or control about a third of the Canadian land mass," and, he said, they went to Beijing to "tell China that Aboriginal Canada was open for business. And to be greeted and hosted at the level we were is quite unbelievable and quite historic. It's an enormous first step."[52]

Helin told Chinese political and business leaders: "The biggest source for uncertainty for developing natural resources in Canada is aboriginal land claims. If aboriginal people are your partners, that uncertainty disappears."[53] Another member of the delegation, Chief Glenn Hudson of Manitoba's Peguis Indian Band explained that the trip was "an important step for us in moving forward. Our future is not only in Canada, but partnering with other countries."[54]

There is an implicit political component to the engagement. China extols the many seeming commonalities between the Chinese people and aboriginals, saying, for example, the two groups have both been on their land for thousands of years, culturally there is a shared respect for elders and tradition, and there may even be commonalities in DNA as the first Canadian came across the Bering Strait from Asia.

It is also implied that both China and aboriginal Canadians have suffered at the hands of Europeans, and China is offering itself up as a sort of postcolonial role model. According to Helin, "Our aim is to lift ourselves up in the same way we have heard China has done in the past few years."[55] This brothers-in-arms appeal is a common and effective tactic often used by China when engaging with the developing world, or with groups within the developed world who have (often legitimate) grievances. In the first case, China tries to set up bilateral deals. In the second, the relationship is essentially sublateral, as the national government of China is bypassing the government of the people it wants to do business with (in this case Canada). Of course China would not allow this sort of sublateral engagement with its own Tibetan and Uyghur citizens.

The relationship between the aboriginal Canadians and the Canadian government is complex, especially when it comes to natural resources and land use. Outside elements know this and are not averse to profiting from the lack of unity and legitimate historic resentment. When it comes to choosing who will get to do business in the North, unless the Canadian government is attentive to the needs and wants of the people who live there, it could get very tricky very quickly. Already there have been bombings of gas pipelines in British Columbia. The reason for the attacks is unclear, but a letter sent to the local paper (allegedly by the perpetrator) seems to imply that a major motivator was a perceived neglect of the health and needs of the local community.[56]

Healthy domestic community relations will become even more crucial as the resource treasures of the North unthaw. China and others are not averse to a warming of relations with Canada, or key Canadian decision makers. Open access to the Northwest Passage makes the creation of a potential beachhead in North America just that much easier.

The current U.S. approach to Arctic shipping, focusing on narrow commercial and "freedom of the seas" issues, is shortsighted. Not only does it make Russian, and possibly Chinese, partnerships more appealing to some Canadians (something even perhaps encouraged by certain U.S. business interests), it also undermines the Canadian legal and military positions even though the United States is not equipped to fill the gap. If the Northwest Passage is made stateless, Canada and, by extension, its allies lose their leverage over regulating who uses it, and for what.

Already it is likely that, for a range of political, security, and other reasons, the North, and the shortcut to Europe, is being tested by Russia and China to see if it's being properly defended. It's not, in spite of Canadian prime minister Stephen Harper's announcements on new military investment in the Arctic.[57] Canada simply can't protect the Arctic alone, militarily or politically. The way the situation is currently being handled by the United States, if Canada wants to assert its claim over the Northwest Passage, it is going to have to shoot over the bow of an American ship (something that will not happen). That is not a U.S. "win." It seems a bit absurd that the United States and European Union are seeking to replace control over a strategic route by one of their closest allies with substantial control by a less cooperative nation like Russia that alone has the military assets and mindset needed for such a power grab. Strategic imperatives demand that the United States shouldn't be trying to weaken Canada; the two countries are too closely joined for that to be good for either of them. They need to be working together to strengthen their overall capabilities as allies.

If the United States and Canada are going to protect North America's northern border (and monitor dangerous traffic on this potentially massive, largely unregulated highway from Asia to the United States and Europe), they are going to need more legal rights as well as military muscle. The logical thing would be for the United States to accept Canada's legal claim and help Canada get on with defending the border. Or perhaps revisit the 1988 agreement in such a way that the U.S. doesn't feel that its stand on freedom of the seas is compromised, but it backs Canada's de facto rights in the area. The United States needn't worry; Canada will not hinder legitimate trade through the region.

If key figures in the United States don't change their position, another option would be for some old friends to come to Canada's aid. The

United Kingdom can spearhead a drive in Europe to help prevent the Northwest Passage from becoming an international waterway—something that would be welcomed by that large section of U.S. strategists and policymakers who understand the value of keeping this critical waterway under the control of one of the United States's closest allies. In return, Canada could look at cooperation with the UK and EU on Arctic resource issues and help ensure that traffic coming toward Europe isn't hazardous.

However, to date, the UK and, to a certain degree, the EU, have badly mismanaged Arctic affairs. For example, when the Icelandic economy collapsed in 2008, that Arctic Council country turned to the EU for help. It was turned down. The UK even invoked anti-terrorism laws in order to seize the assets of Icelandic banks. Iceland then asked Russia for a loan. Russia said it would think about it—raising the possibility of a geopolitical Arctic bridge from Russia to Iceland that excluded other Western nations. The EU assumed it was the only option for Iceland and was suddenly caught out when the Nordic nation turned to other benefactors not so friendly to the West. Realizing its miscalculation, the EU scrambled to reestablish relations with Iceland and eventually came through with a loan. As of this writing, Iceland was considering joining the EU.

The EU seems to be eyeing the Arctic from a primarily commercial perspective. As EU-based oil companies are increasingly being pushed out of nationalistic capitalist countries, such as Russia and Venezuela, they are finding fewer possibilities for expansion and access to supply. One of the rare new, potentially open, areas for expansion and supply is the Arctic. Various elements in the EU are now floating the idea of some form of "global governance" in the Arctic, often in consort with stated concerns over environmental protection. This global governance is sometimes seen as a way of trying to justify an EU role in the region. Occasionally NATO is mentioned as a possible enforcer of "environmental safeguards." As a result, the EU does not support Canada's claim to the Passage. In a familiar scenario, the EU's short-term commercial goals could potentially have a disastrous effect on its security. The EU apparently assumes that in a global governance situation it would hold substantial sway, as it does with other global organizations, such as the World Bank, IMF, and UN Security Council. However, this may not be the case when its global governance opens the door for another oil-hungry power, China, to enter the Arctic with support from Russia.

It would be in the best interest of the EU to support Canada's claim to the Passage. It would not affect EU oil and gas interests in the Arctic; in fact it could give the EU the edge as strict environmental controls could impede exploration by other nations with less developed technologies.

Ideally the United States, supported by the EU, would help Canada get on with defending itself and its allies. Then, once Canada's claim to the Passage is recognized and defendable, it can talk to other countries, including Russia, on a more equal basis about creating and jointly using facilities like search, rescue, and toll stations, and on methods of speeding legitimate, safe shipping and exploration in the northern waters.

The irony is that unless the United States changes its policies, Manifest Destiny could finally become a de facto (if not de jure) reality in the Arctic—but it might be Russia's destiny that is being manifested. In the same way the Suez helped make and break the British Empire, and Panama helped make the United States before it was sold on (or possibly even sold out), environmental change and the Northwest Passage could help ensure that the West remains a major force in the twenty-first century, reinforcing its position and stability. Or it could turn into a whole new vulnerability at a time when there are more than enough vulnerabilities to go around.

PART THREE

PRECIPITATING CHANGE IN ASIA AND BEYOND

HOW CHINA, INDIA, AND THE WEST ARE TRYING TO MAKE FRIENDS IN INTERESTING TIMES

May you live in interesting times.

—Traditional curse

Asia
Courtesy of the Library of Congress, The Central Intelligence Agency

6

TODAY'S WEATHER

INTOLERABLE WITH
PERIODS OF UNINHABITABLE

And on the pedestal these words appear:
"My name is Ozymandias, king of kings:
Look on my works, ye Mighty, and despair!"
Nothing beside remains. Round the decay
Of that colossal wreck, boundless and bare,
The lone and level sands stretch far away.

—*Ozymandias of Egypt*, Percy Bysshe Shelley, 1818

The Asian continent has given the world some of its most important and enduring civilizations, and after a long sleep it is ready to shake off the sands of time and rise again. However, it is a temperamental land that takes as well as gives. In the best of times, some of its regions are unrelentingly harsh. In the worst of times, they are deadly. Already in many places demand is outstripping supply across the continent, and Asia is joining the West in needing a massive influx of outside resources to sustain its growth. The future of Asia, and the new geopolitical order, will be about alliances created to secure supplies and foster stability in turbulent times. We've been here before.

I was walking through the ancient history section of the British Museum with my friend Professor W. M. S. Russell. We had gone through gallery after gallery of stern, imposing carvings of long-forgotten kings when, in a side room, we suddenly found ourselves facing a series of carved plaques depicting some jolly, chubby people enjoying what looked like a pleasant day out. They seemed out of place among the severe Assyrians and stiffly regal Egyptians. It was as though a bunch of good friends ended up having a rather drunken picnic in the middle of a G8 meeting. I asked Professor Russell, "Why do they look so happy?" He said, "Well, they've just invented civilization." And so they had.

The happy people in the carvings were Sumerians. They lived in what is now southeastern Iraq, between the Tigris and Euphrates rivers, from as early as the mid-fourth millennium BCE. They were exceptional hydrological engineers, a trait shared with those from another contemporary crucible of civilization, the Indus Valley. The Sumerians' language is full of subtle distinctions between dykes, weirs, canals, dams, reservoirs, and aqueducts. By controlling floods and irrigating, they built up an extensive system of agriculture, creating massive, positive, man-made environmental change. The surplus of food relative to population meant that, for one of the first times in human history, large sections of society didn't have to think about how their daily bread made it to their dinner plates. They could concentrate instead on making nicer dinner plates—and tables, and houses, and cities. Then they could trade those dinner plates, and more, with neighboring cities that were also fat with surpluses. They developed some of the first pottery wheels, writing, and legal systems. It was enough to make anyone look jolly.

In fits and starts the incredible accomplishments of the hydrologic civilizations of this largely man-made Fertile Crescent spread out until, by the second millennium BCE., there was a ragged quilt of farm fields from Morocco to Kazakhstan, interspersed with grazing land and desert. Some of these city-states had populations of several hundred thousand and were greater than any built in Europe before the sixteenth century— except for those, like ancient Rome, that imported their food from the irrigation-fed granaries of the world, such as Tunisia, Israel, Jordan, and Syria.[1] This expansion through importation is also what made possible most major modern powers, which is why transportation routes are so critical.

In the Fertile Crescent, the extra food and improved sanitation meant populations grew. Many became involved in the new mass industries of weaving, metalwork, masonry, and leatherwork. And still the populations grew, until it started to get a bit crowded. Soon the neighboring city's grass glowed a tempting shade of green. The Sumerians weren't only among the first to develop the city-state, they also were among the first to create the professional soldier caste. Fights between neighbors over the same water sources became common. The word *rival* comes from the Latin for "on the same river."[2]

The region was eventually subject to more man-made environmental change, and, this time the results weren't so positive. The climate had always been unreliable, with frequent droughts and often poor soil. Some of the farming techniques turned huge areas sterile, and with temperamental rains, the water supply situation could become desperate. The core of the problem was too many people, too little food and water, and too few places to secure more supplies. This relative over-population led to cycles of inflation, over-taxation, unemployment, famine, revolts, war, anarchy, and disease. The cities fought among themselves. Nomadic shepherds attacked the farmers at the retreating fringes of the agricultural belt. The shepherds cut down trees for pastures, and their grazing animals ate beyond what the land could regrow, causing widespread erosion. The land, already marginal, dried out even more and desertification spread, causing the inhabitants to become increasingly desperate and rapacious.

The chaos led to the breakdown of irrigation systems, which in turn created stagnant marshes ideal for disease-carrying mosquitoes and the spread of livestock and human illness. When the societies were weakened, invaders, often nomads, attacked and took control. Then the conquerors would settle and merge with the reduced population. This smaller population, living within their means food-wise, would slowly rebuild and eventually grow. Too much. And the cycle would begin again.[3]

Finally, after millennia of dramatic ups and downs, the whole system collapsed and the population crashed. In 800 CE, what is now Iraq had a population of 30 million. At the beginning of the twentieth century, before oil money allowed the large-scale importation of food and the construction of water desalination plants, the population was less than 5 million. One study showed that all the deserts in Iraq were essentially man-made.[4]

What happened in the now un-Fertile Crescent has been repeated in many places all over the planet.[5] Sometimes there are few contributing climate change factors; it largely came down to bad management. At other times climatic changes precipitate or exacerbate the crises—that other great, early complex civilization, which sprung from the fertile shores of the Indus Valley, likely faded as a result of a persistent drought that bled it dry.[6] This time around, at a global level, we are creating vulnerabilities through massive environmental change, such as population growth, leaving us less resilient to the effects of climate change.

The previous sections of this book looked at fairly linear climate change phenomena: rising sea levels and the Arctic thaw. Both those trends may go through ups and downs, but the general vectors are clear: Sea levels will continue to rise and the ice will continue to melt. Other environmental factors aside, that gives us time to plan. However, another consequence of climate change is potentially less predictable. We are starting to see large-scale disruptions to long-standing precipitation patterns as well as increases in extreme weather.

Roughly, the increase in global temperature means the air can hold more moisture. As a result, in some places, the increased evaporation is sucking the land dry, creating droughts. It also means that when it does rain, the clouds can release larger quantities of water, potentially creating snowstorms and floods, leading to erosion and landslides. There are vast regional variations, but the overall effect is a likely increase in unpredictable precipitation and extreme events. We might eventually be heading toward new norms but, in the meantime, it is more difficult to make decisions, such as what sort of crops to plant, how to manage hydro projects, and where to build.[7] In some areas, ocean currents are changing as well, and seasonal rains have stopped coming. Rising ocean temperatures are contributing to hurricanes hitting coasts that haven't seen them in recorded history. Downpours are drowning deserts. In many places, as happened with the Sumerians, we are already pushing the environmental limits through relative overpopulation and ill-advised development models. When erratic precipitation and extreme events are added, areas that are barely holding on may find themselves slipping over the brink.

Signs of potentially dramatic change caused by irregular precipitation patterns are globally evident. In 2008, drought in California resulted in large wildfires, and drought in Australia triggered massive crop failures. In Canada, several snowfall records were broken, and Prince Edward Island suffered the worst ice storm in decades. Record-breaking rainfall flooded Missouri and parts of France. In China, severe snowfall disrupted infrastructure, destroyed crops, and affected millions. In southern Asia, heavy monsoon rains killed about 2,600 people and displaced 10 million in India alone. In Brazil intense rains affected 1.5 million people and killed about 80.[8]

The link between environmental change and human suffering can be seen in Africa.[9] What the U.S. Gulf Coast is to flooding, and the Arctic is to melting glaciers, Africa is to disrupted weather patterns. None of the three is alone in suffering from those changes, but they do exhibit some of the most acute symptoms. One recent study warns that environmental change could threaten the lives of up to 184 million people in Africa alone.[10] Already the effects are tragic. In 2008 Zimbabwe was hit by its worst floods in recorded history, and Algeria experienced its worst floods in a century. In Morocco, tens of thousands were affected by heavy rains and the country suffered severe infrastructure damage. Unusually heavy monsoon rains affected over 3 million people in West Africa.[11] Sometimes, even when it's good news, it somehow ends up bad news: In 2005 there was an excess of corn in western Kenya while a famine raged in eastern Kenya. However, there was no money, means, or enough political will to get the corn across the country, so it was exported to Europe.[12]

Joshua Wairoto of the Kenya Meteorological Service, describes a typical situation, one that the Sumerians may have recognized: "The pastoralists, who look after cattle, and the farmers who grow for subsistence or sale, fight each other over water and grass. The pastoralists believe where there's grass, their cows should go and eat. So the cows eat the green maize of the farmers. Then there is war. When we have severe droughts and the streams dry out you'll have monkeys and other animals fight people for the water from wells. We have conflicts of humans against humans, and humans against animals, and it's increasing. Sometimes it's even cross-border."[13] This rise in conflict also drives the rural poor into cities where, if unable to find work, they are forced to turn to crime. The general urban overcrowding and poor sanitation, in turn, contribute to increasing rates of cholera and dysentery, and the stress on institutions (as well as other factors) makes it difficult for Africans to take advantage of their abundant human and natural resources.[14]

African leaders and scientists know the problems better than anyone and are trying to find solutions. There is vast scope for quick improvements. Development on the continent has been so problematic, with, for example, local soil-appropriate crops being replaced with unsuitable but export-friendly produce, that just a few policy changes could go a long way toward alleviating suffering.[15] Also, Africa is, to a large degree, still in the process of putting in its major infrastructure, giving it a chance to take environmental change into account when planning and thus potentially creating a solid foundation for the future. If it does so, African infrastructure could be stable while sections of the West struggle to grapple with woefully inadequate systems.

Africa faces tremendous challenges, but the continent also has enormous promise, human talent, and resources, producing everything from food to oil to uranium. Those resources are coveted in this era of increasing global scarcity and will be developed. By 2015, Africa is projected to supply 25 to 40 percent of U.S. oil—assuming coastal flooding and storm surges don't make extraction along the Niger Delta increasingly difficult.[16] If Africa manages to plan its way out of the worst of environmental change, and realizes control over even a fraction of its potential, it will start to play a growing geopolitical role. In the meantime, however, Africa's resources are largely being viewed by other nations as prospective sources of surplus to shore up their own domestic shortfalls. Much of what applies to Africa applies to Latin America as well. While so far not as hard hit as Africa by environmental change, Latin America is increasingly being eyed as an essential crutch to support larger powers with needed resources.

Those supplies used to go primarily to the West, and the West is counting on that to continue. However, China is quickly gaining ground. In 2000, China's trade with Africa was around $10 billion. By 2008 it was closer to $56 billion.[17] Earlier, we looked at China's approach to foreign policy and saw that one of the main drivers of nationalistic capitalism is securing resources for the home market. The Chinese Communist Party has long been aware that China is not environmentally able to support a growing population. China's government-mandated one-child policy helped with reducing demand, but not with increasing supply. For that, resources have to be found outside the country, which has resulted in Chinese expansion into Asia, Latin America, the Pacific and, yes, Africa. In Africa, China is involved not only in resource extraction, but also in infrastructure construction, often in the service of resource extraction (but also often to build up the country in general).

India is trying to make friends globally as well, including in Africa and Latin America. As the environmental situation in the West, China, and India fluctuates, African and Latin American allies will become even more important. Potential partners who are planning long term will try to help Africa and Latin America develop, for the benefit of all concerned. Geopolitically, Africa and Latin America may not as yet have the positions they deserve, but through their alliances they could play a key role in determining the stability and global influence of some of the world's great powers. Their help will be needed. We've already seen some of the vulnerabilities the West might be facing, demonstrating how dependent it is, and will potentially increasingly become, on imported supplies. Now we turn to India, China, and Asia in general to see how environmental change might affect these areas, and why alliances of all kinds are going to be so important in the future.

INDIA

In India, at a macro level, climate-related loss has been growing. According to Indian government estimates, in 2006–2007, 2.6 percent of the country's GDP was spent on adaptation to climate variability, compared to approximately 2 percent in 2002–2003.[18] As India's lifeblood monsoon literally veers all over the map, the economic impact has been punishing. As of 2005, around 18.6 percent of India's GDP came from agriculture, and the sector as a whole employs around 60 percent of the country's workforce.[19] That means a huge section of the economy, and the country, is directly affected by environmental change.

As an example, in 2002, the monsoon failed, causing a seasonal rainfall deficit of 19 percent that devastated agriculture and knocked more than 3 percent off India's GDP.[20] The social effect of increased poverty in the already suffering countryside, accompanied by the resulting migration to the cities, has been compounded by a failure of government to deal with the problem in a cohesive and substantial way. The tragedy of farmers committing suicide due to debt is now a regular theme in the press. Meanwhile, deforestation and unsuitable land use risk creating more droughts, floods, and landslides, making a difficult situation untenable.[21] As a result of this (and possibly of hoarding and market manipulation as well), in 2006, the once proudly food self-sufficient India imported wheat for the first time in seven years.[22] By 2008, the situation had deteriorated into a crisis for many, with rising prices triggering social and political discontent—though, as India is a democracy, much of that energy can be dissipated through the safety valve of the ballot box, an option not available in more brittle authoritarian countries such as China.

As elsewhere, India's shifting climate patterns highlight and exacerbate its existing problems. While India's basic infrastructure is improving relatively quickly, it is often tenuous in places, with overstretched cities experiencing problems with safe drinking water, power, and sewerage. Luckily though, unlike China, which has the vast majority of its cities, infrastructure, and industries located along its low-lying, vulnerable east coast, many of India's major centers, such as New Delhi and Bangalore, are inland. However, India does have some major industrial and population centers along the coast, and studies show that a sea-level rise of three feet could put up to 19 percent of what is now Mumbai under water, and affect about 40 percent of the population of Chennai.[23]

Goa could lose up to 5 percent of its total area, and the states of Gujarat and West Bengal could lose the most land.

As with the other places we've seen, coastal areas that aren't flooded might suffer from salt water infiltrating freshwater aquifers, erosion, and damage to infrastructure. Both increased floods and increased droughts are expected. Some studies predict that the rainy season may bring more water—up to 30 percent more in central India—and the Krishna, Ganga, and especially the Godavari river basins may all see increases in extreme rainfall. If so, there will need to be a large-scale implementation of flood controls and rainwater capture, otherwise it is likely that the added water will initially create floods but will then run off and won't be there when needed in the dry season.

The Bay of Bengal is predicted to get more cyclones, especially in the post-monsoon season, and the winds of those cyclones are predicted to be faster and stronger. Temperatures are expected to rise by up to 7.2 degrees Fahrenheit by the end of the century, increasing the transmission window for cold-sensitive diseases like malaria. Production of wheat and rice is expected to fall at the same time as the population grows.

All this will likely result in an added burden to the power supply as air conditioners, pumps, irrigation systems, and construction crews fight to maintain the status quo. Temperature increases can also weaken building material, and sea-level rises and increased rainfall can cause erosion, flooding, and waterlogging, resulting in structural damage and increased risk of collapse. Some existing roads, railways, and ports may be vulnerable. Meanwhile, disputes between Indian states, already concerned over power and water sharing, will only get worse as water supplies become even more erratic and power, especially hydro, becomes unreliable.

Already unpredictable rainfall has complicated the management of some of India's many dams (India is the world's third largest builder of dams).[24] Dams usually serve three purposes: flood control, irrigation, and power generation. Most are designed to store water from the rainy season to use for irrigation and generate power in the dry season. Those plans rely on predictable rain patterns. However, if the reservoir fills in the rainy season and then, owing to changing precipitation patterns, the rain keeps falling well into what should be the dry season, the reservoir can back up and risk inundating villages upstream. If in order to prevent that from occurring, the dam's floodgates are opened, the released water can add to the already swollen river and flood the cities downstream.

It was just such a downstream flooding that happened in August 2006 to Surat, an Indian city with a population of more than three million people and a thriving economy as one of the world's largest diamond-cutting centers. Unseasonably heavy rains overwhelmed dam management and led to the sudden release of water from an upstream dam. The resulting floodwaters covered around 90 percent of the city and destroyed nearby villages. More than a hundred people are known to have died, hundreds more went missing, and disease spread as thousands of animals drowned and rotted in the waters. The financial cost was at least in the tens of millions of dollars, and the cost of the loss of rare manuscripts from the city's academic institutions was incalculable.[25]

The poor planning that contributed to the destruction in Surat is not an isolated event. Some Indian dam managers make decisions based on monsoon schedules that assume regular 35-year rainfall cycles. Others are political appointees with little dam management experience. A few just don't show up for work. Locals know the potential cost of a bad dam manager and anger against dangerous mismanagement can sometimes boil over. After a different damaging flood, the man who ran the dam was killed in a "terrorist" incident.[26] Clever hydrological engineering and predictable climate patterns can create a Sumerian or Indus Valley civilization. Poor planning and/or bad management, combined with erratic rainfall, can drown or starve the best and brightest.

Luckily, in India, an unusually strong social network and remarkable local innovators have the potential to combine to mitigate the worst effects of environmental change. Good planning can go a long way. Many interesting ideas are already being tested around the country, such as micro-insurance pilot projects for farmers that can help sustain them through bad years, keeping them out of the cities and out of that particular cycle of poverty.[27] There are also regional rainwater harvesting projects and new sewage system designs. A little can go a long way. Disaster mitigation and preparedness projects in one Indian state gave a cost/benefit ratio of close to one to three.[28]

As of now, most adaptation initiatives are local, which can mean they are suited to on-the-ground realities but that they may not be properly supported financially. The central government is just starting to grapple with the new realities. In 2006, Indian prime minister Manmohan Singh inaugurated the first India Disaster Management Congress.[29] It was an important step, but by the time there is a disaster it is too late, the damage is done. Ideally, disaster *prevention* would have a higher priority than it does now. For example, greater emphasis can be placed on more state- and national-level initiatives, such as: A cohesive re-examination of India's agriculture and water supplies, taking into account environmental change; ensuring that farmers are informed about predicted impacts in their regions; ensuring that the choice of crops is appropriate to the changing environmental conditions; ensuring that groundwater recharging is systematically incorporated in new developments, and retroactively fitted into existing ones, when possible.

There are signs that this sort of government-led sound management is starting to gain traction. In a ground-breaking move, the Indian government is considering mandating that future major infrastructure investments be climate-proofed. That would mean assessments are done to ensure that, as the environment changes, new airports won't flood, new railways won't erode, and new highways won't buckle. In a few decades, this could potentially give Indian infrastructure (and hence economic stability) an advantage over the West, where such assessments are still uncommon.

Hopefully there will be an increase in this sort of leadership, drawing on the innovation and understanding of those on the ground. Overall, the central government should ideally approach environmental change as a major assault on India that could devastate it economically, socially, and physically, much like a war would do. This is not an overstatement because, as if India's domestic environmental problems weren't enough, the ones that will likely come spilling across its borders are horrific.

BANGLADESH

Apart from the effects of relative sea level rise, storm surges and cyclones in the Bay of Bengal are predicted to increase, perhaps not in number but in intensity, resulting in repeated devastating floods.[30] What other countries consider serious flooding happens in Bangladesh on a regular basis, with annual water levels often surging between 5 and 78 inches. It can take an inundation of more than 50 percent of the country for a flood to be considered "heavy."[31] There are already Bangladeshi refugee camps along the tense Indian border and forecast changes could swell those numbers by millions. There are concerns that extremists keen to destabilize India (and other countries) are courting these poor and desperate refugees, training them, and encouraging them to infiltrate India. In part, as a result, India is building a fence along its border to try to contain the situation. As the refugee numbers increase, putting more strain on already stressed areas, the region will only become more difficult to manage.

HIMALAYAS

While too much water may be the primary worry in the Bay of Bengal, it is the potential lack of water that concerns nations counting on the Himalayan watershed. The massive range is home to more than nine thousand glaciers, and is one of the largest storehouses of fresh waters outside the Polar regions.[32] It provides water directly to Bhutan, Nepal, Afghanistan, Bangladesh, Pakistan, China, and India, and is the source of three of the world's largest water systems. One of the *relatively* minor rivers, the Mekong, starts in the Tibetan Plateau and then flows through China, Myanmar, Laos, Cambodia, Thailand, and Vietnam—a total of 2,700 miles—to the South China Sea. Along the way, it waters 60 million people. India's sacred Ganges River also starts here, and runs through China and Nepal before flowing through India and then Bangladesh. In all, the Himalayan watershed rivers link close to half the world's increasingly water-starved population, and each country is dependent on flow from the one upstream, never a good situation, as the rivals from Sumer could attest.

The Himalayan water supply is facing the twin threats of glacial melt and changing precipitation patterns. Already there are problems with the water flow. In 2002, the Indian water resources minister said that 22 percent of Indians faced "absolute water scarcity,"[33] and according to the *Stern Review*, 23 percent of China's population, or around 250 million people, live "in the western region that depends principally on glacier meltwater. Virtually all glaciers are showing substantial melting in China, where spring stream-flows have advanced by nearly one month since records began."[34] The Chinese Academy of Sciences estimates that by 2050, as much as 64 percent of China's glaciers could be gone.[35]

The immediate impact of that melt is localized flooding. The Katmandu-based International Centre for Integrated Mountain Studies and the United Nations Environment Programme (UNEP) have shown that around 50 lakes in Nepal, Bhutan, and China have formed as a result of melting glaciers. Glacial lakes can be unstable and liable to burst their banks, as happened in Nepal in 1985, when one outburst washed away communities and a hydroelectric installation.[36] It is also possible that in areas that are already susceptible, the added geological stresses caused by the new lakes could be the "last straw" that triggers an earthquake. Not surprisingly, the melt is also disrupting hydro projects. The flip side is that once the melt is done, those same regions (and the ones downstream) will suffer drought and power shortages. Engineering megaprojects that might help in the short term could compound the problem in the longer term.[37] Regardless, one country that is pinning many of its hopes for the future on exactly that sort of project is China.

CHINA

Environmental change in China, as elsewhere, consists of many complex and interrelated factors. The one factor that seems to have most caught the attention of the Chinese government is water scarcity. The Chinese Communist Party is putting an enormous amount of effort into water security, and so it is a good place to start when trying to understand the best-case scenario for the CCP's ability to grasp and adapt to environmental crises in general.

China is ahead of many of its neighbors in its determination to secure water supplies in any way it can. Control over the Himalayan watershed may even have been a factor in the Tibet takeover, and a desire for access to the water from Siberia's gushing rivers may be one of the many driving components of Sino-Russian relations.

The reasons for China's focus on water are easy to understand. Approximately 18 percent of China is desert. Around 78 percent of that total is natural and the rest was man-made by the sort of conditions the Sumerians would recognize, with farmers and pastoralists reducing around 154,440 square miles of previously productive soil to desert.[38] Across the country, vast resettlement programs have been initiated, with hundreds of thousands already relocated from some of the most parched regions to brand-new communities.[39]

One of the driest areas is China's north, where close to 200 million people are in danger of water starvation. The Gobi desert is just 75 miles or so outside Beijing, and, due to poor land management as well as climate change, it is moving closer all the time. According to one 2008 study, the two main reservoirs for the city of 16 million people were below 10 percent capacity.[40] Chinese hydraulics engineer Professor Liu Zihui has said, "If the water supply stopped, it would be a disaster for Beijing. A crisis like that would affect the stability of people's lives. The stability of our society."[41] Beijing is also frequently choked with dust storms, just one of which, in 2006, smothered the city in around 363,762 tons of gritty dust in a single night.[42]

The government is concerned. It is also staffed by an unusually high number of engineers, with Chinese president Hu Jintao himself a hydroelectric engineer. The prevailing ethos seems to be that with the right engineering, man—or the CCP—can conquer nature. The results are engineering plans of staggering proportions. For example, the government is already working on the largest hydraulics project in the history of humanity, a $63 billion canal that would bring water from the south to the increasingly desertifying north. The canal is a Mao-era dream that is projected to take 50 years to build and will stretch about 2,175 miles. Pumps will move the water uphill, and some sections will tunnel through mountains. Professor Liu is working on the project and his attitude exemplifies the man-over-nature approach. As he explains, "I don't feel we are conquering nature. We think nature itself isn't very fair. God isn't fair. Why is that? He's given Southern China so much water but given the North so little. It's good land—nice flat land—up there. But it's got so little water. So we say, as God isn't fair, we are trying to balance out God's unfairness."[43]

Unfortunately, God is in the details. On paper the big engineering projects might look good, provide ample opportunity for financial and political gain, and serve to absorb some of the excess workforce (predominantly male due to the one-child policy and a cultural bias toward boys). However, it is unlikely that this sort of megaproject will solve China's water problems. According to some projections, once the canal is done, given the country-wide rain deficit, melted glaciers, leakages, and evaporation, it may only be able to deliver around 5 percent of the north's water deficit, while taking proportionately more than that out of other areas that need it and, in the process, worsening a growing North-South social rift.[44]

Another problem with the canal plan is that not only does China have a water deficit, but it is poisoning the precious water it does have. The Chinese government's own numbers show that more than 50 percent of the rivers in China are graded too dangerous for any sort of human use, including washing clothes. A third are so toxic that they are off the scale. One river, the Huai, provides water to around 100 million people. As of 2006, every day half a million tons of untreated human sewage were dumped straight into the river, as well as millions of tons of toxic waste, including ammonia, cyanide, and arsenic from tanneries, industrial sites, mines, and chemical works. The river water is then used for irrigation, infiltrating the ground water and seeping into the crops. The result is "rivers of death," bordered by villages with astronomical disease and cancer rates.[45] There is no guarantee that, by the time the south-north canal accrues flow from various tributaries the length of China, the water will be usable in any form.

There are other options. Water shortage is essentially a problem of power shortage. There is a lot of water, several oceans full; it just has salt in it, and desalination plants take power. The canal would take a gigantic infrastructure investment, and then a huge annual outlay to drive the water north. Given the scope of the project, it is possible that, with newly available technologies, the money destined for the canal would be better invested in desalination plants in the north. Desalt plants may not look as dramatic as the Great Canal of China, but they could be in operation quicker, are strategically more secure, don't steal water from other areas, and, as the technology is refined, could end up as a comparatively affordable long-term solution (this is the route that Israel is starting down in the hope that it will ease its water problems with its neighbors).[46] If China has an overwhelming social, political, and economic drive for massive make-work projects, it might be better off focusing on ones that markedly increase stability in changing conditions. For example, instead of a 2,175-mile south-north canal, the CCP might want to start thinking about extensive coastal defenses to protect its expensive seaside real estate and infrastructure from rising sea levels and storm surges. China needs to consider solutions that are designed not just for today's problems, but for tomorrow's crises.

Problems caused by a narrow focus on big fixes that produce, at best, mixed results, is a long-standing issue in China. The textbook case of Chinese environmental policies gone awry happened under Chairman Mao Zedong. During his tenure millions died as a result of famines triggered by poor policies. However, one directive stands out for its complete misunderstanding of the basic dynamics of agriculture.

Mao decided that sparrows were a menace to crops and must be eliminated. He decreed that, during a given period, the entire Chinese population should go outside, bang pots, and generally make as much noise as possible so that the sparrows would be too scared to land and eventually fall from the sky in exhaustion, making those not already dead easy to catch and kill. The plan worked well. Too well. Not only sparrows, but a wide range of birds also died, resulting in a massive boom in locusts and other pests that then ravaged crops. As a result, tons of toxic pesticides were poured onto the land; from there they leeched into the water systems and affected drinking water and crops. In the end, the Chinese government sent a top-secret request to the Soviets for a resupply of 200,000 sparrows. (Luckily, in one of the few agricultural mistakes avoided by North Korea, President Kim Il Sung sidestepped Mao's pressure to kill all North Korean sparrows as well. Allegedly he managed it by drafting a "three-year plan for punishing sparrows," which was discretely never implemented.[47]) China is lauded for its long-term planning; however it is worth bearing in mind that just because the plans are long term doesn't guarantee they are any good.

Today, as with the south-north canal, the drive for large-scale interventions continues in China. There are smaller-scale initiatives as well, though many, even if well conceived, suffer from a problem of implementation. There is a Chinese saying: "The mountains are high and the Emperor is far away." While the Chinese Communist Party seems suited for designing and implementing focused and cohesive foreign policies, and ordaining massive domestic programs (for better or worse), its control wanes at the increasingly restive local level. The countryside in particular has its own concerns, which are handled largely outside the purview of the central government. One reason is that local government, funded in large part by local industries, normally finances the local courts. As a result, if a local court finds a local business is polluting and orders it to cease production, the local government will stop receiving tax revenues and there will be job losses. Therefore, even with the strictest pollution regulations, there is likely to be habitual collusion between the business community, local government officials, and the court system.[48]

In China, local-level environmental programs also come up against sheer survival. The problems are legion: Often the land is poor; the water, if available, is polluted; local officials expropriate land for personal profit; there is no functioning, affordable legal system through which to seek redress; hundreds of millions of farmers can't afford health care; the list goes on. The situation is dire. It's hard not to cut down trees for fuel if you need to make a fire to boil safe drinking water for your family—even if you know that cutting down the trees will cause erosion and siltation that will make the water quality even worse as well as possibly contaminate your meager crops. The situation is reminiscent of the sort of dynamic that created such destructive misery for the Sumerian peasants—and for the same reasons. There are essentially too many people for the available regional resources. The Chinese government knows it. In one of its most famous large-scale plans, it has tried to mitigate demand through the one-child policy, but to secure additional needed supply it has no choice but to actively try to obtain resources from abroad.[49] Hence the drive with which China pursues its nationalistic capitalism policies.

Ever since ancient Sumer, the potential end results of relative resource scarcity have been seemingly foreseeable, and were described in detail in 1977 by Professor W. M. S. Russell, the man who introduced me to the Sumerians, and his wife and colleague, Claire Russell:

> The economic effects included price inflation and fall in real wages (which can be shown in many times and places to depend closely on population growth), unemployment, and often grandiose building projects (designed to absorb labor) which further depleted resources. The political effects included reduced freedom of the individual and a tendency to tyrannical government. The cultural effects include narrow specialization, distrust of new ideas (especially if simple and wideranging), superstition, intolerance and restrictive censorship. The social effects included greater inequality between classes, greater difficulty in moving from lower to higher classes, social tension and a tendency to redirect resentment to defenseless minorities. The behavioral effects included increases in all kinds of violence, involving violent crime, class conflict and persecution of minorities: the usual protective attitudes to women and children were impaired.[50]

China is not alone in facing these pressures, and one of the many differences between ancient Sumer and China is that the Chinese government realizes some of the dangers and is trying to use its authoritative powers to change course. However, its approach has weaknesses and already there is unrest. According to China's own numbers, there were around 87,000 riots, protests, and demonstrations around the country in 2005, the last year such numbers were available. Premier Wen Jiabao acknowledged this "affects the stability of the countryside and the society, and it must be clearly recognized by all levels of government and party committees."[51] What hasn't been so clearly recognized is that environmental change is going to add new stresses to an already difficult situation.

Generally, China has the opposite problem to the one India has. Whereas India benefits from grassroots initiatives and understanding of the problems but suffers from a lack of cohesive central support, the Chinese Communist Party applies its massive levers of state to challenges, sometimes without a real grasp of the on-the-ground realities. As their environments change and become more difficult to manage, both India and China will increasingly join the West in trying to shore up home deficiencies by securing resources and geopolitical support from abroad. However, even with development in Africa and Latin America, there is only so much "abroad" to go around, and those who already have access are not going to give it up easily. We are entering an era of new domestic vulnerabilities, new alliances, and a refocusing of strategic interests. India and China have the shared goals of stability, growth, and increasing geopolitical influence. How (and if) one, or the other, or both accomplish those goals could reshape the world—and might mean the difference between the blossoming of a renewed era of civilization or the creation of a new Ozymandias.

7

THE STORY SO FAR

A weak people means a strong state and a strong state means a weak people. Therefore, a country which has the right way is concerned with weakening the people.

—Sun Tzu, *The Art of War*, classic Chinese
text on strategy, circa 403–221 BCE[1]

When a people are impoverished, they become greedy; when they are greedy, they become disaffected; when disaffected, they either go over to the enemy or kill their rulers themselves.

—Kautilya, *The Arthashastra*, classic Indian
text on strategy, circa 150 AD[2]

China and India often have different ways of dealing with the same challenges, and one of the biggest challenges they will soon face is how to mitigate and adapt to environmental change. Both will suffer domestic damage and dislocation, and will join the West in trying to develop and maintain international relationships that can supply needed resources and support. The methods China and India use to achieve those goals, however, are likely to be markedly different from each other. As with every nation—and perhaps even more so with China and India, which both claim thousands of years of history—Chinese and Indian policies did not spring from a vacuum, but rather evolved from each country's own historical senses of nationhood. This short section outlines key points in China and India's recent past—a period of colonization, emancipation, and growth—in order to give a sense of the two countries' current national imperatives, as well as offer an indication of the sort of alliances they will likely be looking for.

In the West, colonial maneuverings in Asia are frequently glossed over, or romanticized as Great Games. In places like China and India, the memories of those periods still sear—and play an important role in shaping current and future foreign policy. As of 2008, the average age of the Indian Council of Ministers was just over 60, or around the same age as the country itself.[3] Indian prime minister Manmohan Singh was a teen at Independence. The president of China, Hu Jintao, came of political age during the Cultural Revolution, which began around 1966. Many policy makers in both countries know first hand, or through immediate relatives, the reality of colonization, severe unrest, and starvation.

In the nineteenth century, the two countries were both also militarily subjugated by European powers and, in the case of China, by Japan as well. Those events are still frequently referred to in public discourse (more so in China than in India).

For China one of the colonial traumas most often mentioned is the Opium Wars, beginning in 1839, during which the British deliberately fostered opium addiction in the Chinese population in order to weaken the nation and forcibly gain access to trade goods.[4]

In India, a key moment was 1857. Existing discontent sparked into rebellion when the (British) East India Company introduced new rifles that were likely lubricated with a combination of pig and cow fat. They were unacceptable to the Indian troops, as Muslim soldiers were not allowed to touch pigs, and Hindu soldiers revered cows. During the uprising, some Indian soldiers killed their commanding officers as well as other British residents. The British soon retook control. The reprisals were horrific, and included shooting hundreds of live Indian soldiers out of cannons.[5] The British called this event the Indian Mutiny. Many Indians call it the First War of Independence. India is also still suffering from the hurried dissection of British India in the months leading up to Independence in 1947. This Partition led to British India being cut up into secular India and Muslim Pakistan, and has led to decades of conflict over control of the border region of Kashmir. Making things even more difficult for the new states, Pakistan itself was physically divided into West Pakistan (the modern country of Pakistan) and East Pakistan (now Bangladesh).

Terrible times, such as the Opium Wars in China (1839–1842 and 1856–1860), the events in India of 1857, and Partition (1947) still live in the hearts and minds of many Chinese and Indian strategists. They are touchstones, motivators, points of reference. They are the reason some Indian and Chinese nationalists don't even like visiting Western capitals. While many Western leaders think the world has moved on, at least some of the geopolitical drive in China and India comes from a desire to ensure that the colonial experience is never revisited. For example, the Chinese Communist Party's identity is still overtly bound up in its role of "uniting all of mother China after 150 years of humiliation at the hands of foreigners."[6]

Though their national pain may have grown from similar roots, China and India branched away from each other in their approach to achieving immediate post-independence national security. Broadly, China opted for a more centrally controlled, assertive model. India chose a more international, consensus-based, defensive model. While China took control of Tibet in the 1950s and laid claim to Taiwan, India tried to position itself as a moral leader in the global non-aligned movement. The two policies did not sit comfortably side by side. As Indian national security advisor J. N. Dixit wrote in the 1950s, "Mao Tse-tung and Chou-en Lai did not quite share [Indian Prime Minister Jawaharlal] Nehru's vision of a great era of Asian cooperation being structured on the basis of Sino-Indian friendship. The Chinese were hard-nosed and focused on their territorial aspirations and strategic interests. They firmly believed, and still believe, that their destiny is to be the most important Asian power and to become one of the great powers of the world, regardless of their claims of 'non-ambition' off and on. This perception was in total contrast to the Indian policies of what I would call 'emotional positivism' toward China."[7]

Given the two countries' differing approaches and long, shared border, it is not surprising that the two views of foreign relations soon came to a crashing head. While India was one of the first countries to recognize communist China, it had also accepted the Dalai Lama and his followers when they fled Tibet in 1959 following the Chinese takeover. China's leadership thought Nehru was, in the words of Chinese prime minister Chou En-lai, "getting very cocky."[8] As an added impetus, there had recently been devastating and demoralizing famines in China, caused in large part by poor central government policies. Mao decided that winning a quick border war would improve morale at home and keep India in line. On October 20, 1962, China invaded India. Chinese forces made quick advances, stunning India. On November 21, China declared a unilateral ceasefire.[9]

Though Nehru had attempted to position India as a global moral force, no nation came to India's aid during China's strike. Nehru and India were left shocked and humiliated. This led to a marked shift in India's foreign policy, and the country started to concentrate in earnest on building defenses. Nehru became convinced that technological development was key to defense development. The sciences took a front seat. He also tried to improve relations with the United States, as India's Soviet ally had proved unreliable by staying out of the fray in 1962. At first the United States seemed interested, but soon U.S. policy toward India changed considerably.

The reason for the change is still in force today, and is one of the stumbling blocks for a full alliance between India and the West. In the 1960s, the United States joined Britain and China in deciding to back Pakistan. Each country had its own reasons. Ever since Partition, Britain considered Pakistan its main strategic partner in the region. According to Narendra Singh Sarila, a former personal secretary to the last British viceroy, Lord Mountbatten, two of the main reasons the British nurtured the idea of an independent Pakistan was to gain a "forward defensive glacis" against the Soviets, and to have a lever of control over Middle East oil.[10] Britain still relies on Pakistan, now with combating terrorism as well. In November 2006, British prime minister Tony Blair visited Pakistan and Afghanistan for talks on how to handle terrorism. Notably, he didn't visit India, which for decades has been fighting Wahhabi extremists—often funded by Pakistan and its ally Saudi Arabia. More recently, in early 2009, British foreign secretary David Miliband created consternation in New Delhi when, on a visit to the Indian capital, he reportedly pushed for Indian concessions to Pakistan on Kashmir.[11]

In the case of China, the reasons for the country's relationship with Pakistan included gaining access to the Middle East and to ports on the geostrategic Indian Ocean, as well as encouraging Pakistan to aid terrorist attacks in India in order to destabilize it, making India less of a competitor to China.

Given the growing relationship between China and Pakistan in the late 1960s, the United States found Pakistan a useful backdoor into China during the period in which official relations were impossible. As a result, President Richard Nixon and National Security Advisor Dr. Henry Kissinger were willing to go to great lengths to shore up Pakistan in order to keep their access to China. This resulted in one of the most unfortunate touchstone events in modern U.S.-India relations.

By 1971, the odd geographic construct that was Pakistan was falling apart. Many of the citizens of East Pakistan resented that the culturally different people of West Pakistan were running their affairs and there were rumblings of discontent threatening the stability of northeastern India. In November 1971, Indian prime minister Indira Gandhi went to Washington to discuss the situation, but there was little useful diplomacy. Declassified Oval Office tapes of the day after the talks reveal Nixon and Kissinger discussing what transpired. The sort of language used still rankles. Nixon said, "We really slobbered over the old witch." Kissinger said, "The Indians are bastards anyway," adding that Indians "are the most aggressive goddam people around there," and are "slippery, treacherous people," whereas "the Pakistanis are straightforward and sometimes extremely stupid. The Indians are more devious."[12] While Indian policy makers at the time may not have known the exact language used, they were certainly aware that the United States was not entirely supportive.[13]

Soon the situation deteriorated further. It had been a particularly bad flood year, and India was already hosting tens of thousands of environmental refugees fleeing across the border from East Pakistan. Soon millions more fleeing the repression of the West Pakistan troops joined them. In a portent of things to come if, as projected, environmental change creates million of Bangladeshi refugees, India became very concerned that its northeast was on the verge of being destabilized. India declared that this was no longer an internal Pakistani affair. It armed and trained refugees and sent them back to East Pakistan. India also sent its own troops. West Pakistan bombed Indian airports. India bombed West Pakistan.

To protect its ally, Pakistan, and to bolster relations with China, the United States became heavily, if covertly, involved.[14] In spite of United States and Chinese support, the war ended with East Pakistan becoming independent Bangladesh.[15] Nixon was so upset that he said, "I don't want the Indians to be happy. [. . .] I want a public relations program developed to piss on the Indians. [. . .] We can't let these goddamn sanctimonious Indians get away with this."[16] India was well aware of how it was viewed by the U.S. administration.[17]

A postwar memorandum prepared for Dr. Kissinger by the CIA's Office of National Estimates summed up the feeling in India: "The basic fact is that the Indians are suspicious of all great powers—even the Soviets—and chafe under their dependence on the more developed countries. Mrs. Gandhi's reaction to our actions during the war has further reinforced her inclination to seek greater independence of action."[18] The assessment was correct. In the same way the Suez debacle forced a shift in policy for the UK and France, India's humiliating loss to China in 1962 (in which it was not supported by its nominal allies, the Soviets) and veritable isolation (tinged with active U.S. hostility) during the Bangladesh War made the country even more determined to be able to protect itself—and it did something about it.

In 1974, 12 years after the surprise attack from China and 3 years after its third war with China- and West-supported Pakistan resulted in the independence of Bangladesh, India exploded a nuclear device. It became the world's sixth openly nuclear power. The tests earned India technological and economic sanctions and rebukes from the West. In 1998, India tested again. The 1998 blasts garnered the predictable admonitions, but the major powers also realized that India could no longer be ignored, and soon a flood of foreign leaders came to Delhi looking to make deals. Technologically advanced defense and a booming economy were starting to work where emotional positivism had failed.

Another factor in recent Asian history has been, and is, the Soviet Union and Russia. After the disintegration and confusion of the 1990s, Russia has reemerged as a global petropower. Within Asia, Russia's role is largely based on the export of weaponry (which ties the recipient into the security apparatus of Russia) and resources (including large fossil fuel deposits, uranium, crops, and, potentially, water). Russia is an important nation with strong international connections, but it is increasingly being pulled into the anti-West position of other nationalist capitalist countries, and its ties with China are growing. However, Russia is not actively expanding its global reach the way China is, except along its borders and in the Arctic, where the potential trade routes, fisheries, and fossil fuel reserves augment Russia's existing strategic and economic strengths. Generally though (and given the scope of this book, general is the best one can offer), China is becoming a much more dynamic international player than Russia, and India is crucially important as it is a potential "swing vote" in the new balance of power. So, for now, we will concentrate on China and India.

Today any geopolitical calculus must factor in China and India. Those two economic, population, and military powerhouses, along with Russia, are shifting the fulcrum of the world eastward and realigning the balance in new ways. The twentieth century has set some vectors, such as China's and India's overwhelming pushes for strategic independence, the largely thwarted desires of India to gain acceptance from the West on equal terms, the mutual suspicion between China and India, and the support of Pakistan by both China and the West. However, just as the climate system is in flux, so are relations between the great and emerging powers. Once geophysical changes are added into the equation, some of the existing vectors may be reinforced, and others deviated. What happens next in Asia may determine what happens next in the world.

8

INTERESTING TIMES, NARROWING OPTIONS

"It's not what your country can do for you, but what your country can steal from other countries."

—Comedian Jon Lajoie[1]

The United States, China, Russia, and India are likely to dominate geopolitics in the first half of the twenty-first century. The EU will play a role as well, but it will face increased stress at home as environmental change takes its toll on regional treaties, domestic politics, and economic growth. The EU is better designed for sharing the spoils in good times than for sharing the burden in times of scarcity. Already there are potential flashpoints around fisheries quotas, water sharing agreements, and even emergency services. Moreover, the EU unfortunately carries the legacy of its colonial past, which may restrict its reach in several countries in the developing world. Individual European nations may be pivotal in specific areas, but unfortunately it seems unlikely that a strong and cohesive European foreign policy, backed by a viable military, will emerge soon. An example of the challenge of always presenting a united front was seen in the differing attitudes of Poland and France toward the 2003 U.S. invasion of Iraq.

Meanwhile, the thing to note about the United States, China, Russia, and India is that three of the four are in Asia. Russia increasingly thinks of itself as also an Asian nation—as shown in 2008, when newly inaugurated Russian president Dmitry Medvedev chose as his first official visits Kazakhstan, in central Asia, and China. Russia has a fitful but strong relationship with China, and on that visit President Medvedev said: "Russian-Chinese cooperation has today emerged as a key factor in international security, without which it is impossible for the international community to take major decisions."[2] They are perhaps not quite there as yet, but this new "cooperation" must be taken seriously. Asia is no longer a mere arena for the "real" powers to fight proxy wars. The chess pieces of the Great Game have outgrown the board and are now playing the players. Understanding these new realities and relationships will be critical for fostering stability in turbulent times. In that context, it has been a challenging few years for the United States, and it is worth taking a look at how U.S. foreign policy is faring in the world generally, and in Asia in particular.

In spite of gaining ground after the Cold War, and the burst of geopolitical empathy following the tragedy of September 11, 2001, the United States has found it increasingly difficult to maintain influence in Asia, especially following the Afghanistan and Iraq wars. There is a growing movement away from overt alignment with the United States, and U.S. strategists know it. A 2003 U.S. Defense Science Board Task Force research paper concluded, "During the Cold War, US bases on foreign soil did cause considerable friction, but such friction was, for the most part, bearable to Allied political leaders. However, since the Cold War the situation has changed dramatically. The existence of a substantial American presence on land bases in the Middle East has contributed to political unraveling in that region and provided a propaganda base for those opposing America's presence."[3]

As a result, in spite of large U.S. military expenditures for building bases in the Middle East, when it came time to use those bases, for example, for the war in Afghanistan, host countries often refused permission.[4] The task force findings are blunt: "The political reality of the post–Cold War era is that US allies are less dependent on the United States for their security than during the days of the Soviet Union. In fact, in the current war on terrorism, the United States has become more dependent on allies and friends for intelligence and cooperation in addressing a global, distributed threat than it ever was during the Cold War."[5]

A problem for the United States is the perception that its security establishment has a tendency toward expediency and will use groups when convenient and then abandon them once no longer needed. One example of this is when the United States first armed Islamic extremists to defeat the Soviet Union in Afghanistan and then, once that was accomplished, pulled out, leaving the trained and armed militants to focus on other targets, including, eventually, the United States itself. From the Arctic to the Pacific, I've had people tell me that they think the United States is an inconsistent ally caught up in short-term objectives. It doesn't matter whether it's true or not (or which nations benefit from spreading that sort of impression); what matters is that it is starting to be believed and nations are acting accordingly.

There is growing, increasingly confident, increasingly nationalistic capitalist, anti-U.S. (and often anti-West in general) feeling in some sectors of the developing world, especially following the financial crisis that started in 2008. Even within the West, there is concern. For example, the U.S. Defense Science Board study on seabasing found: "The reluctance of France and Germany to support U.S. policy over Iraq was a signal that the United States can no longer rely on European support for many of its policies. Such attitudes will inevitably translate at some time in the future to an unwillingness to provide access to America's bases in Europe during the course of a major crisis."[6]

Even the strong relationship between the United States and the UK is occasionally strained. The two countries worked together on a multibillion-dollar fighter jet that would be used by both militaries and sold to other countries. The United States, however, refused to release all the technical details to the UK, meaning that the UK's fleet could not be operationally independent.[7] That did not go down well in London, and, in justifying his 2006 decision to reinvigorate Britain's nuclear weapons program, Prime Minister Tony Blair said in parliament that part of the reason was that "the independent nature of the British deterrent is again an additional insurance against circumstances where we are threatened but America is not."[8]

Meanwhile, as the United States finds relations with even its closest allies increasingly complex, new and renewed organizations are restructuring military, political, and economic alliances in order to shore up regional positions and sideline the West. A case in point is the Shanghai Cooperation Organization (SCO), founded in 2001. While not explicitly (or effectively) a counter to NATO, the member countries are China, Russia, Kazakhstan, Tajikistan, Uzbekistan, and the Kyrgyz Republic. Iran, Pakistan, Mongolia, and India are observers.[9] The countries have a shared goal of regional stability and economic cooperation. Both Beijing and Moscow define such stability as the removal, or at least the diminution, of Western influence in the region. Russia, for one, is touting the SCO as a potential energy cartel, and, as access to food and water becomes even more important, they might be included in the SCO remit as well.[10]

There are also moves to insulate emerging economies from reliance on West-dominated structures such as the International Monetary Fund (IMF) and the World Bank. In 1997, speculators were alleged to have caused widespread damage to the "Asian Tiger" economies, collapsing currencies in Thailand, Malaysia, and Indonesia, and provoking a plague of bankruptcies. The IMF offered bailouts only on the condition that the governments make sweeping changes to the way they do business, often through giving multinationals increased access to protected economies. To try to avoid that sort of perceived interference again, in 2007 China, Japan, Korea, and other Asian countries announced that they were going to pool their financial reserves so that they could solve problems on their own, without having to resort to the IMF.[11] And following the onset of the financial crisis in 2008, countries such as China have demanded greater power in the traditionally Western-dominated economic institutions and have suggested that the U.S. dollar be abandoned as the favored global currency.

Some nationalist leaders are taking advantage of anti-West feelings for political gain. One poster boy for this brand of rabble-rousing has been Venezuelan president Hugo Chavez, a strong nationalistic capitalist riding high on fossil fuel reserves (Venezuela is the fourth largest foreign supplier of oil to the United States). Chavez made a point of visiting Iran to show support in the face of U.S. sanctions, and has been a strong proponent of building up another non-Western institution, Mercosur (the main South American trading bloc), into a major economic and political force in South America, and beyond. In 2007, President Chavez declared his intention to take Venezuela out of the World Bank and the IMF.[12] It is telling that his 2006 melodramatic declaration on the floor of the UN—that he could still smell the sulfur left after the visit from "the Devil," U.S. president George W. Bush—elicited more chuckles than boos.[13]

Around the world the United States, and often the West in general, may be in danger of being sidelined, or perhaps sidestepped. Apart from the overt political and economic shifts, it is also happening in myriad little ways. For example, one of the West's big selling points has always been its educational institutions. Attracting the world's best (or at least best-connected) students gave the West a chance to introduce future generations of global policy makers to some of the many very good things about the West, such as open debate and the ability to run daily errands without fear of being shot, arrested, or extorted.

However, increasingly self-confident countries are now simply importing the education rather than exporting their children. Qatar, for one, decided that it wanted its own medical, design, computer, business, government, and engineering schools. So it asked top English-language universities to put in bids to create branches in Qatar that would be comparable to ones at home. The result was a modern, sprawling Education City. Here, students, primarily from Qatar but also from all over the Middle East and beyond, can take classes from Cornell Medical College, Texas A&M, Georgetown University, Carnegie Mellon University, and Canada's College of the North Atlantic. Their degrees have the same value as if they were awarded in North America, but the students earn them without their parents worrying about the perceived cultural risks of four years in the West.[14] A similar model is being developed in India.[15] Even people who have gone through the U.S. education system are reexamining their options. One 2007 study estimated that 60,000 previously U.S.-based Indian IT professionals had moved back to India in the past four years.[16]

One of the biggest problems for the U.S. image and position abroad, aside from the U.S. role in the current financial crisis, is the U.S. legacy in Iraq. The highly respected Iraq Study Group (ISG) reported in December 2006 that perceived failure in Iraq "could diminish America's credibility and influence in a region that is the center of the Islamic world and vital to the world's energy supply. This loss would reduce America's global influence at a time when pressing issues in North Korea, Iran, and elsewhere demand our full attention and strong U.S. leadership of international alliances."[17] Response to the report from the Arab world was unequivocal. Abdel Moneim Said, head of Al-Ahram Center for Political and Strategic Studies in Cairo, said, "This report is a recognition of the

limitation of American power. In the short term, America will highly suffer the loss of its reputation and credibility in the region."[18] And a lot of
work will need to be done to secure the U.S. reputation in the long term.
According to U.S. Senator Jack Reed, chairman of the Senate Armed
Services Subcommittee on Emerging Threats and Capabilities, Arabs are
"trying to figure out what the Americans are going to do, and trying develop their own plans. They're trying to figure out their Plan B."[19]

One reason the West in general, and the United States in particular,
seems to be having such a hard time is that, as with the Northwest Passage, short-term interests sometimes jump in the way of long-term security plans. Another reason is persistent intelligence failure. The serious
deficits in the U.S. intelligence establishment became clear in the les-
sons-learned phase of post-9/11.[20] In spite of widespread acknowledge-
ment that something had to be done to improve intelligence gathering,
in 2006 there were still fewer than ten analysts at the Defense Intelligence Agency with more than two years experience in analyzing the Iraqi
insurgency.[21]

It is hard to underestimate the difficulty and importance of getting,
and understanding, reliable intelligence. Acquiring solid on-the-ground
information, especially in areas with limited electronics (or even electricity) often has to do with access and the ability to blend in and be accepted. According to the ISG, this was a persistent problem in Iraq. As
of December 2006, the U.S. embassy in Iraq had a staff of around 1,000.
Of those, 33 spoke some Arabic and, in all, out of the whole embassy,
only 6 were fluent.[22] There was no report on how many could speak
Farsi, the national language of Iran, which was likely being heard more
and more on the ground, but it is unlikely the numbers were much better. There are similar problems elsewhere in the Gulf, and in many other
non-Western countries.

Compare that to the potential person-to-person information-
gathering networks of countries such as China (with its large numbers of

workers on the ground, and political access in countries around the world), Pakistan, India, and even Bangladesh. For example, there are millions of South Asians working in the Gulf. Qatar alone has a population of around 900,000, more than 50 percent of whom are foreign workers, mostly from South Asia. In the capital, Doha, three out of every four people are foreigners with temporary residence.[23] They work in every facet of society, including as drivers, doctors, accountants, construction workers, teachers, and nurses, and many of them speak Arabic and attend local mosques.

If information was needed on the nocturnal habits of a Qatari general, then, given the choice between getting information from a Harvard-educated "NGO worker" who buys him drinks in the local illegal bar or a Bangladeshi driver who takes him to his appointments, most would go with the driver. That difficulty to blend in, coupled with perceived inconsistent support to allies, both individual and national, partially explains why the United States, and some other Western countries, are having difficulties gaining, and even retaining, ground in some parts of the world.

Though the United States is a vitally important global power, it seems to be finding it harder to make unilateral headway. For example, since the fall of the Soviet Union, the United States has been trying to gain purchase in the resource-rich and geostrategic newly independent states of the former USSR in Asia, the so-called 'Stans: Tajikistan, Turkmenistan, Uzbekistan, Kazakhstan, and Kyrgyzstan (also known as the Kyrgyz Republic). Not only is the region strategically located between Russia, China, and the oil fields of the Middle East, but some of the states have copious fossil fuel reserves of their own. Even the ones that don't, like the Kyrgyz Republic, have been the subject of American interest, and the difficulties the United States has had there are instructive.

As of 2009, the Kyrgyz Republic had the unusual distinction of hosting both a Russian and American military base, with the U.S. base being primarily used for operations in Afghanistan. In 2005, the Kyrgyz Republic experienced a relatively bloodless "uprising" that deposed the country's president. It was a curious event, one that was widely believed to have been "encouraged" by Washington in order to install a leadership that would allow the U.S. base to stay for the foreseeable future.[24] The Kyrgyz base had become particularly important to U.S. strategy because American criticism of the government in neighboring Uzbekistan contributed to the Uzbeks demanding that the United States pack up its base there and leave the country. However, whatever advantage the U.S. gained with the Kyrgyz regime change was short lived. The new government soon asked the U.S. military to leave. Both Secretary of State Condoleezza Rice and Secretary of Defense Donald Rumsfeld had to visit the capital, Bishkek, before the base was grudgingly allowed to stay.

As a result of the instability in the government, created in part through these extreme pressures, some in the political class in the Krygyz Republic started to grow impatient with perceived interference. Washington's apparent attempt to install a friendly government destabilized the region enough to bring rival factions together against the United States itself. One Kyrgyz diplomat told me bluntly, and in faultless English, that the Kyrgyz Republic's political future lay with Russia. Echoing what I had heard elsewhere, he said he didn't think the United States was in it for the long haul, and the Kyrgyz Republic needed a reliable alternative to China, especially as trade between the Kyrgyz Republic and China increased.

The Kyrgyz Republic seems to have made its choice. Russia is already saying its Kyrgyz base "is here forever" and is upgrading the installation. The Kyrgyz gave Russia its site for free. Meanwhile, in June 2009, after initially announcing the U.S. base would have to leave, the Kyrgyz allowed the base to stay, for $180 million.

In contrast to U.S. difficulties in Central Asia, there is a military consolidation by Russia and a growing Chinese economic role, as evidenced by the SCO. As food and water supply problems increase, neighbors will be tied even closer together through trade and water sharing. Nations concerned about options, if not balance, are now finding India an interesting option. India has a base in Tajikistan, a defense agreement with Mongolia, and is playing a key role in the reconstruction of Afghanistan.[25]

All in all, globalization is making many of the Asian, and other emerging countries, increasingly, and effectively, interdependent and, as a result, more resistant to Western pressure. It used to be easier to pick off an unfriendly regime. Now it's more like pulling at a lose thread. Tug hard enough and it all unravels. The tiny Kyrgyz Republic, with just five million people, is much more than just the Kyrgyz Republic. It has friends in Moscow, wannabe friends in Beijing, extremists with ties to Afghanistan, burgeoning relations with India, and more. The Kyrgyz Republic has options. Nations that come in with money and short-term objectives may trigger undesired responses. However, as I proposed with the Arctic, if the United States starts building equal and long-term relationships with allies, ones that take into account changing security, political, and environmental realities, it can have a lasting and influential role in Asia. And having a long-term plan for Asia is crucial because, in many ways, Asia is the future.

Combined, China and India alone have around a third of the world's population and are booming economically. In 2008, according to the IMF, the country with the largest purchase power parity was the United States (with 14,264,600 international dollars).[26] Second was China (8,223,494, including Hong Kong). A distant third was Japan (4,354,368), followed by India (3,288,345). Number five, Germany, was around 2,910,490. At least by this measure, together, China and India are closing in on being wallet-to-wallet with the United States, and both have been growing much faster than most countries in the West, especially following the financial crisis.

Both China and India are planning for the future. Together, they graduate more than half a million engineers and scientists a year. The U.S. graduates about 60,000 (and a proportion of those are from China and India).[27] Both China and India are nuclear states with large, well-trained and well-equipped militaries. Both have extensive intelligence-gathering networks. They have also been politically and economically dominant before, have thousands of years of civilization and archives full of accomplishments that start well before Europeans had thought to move out of caves and upgrade to mud huts. They both face serious domestic problems, but, geopolitically, they are strong and getting stronger and believe reasserting their historic roles is their due. Their rise, however, is not inevitable and could depend substantially on how they handle environmental change. Already China is having problems.

Many pundits take the continued growth and increasing dominance of China as a given. It isn't. Apart from its penchant for dubious megaprojects, as described earlier, there are other serious fractures in the system that will exacerbate, and be exacerbated by, disruptive environmental change.

There are a myriad of theories about what, if anything, is China's fatal flaw. Some think, rather convincingly, that its banking, financial, and legal systems are its Achilles' heel. Others argue corruption is rotting the ship of state. Some are convinced that a bloom of democracy will suddenly blanket the countryside.

One factor that cuts across all those issues is the Chinese Communist Party's self-destructive obsession with controlling the lifeblood of a healthy body politic: the free flow of information. The CCP treats information the same way it treats water, as something that has to be controlled, dammed, diverted, and made useful to the state. In the process, information often ends up poisoned and, worse than useless, dangerous.

There are nearly habitual occurrences of systemic censorship and the distortion of facts. Some examples:

- History is rewritten to fit political goals. For example, the researchers in the government-sponsored Northeast Project (run by the Centre of China's Borderland History and Geography Research) have declared that, far from having a long and independent history, parts of Korea used to be Chinese territory.[28] These statements are relevant because they are the same kind that justified claims over Tibet and Taiwan and are increasingly being used to legitimize a potential Chinese encroachment on India, Russia, and Mongolia.

- Workplaces falsify information with an efficiency that would have been the envy of the Soviet Union. According to a report in the *International Herald Tribune* about widespread cover-ups in industry, "Some factories use specially designed software to churn out fictitious employee work logs. Factory managers share tips in Internet chatrooms and hire consultants who coach them on how auditors operate. Less innovative are the cheat sheets that factory supervisors hand out to their employees with questions that auditors are likely to ask—and the preferred answers. (Do you work on Sundays? Answer: Never!)"[29]

- Information fraud is endemic in the Chinese research community. A study by China's own Ministry of Science on 180 PhD candidates resulted in 60 percent admitting to plagiarism, and an equal percentage admitting to paying bribes in order to get their work published.[30]

- Search engines and Internet service providers are told to block posts containing words like "democracy" and "human rights."[31]

- In 2008, the Chinese government tried to cover up the fact that a popular brand of baby milk was contaminated by melamine so as not to cast a pall over the Beijing Olympics and for the sake of "social stability."[32]

The Chinese press is in a category all its own when it comes to unreliable information.[33] The government regularly issues directives and intimidates and censors journalists. Domestically, newspaper editors receive regular lists of banned topics, and all foreign news agencies that want to distribute information in China must first have it approved by the state media. According to one newspaper editor, the media's role is primarily to "entertain and promote consumption."[34] The controls extend to the seemingly minute, including: a newspaper cartoonist suspended for drawing a caricature of President Hu; a Chinese filmmaker who was banned for five years from making movies in his home country because he entered a film in the Cannes festival without requesting the government's permission first; and a concert in Shanghai where the Rolling Stones were asked not to play songs with suggestive lyrics. The Stones complied. Almost everyone complies, including Yahoo!, which provided the Chinese government with user information that contributed to the cases that resulted in the convictions, with jail terms, of at least three Chinese journalists.[35]

At every level of society, except perhaps the very top, open discussion is impossible. This censorship, and equally potent self-censorship, makes it difficult for the Chinese government to know what is going on. China tries to get around its information flow problem by having some members of its national news service, Xinhua, file two reports: an official one for the newswire and a more "complete" one for the political elite. The second sort, known as "internal reference materials," is classified and is designed for decision makers only. According to one former high-ranking Xinhua official: "The ministers and provincial leaders no longer read the official press. The first thing they do each morning is to read the internal reference reports."[36] In effect, China's leadership is relying in part on a spy system based on far-flung journalists, combined with honest reporting by local officials, to gauge the state of the nation. There are obvious problems with that system. Given that Xinhua reporters are not particularly well paid, they are susceptible to bribes from those same local officials. Together, a corrupt town official and a compromised Xinhua reporter can impede accurate information from getting out of a region.

This sort of breakdown in the flow of information is likely what happened with the coverage of the Chinese mining industry, triggering a national crisis. In the first half of 2005, around 2,700 miners died in accidents. It seems the central government had no idea how bad it had become out in the field. Corrupt local officials colluded with mine operators and, presumably, local reporters to cover up the deteriorating situation in the mines. By the time the central government realized the depth of the problem, it was forced to shut down nearly a third of the country's tens of thousands of coal mines in order to reassert control.[37] It indicated a massive intelligence failure—and a very public and costly loss of face in an energy-depleted country. Given the extensive effort to procure fossil fuels from places like Africa, the fact that the CCP couldn't secure domestic supply was an indication that something was wrong with the system. It doesn't bode well.

The obvious solution would seem to be a more open society, one that would allow a freer flow of information. But that would cause its own problems for the CCP. Conventional wisdom assumes that, as a country becomes more affluent, it's not long before democracy comes bounding along like an eager little puppy. In China, barring severely disruptive events (such as, potentially, a widespread ecological collapse that the government fails to satisfactorily address), a change in government is unlikely to happen, at least in the short term. One of the reasons is that with the way the Chinese authorities have structured the economy, growth is tied to strong central rule. The security apparatus ensures that labor unrest is kept to a minimum, the development of industrial infrastructure is pushed through with little regard to the wants of civil society, and through various centrally controlled economic levers, the cost of products are manipulated in order to be competitive in the world market.[38] Also, the continuation of China's nationalistic capitalism abroad dictates the need to stay in tight command at home. Loosen that control and the whole structure may start to fall apart.

Under the current system, in order to keep growing economically, or even just remain stable, China needs to stay authoritarian. And it is also increasingly bureaucratic. That means the government will continue to have problems with controlling information flow and assessing the true state of affairs in the countryside. This could increasingly undermine the nation, and potentially the CCP's legitimacy with the population, as environmental change results in centrally decided agriculture and water policies that are completely out of step with the on-the-ground reality. The CCP's mismanagement of the SARS outbreak in 2003—in which it ordered infected patients to circle Beijing in ambulances so that there would be a smaller number of cases on the hospital wards when World Health Organization inspectors came by[39]—is a small but symbolic example of the system's inability to handle sudden, complex crises, and its instinct to paper over the cracks. As the whole foundation starts to waver, in part as a result of encroaching environmental change, the government's inflexibility and culture of misinformation and secrecy could dangerously add to the instability. And subsequent grabs at big fixes may only make things worse.

There is a possibility that recurring droughts and floods in the countryside could become so intolerable they could lead to uncontrolled internal desperation and migration. In addition, in one area where it has loosened up control, the Communist Party has let developers in coastal cities build extensively. The result is the same as elsewhere when long-term planning takes a backseat to short-term money making in a volatile system: Expensive and critical infrastructure has been placed in vulnerable areas. Many of China's glittering, economic powerhouses, such as Shang-hai, are extremely low-lying and right on the coast, making them suscep-tible to rising sea levels and increased storm activity. Much of coastal China, home to most to the country's wealth creation, has the potential to go the way of Katrina-hit New Orleans. One big typhoon could cause a sudden shock to the Chinese economic system with billions in damage. Already mass evacuations caused by typhoons and storms are common along China's coast, with a million people evacuated in July 2005,[40] 500,000 evacuated in September 2005,[41] more than 630,000 evacuated in May 2006,[42] and close to 2 million people (300,000 from Shanghai) evac-uated in 2007.[43] In July 2008, 600,000 were evacuated and Shanghai closed all ferry stations. In September 2008, 460,000 were evacuated. In August 2009, another million were evacuated south of Shanghai. (The United States could learn from China how to execute well-coordinated, efficient evacuations.) With environmental change, more people will move from the suffering and desertifying countryside to the coastal economic centers, and the potential for crisis-related instability will only worsen.

Currently in China, given the relatively recent memories of chaos and starvation during the late 1960s and 1970s, there is a certain will-ingness to go along with an authoritarian regime if it is at least provid-ing stability, food, and the possibility for advancement, if not for you, then for your child. Should the government persistently fail in providing those essentials, the floodgates could start to buckle. Given the infor-mation flow problem, the situation could get surprisingly bad very quickly. The government is likely to respond aggressively, both domes-tically and internationally. Severe unrest would almost certainly result in the government using extreme force to try to quell dissent.

Meanwhile, the CCP policy of arming friends and neighbors to fight proxy wars against competitors could come back to haunt it. As the United States found when the militias it fostered in Afghanistan eventually turned on their erstwhile backers, by creating instability for others, China has risked destabilizing itself as well.[44] The CCP is constantly being tested, and if it ever starts to look weak, the assaults could begin in earnest both at home and abroad. If China fragments, or is too weak to protect its interests, it could lose carefully cultivated diplomatic and strategic ground in Central Asia, the Pacific, South America, South China Sea, Africa, and, of course, along its complex borders—especially as resentment builds with Himalayan neighbors over water sharing issues.

However, while many don't want China to get too strong, none of the major powers wants China to collapse completely. Too many in the West have economic interests tied to China, and too many regional countries, such as Russia and India, don't want extreme unrest on their doorstep. What they want, ideally, is a lasting peace. As a result, while there will be the inevitable maneuvering for advantage, China will likely get room and time to try to sort itself out. It may need to retrench, and lose ground internationally, in order to focus more attention on internal problems, but it is unlikely to completely crumble in the short term.

Whether China can continue with its expansion plans is another question. The cost of environmental change and the CCP's inability to deal with the problem is increasing. The Chinese deputy minister of the Environmental Protection Agency estimates that the loss to the Chinese economy caused by the environment is already around 15 percent of the GDP.[45] Other Chinese government numbers estimate that it would cost the equivalent of $84 billion to clean up the pollution created in 2004 alone.[46]

The CCP may have realized it has a problem, but it has yet to "mainstream" the solutions by, for example, ensuring that its plans will still be viable as the climate changes. That blind spot, exacerbated by a poor grasp of the changing environmental realities on the ground, is evident in megaprojects such as Dongtan, China's proposed multibillion-dollar "eco-city." The plan was for the new city to be entirely self-sufficient in water, energy, and most food, with a zero-emission transport system.[47] Unfortunately, the location the Chinese government has chosen for this low-carbon vision of the future was a low-lying alluvial island off the coast of Shanghai, one of the areas almost certain to be hit by rising sea levels and storm surges. It's not building utopia, it's building Atlantis. This is a classic case of focusing on our impact on the environment while ignoring a changing environment's impact on us, giving rise to potentially disastrous consequences.

Heading off expensive, dangerous, and disruptive environmental change will take a cohesive, systemic approach. It requires accurate ground-level information in order to assess the real vulnerabilities, flexible and innovative projects to counter them, and political will to follow through. While the CCP certainly has political will, it is currently lacking in the first two components. Interestingly, the same sort of long-term, meticulous, hard-nosed focus that the CCP is using to take on perceived external threats would go a long way toward countering internal environmental ones. Authoritarian regimes benefit from having an enemy. It gives justification for "strong measures" and a military build-up. While the specter of an independent Tibet or Taiwan is often rattled about in the Chinese press as a national "motivator," once water and food shortages begin in earnest, survival and affordability will be the most immediate daily threats for the Chinese people.

If the CCP declares environmental change in general, and climate change in particular, an enemy of the state, it might solve many problems in one go. Environmental change is a convenient foe because the public is already sensitized to the danger. Additionally, the climate change component can be highlighted and the CCP can use the *Stern Review*, and other publications, to lay the blame firmly at the feet of the West and its century of unbridled emissions, while at the same time pointing to the difficult sacrifices China made for the environment through its one-child policy. There are already some indications that this might be a natural course for the CCP to follow. Following the destructive earthquake in Sichuan province in 2008, Chinese soldiers were used to divert water from an unstable lake. The entire procedure was framed in military terms and, once successful, the local Communist Party chief declared that a "decisive victory" had been won.[48]

If at all successful, China's "war" on environmental change could promote stability in the countryside, foster a national sense of purpose, rein in badly performing local governments, take some of the stress off relations with Himalayan neighbors, offer new areas for research and development that China could then export, and mitigate some of the country's inevitable large-scale economic losses. But that's a pretty big "if."

For now, China is covering over domestic problems, relying on monolithic megaprojects instead of varied and flexible regional responses, and actively trying to expand its global reach through nationalistic capitalism to provide resources for shortfalls at home. The CCP seems to be working to a plan, but it looks like that plan doesn't take into account the real domestic impact of environmental change. And, just as big a problem geopolitically, it also doesn't seem to know what to do about our other increasingly important factor, India.

India's advances in defense aren't only for show. To understand the full motivations and the real intended audience for its nuclear tests, it helps to take a look at India's borders. India is situated in a rough corner of the world. Apart from nuclear China and Pakistan, India also shares boundaries with Bangladesh (which has signed a nuclear agreement with China, has Pakistan-funded militants seeping through the porous Indian border, and is often flooded, sending shoals of refugees toward India), the military dictatorship of Myanmar, and unstable Nepal. It is also a short boat ride from the problems of Sri Lanka (which, in 1991, resulted in the assassination of former Indian prime minister

Rajiv Gandhi), and is just a short hop from the narco-terrorism of Afghanistan.

India feels under siege. China helped to create Pakistan as a nuclear state in order to contain India, in the same way it helped North Korea go nuclear in order to concern Japan (and ultimately the United States).[49] The United States equipped and trained an army of extremists to bring down the Soviet Union in Afghanistan, and once it succeeded in 1989, it pulled out, leaving India with an influx of Pakistan-based fanatics ready to "liberate" Kashmir next. All the while, from its point of view, India acted as a responsible world citizen. It didn't proliferate its nuclear power (unlike Pakistan and China); it tried to warn and work with the United States to contain global terror (a threat it could see developing from its unfortunate vantage point as a target of terror); and in the 1990s it started the slow, painful, but necessary process of opening up its economy.

India can be frustrating and complicated, with a Byzantine bureaucracy and endless shifting internal political alliances, and it has crushing domestic problems. But at its core, India is more in line with what are deemed "Western values" than many other major powers in the region. It is democratic, officially secular, and enjoys a lively press. It is also accessible, with one of the largest numbers of English speakers of any nation in the world. It is a natural ally of the West.

However, in spite of rhetoric to the contrary, Western leaders have been slow to fully implement this option. In many chancelleries, India is still not treated as an equal partner with its own operational realities. For many in India, a particularly difficult period was the negotiation of the U.S.-India nuclear deal, first officially proposed in 2005. The deal— while certainly not the only important bilateral U.S.-India negotiation— is the modern touchstone of U.S.-India strategic relations and it bears some examination.

At first, under President George W. Bush, it seemed like India might be seriously considered as a key ally. After India's first nuclear detonations in the 1970s, sanctions had been imposed on the country, but domestic research had continued and India made huge strides toward developing an indigenous fast-breeder thorium-based power reactor. As India has an abundant domestic supply of thorium, this would allow the country another energy source outside the increasingly heated global battles over hydrocarbons and politically controlled nuclear fuel. All of this was regarded by India as legal since it had never signed the nuclear Non-Proliferation Treaty. However, the sanctions were still an impediment to partnership with the West.

On July 18, 2005, the United States seemed ready to acknowledge the reality of India's indigenous nuclear program. In 2006, President Bush visited India, military cooperation was deepened, and India was officially touted as an important strategic partner.[50] The two countries agreed in principle to an equal partner–style nuclear deal. The draft agreement would give India what it wanted: legitimacy in the eyes of the West as a mature, responsible nuclear power and a lifting of sanctions. The United States, and the West, would get a new customer for high-tech products and a strong ally for the turbulent times ahead.

However, it wasn't long before the U.S. non-proliferation lobby began work on the document. Soon the deal included a range of limiters that many in India thought were designed to hinder India's indigenous nuclear program, making it reliant on imported nuclear fuel and opening its installations to inspections (and their industrial and strategic by-product, espionage). The result was an unprecedented public revolt by India's highly respected nuclear scientists. One previously pro-U.S. Indian strategist told me: "In this era, the worst thing a country can do to itself is to be a friend of the US. They get destroyed—by the US itself."[51] Another, who had worked closely with the United States before the nuclear deal, told me, "The nuclear deal was a terrible thing for me personally. I thought we were making progress, but I realized they still think I am some little darkie Sambo."[52] It doesn't matter whether one thinks he's right, what matters is that he thinks he's right. As risked happening with Iceland over the loans, and Canada over the Northwest Passage, that frustration made India contemplate its other options: A stronger alliance with Russia and China—or perhaps sitting on the sidelines if a face-off comes.

India's assessment of the value of these other options was colored by its perception of history. At the time the deal was being rewritten by the United States, influential India strategist Professor Madhav Das Nalapat said:

> The Western attitude toward non-Western civilizations—that it is the navel of the universe, that it is a permanent fact of life, that history started 450 years ago and the rest is just a postscript—is going to kill the West. The Chinese are feeding on Western arrogance and ignorance. For them it's manna. But for regional leadership, and beyond, China needs India. So does the West. We are the swing vote. The ideal situation is that the West, with India's help, has leadership for two more generations, with the Chinese, Africans, and Latin Americans becoming equals. Forget Western dominance, that is over. But the India-West relationship has to be based on equality. And nuclear rights have to be a touchstone of that relationship. We are not being judged the same as Britain and France, we are being put in the same category as Burundi and Botswana. Accepting India on its own terms is very important. Ultimately, the West themselves have to decide the terms of engagement. I love Western civilization but if I'm treated as an untouchable, I'll behave like the way they think one behaves. And if an equal partnership is closed, I'll work for the second option, a partnership with Russia and China.[53]

The West will need to understand and react to the motivations, potentials, challenges, and realities of a changing Asia if it is going to head into a period of increased stresses with strong alliances. Simply put, to many, even the Kyrgyz Republic, it seems that the West is no longer the only option.

India's option to work more closely with China (both already have strong ties with Russia, their primary arms supplier[54]), or, at least, to limit hostilities, took a step forward in November 2006, when Chinese president Hu Jintao visited India and Pakistan. Several important things did—and did not—happen.

These are complex countries with shrouded and proprietary operating systems, so the real messages are often in the details. Even before Hu arrived, India and China needled each other in their own ways to reinforce the point that they can cause each other a lot of trouble. In the lead-up to the visit, China's ambassador to India made a rather stunning claim that one entire Indian state, Arunachal Pradesh, was "Chinese territory."[55] Perhaps not coincidentally, Hu and his entourage then found they had to scramble for accommodations as all hotels in the Indian capital suddenly reported that they were all booked up. Then attendance numbers for President Hu's public events were inexplicably low, and widespread demonstrations by Tibetans based in India were featured in the press. Point, counterpoint.

In the end, after the requisite amount of will-he/won't-he foreplay, there was progress, building on earlier growing bonds. In 1990, trade between India and China was around $250 million. By 2006 it had reached around $20 billion. On his visit to Delhi, Hu promised to raise it to $40 billion by 2010, with China hoping to become India's largest trading partner in the not-too-distant future.[56]

In a move that likely caused a few tremors in Washington, London, and Brussels, India and China also agreed to start working together on bids for hydrocarbon assets in Africa, Latin America, and possibly Central Asia. Both countries already have strong ties in the regions and have already jointly acquired fields in Syria, Columbia, and the Ivory Coast.[57] The trip showed that China is paying more heed to India's concerns, or at least trying to look as though it is paying more heed, in large part to try to show India the potential of a future that doesn't involve a growing alliance with the West.

However, any relationship between India and China is bound to be bumpy. There are a cartload of inherited and deliberately created problems. The potential stumbling blocks are numerous and wide-ranging. For example, Bangladesh, wary of becoming a vassal of India, quickly found itself being wooed by Beijing, which covets the country's offshore hydrocarbons, fresh water, and its ability to make India nervous. China is already the major arms supplier to Bangladesh and is planning on working with the country on nuclear plants.[58] Considering that India is already seeing an infiltration by extremists coming in from Bangladesh, and that environmental change is bound to make the situation more severe, China's role increases even more the chances of the India-Bangladesh border becoming a potential flash point. The same is true of the flow of arms to Maoists in Nepal from China's Yunnan province.[59] This affects India directly as there are likely ties of weapons and drugs smuggling between Nepali Maoists and extremists groups across the border in India.[60]

Another problem, as already mentioned, is that China set up Pakistan's nuclear weapons program in large part to tie down India. It may just be coincidence, but Pakistan is also involved in large-scale counterfeiting of Indian currency.[61] China also helps Pakistan with critical tactical equipment, such as communication anti-jamming devices, that help infiltrators cross into India (which in turn has led to some Chinese firms being barred from investing in key Indian infrastructure projects).[62] Then there is the matter of Chinese firms being regularly charged with "dumping" underpriced products in the Indian market.[63]

China is also setting up ports (and possibly naval bases) in many of the countries that ring India, in an effort to hem India in and consolidate control over the Indian Ocean—a major sea lane that leads to the Suez Canal and the oil fields of the Middle East.[64] Two-thirds of the world's oil, and half of Asia's trade, passes through the Indian Ocean.[65] It is a vital trade route, complete with chokepoints. Given what we've seen about China and maritime ambitions, it's not surprising to hear James

Mancham, the founding president of the Seychelles, say: "China is the most active foreign government in the Seychelles. The Americans have a short-term policy. The Chinese have continuity, strategy and their own plan. [. . .] they attach great importance to maritime routes."[66]

The persistent areas of friction are not sustainable if India and China are going to work together in any meaningful way.[67] Clearly, in this tightly interlinked region, there are more than a few obstructions that will have to be cleared away if India decides to move closer to China. While India doesn't get the respect and support it craves from the West, Indian strategists know that in a China-dominated world, they will also play second fiddle.

However, there are at least two reasons for China to start working toward a more equitable relationship with India. The first is that India has come a long way since its emotional positivism of the 1960s and is starting to act with the same hard-nose nationalism, and indeed nationalistic capitalism, that China perfected long ago. India is making it very clear that, if China continues to make life difficult for India, India might decide to return the gesture. Another reason China needs India is that large-scale environmental change is going to put painful pressures on the region, for example over Himalayan water supplies, and if China is not careful, that added stress could unravel carefully made alliances.

Some of the most complex geopolitical borders come together in the Himalayas. The potential changes in water flow mean that the entire Himalayan region is vulnerable to increasing tensions over water and hydropower supplies. The region is already a front line. For example, it is home to the Siachen glacier, a contested frontier between Pakistan and India that is often called the world's highest battlefield. In a new world where fresh water may become as valuable oil, the soldiers will be standing on what is potentially a very valuable asset. Siachen is one of the largest freshwater glaciers outside the polar areas. If the soldiers were camped on a frozen lake of oil, the value of the position might be a bit clearer to decision makers.

Any accurate political and military analysis of Siachen, or the rest of the Himalayan region, must now include hydrological, glacial, and climate studies to see where that glacier melt is flowing, if it can be diverted, and what the terrain might look like in the years to come. For example, supply lines may change as the ice and permafrost melt. From a military point of view, aside from climate-smart terrain surveys, a reevaluation of training and equipment will have to be done with the new realities in mind. For example, it is likely that the military will become involved in an increasing number of extreme weather-related emergencies and that their future operating environment will often be soggy and desperate. The situation in the Himalayas is currently kept in check by a complex system of treaties and politics, but environmental change will add a new component to the delicate balance. One Indian strategist, on being told that China is talking about damming and diverting one of the major rivers that waters India, countered, "China will spend four billion dollars building the dam, and 'someone else' will spend four hundred thousand dollars blowing it up."[68]

Assuming China behaves logically and truly respectfully toward India in its foreign policy, the question is, when China comes calling, how far will India let China in and what will the West do to counter? India is the West's to lose, but the West has yet to fully appreciate that advantage. Meanwhile, China is starting to learn how to woo. When the U.S. nuclear deal looked as though it might falter, both China and Russia offered India uranium. China could also offer the possibility of containing Pakistan and Bangladesh and become an ally (or at least not an enemy) in the control of narco-terrorism.

At minimum, China needs a complacent India to continue to expand its reach, and the West needs a friendly India to maintain a measure of stable influence in Asia and, increasingly, globally. The crux of the situation was put in print by Professor M. D. Nalapat. When Chinese president Hu Jintao visited India in November 2006, Professor Nalapat wrote "[Hu] has the opportunity to forge a new course, one that accepts India as an equal. Should he do so, then within a decade, India and China together will emerge as the centre of gravity in Asia. Within twenty-five years, in the world. [India's] strategic support is crucial to the continuation of the Chinese success story. Only an India-China partnership can ensure the security that China needs to expand its capabilities. A sullen New Delhi can make conditions difficult for Beijing across Asia, including within China itself."[69] The United States also needs India, especially as it tries to recover from the foreign policy fallout of the wars in Afghanistan and Iraq.

Surprises aside (and surprises are to be expected), there are three likely ways forward in Asia. First, things can muddle along as they are, with competing interests distracting and disabling responses to critical issues such as environmental change, resulting in a draining economic, political, and security cost for everyone, including the West.

Second, there could be some sort of loose alliance or understanding between India, China, and Russia, whereby India sits out confrontations between the West and the region. Such an alliance might squeeze the West out of Asia, then Africa (where both China and India are becoming entrenched), and finally Latin America (where China and India are welcomed by the growing number of nationalistic capitalist countries).

Or third, India and the West can form an alliance in certain sectors (possibly even allowing for India to work with non-Western allies, for example Russia, in some areas beneficial to all concerned, such as Afghanistan). This becomes more likely as the West starts to treat India like an equal partner, understanding and accepting India's operational parameters and limitations. This arrangement could potentially go a long way toward fostering stability in a time of change.

To a large degree, India is the swing vote that might shape the future of geopolitics for the next long while.

Current rival poles of influence need India's weight to create enough gravitational pull to be dominant. Not only is India an economic and military powerhouse with a young and increasingly educated population, but with good management it could end up more resilient to environmental change than many other great powers, including China.

From India's point of view, it might be best to avoid committing to an alliance for as long as possible, negotiating concessions from all sides before finally settling with the West in areas of mutual interest. From the West's point of view, the sooner the better. Heading into this new era of change and scarcity, partnerships with stable allies are critical. Nations that don't want to go the way of Ozymandias are going to have to move quickly to build strong, multifaceted networks that supply them with needed resources and geopolitical backing.

In this race to build extensive and stable relationships, some countries are already losing ground, while others are forging ahead. One region where the tactics of some of the world's major nations are clearly on display is the Pacific—an area of potentially vast resources and geostrategic importance. So far, however, few have fully realized how soon the typhoon of environmental change could sink some of the best-laid plans.

PART FOUR

THE TURBULENT PACIFIC

HOW RISING SEA LEVELS COULD WASH AWAY WHOLE COUNTRIES AND SWAMP THE GLOBAL SHIP OF STATE

When you're drowning, you don't say "I would be incredibly pleased if someone would have the foresight to notice me drowning and come and help me," you just scream.

—John Lennon (attributed)

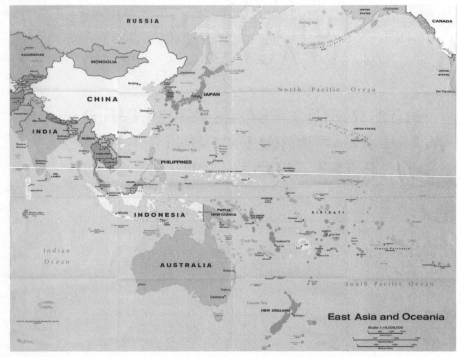

The Pacific
Courtesy of the Library of Congress, The Central Intelligence Agency

9

BUILDING A
GEOPOLITICAL ARK

We can do nothing to stop climate change on our own and so we have
to buy land elsewhere. It's an insurance policy for the worst possible
outcome. After all, the Israelis [began by buying] land in Palestine.

—Mohamed Nasheed, president of the Maldives, 2008[1]

When the islands that make up the Pacific country of Tuvalu die, it won't be a dramatic Hollywood ending, with
monster waves snapping trembling palms and civic build-
ings floating out on the tide. No, it's more likely to be a slow, painful, incremental death. The coral reefs, those natural breakwaters, will bleach
and die. Seawater will rise up through the ground, as it already has done
several times this decade. The earth will become squishy. Then wet.
Soon clear water will seep up, covering everything. Ankle deep. Then
knee deep. But this time, unlike all the other times, it won't subside. The
poisonous salt water will contaminate the lifeblood of the islands, the
underground freshwater system. With no fresh water, the plants, whose
tenacious grasp holds the soil together, will wither and lose their grip on

the earth. The land that was Tuvalu will just wash away. And Tuvalu will be gone.

In just about every climate change scenario, the low-lying atolls in the Pacific disappear beneath the waves. The only variation is when. Most forecasters agree that they will be gone by the end of the century; many think it will happen much sooner. Already the village of Lateu in another Pacific island nation, Vanuatu, has had to be disassembled and moved inland to escape increasing "king" tides that were flooding the community four to five times a year. The UNEP declared that Lateu "has become one of, if not the first, to be formally moved out of harm's way as a result of climate change."[2] Meanwhile, in spite of building sea walls and planting mangroves, continued flooding means all 2,000 or so people on the Carteret Islands in Papua New Guinea will be relocated to another island a four-hour boat ride away. The Carterets are predicted to disappear completely by 2015. Two islands in the central Pacific Republic of Kiribati beat them to oblivion in 1999. The Red Cross estimates that since the mid-1970s, the number of people in Oceania affected by the increasingly erratic and strong weather-related crises has increased by a factor of 65.[3]

As with other environmental change factors in the United States, Europe, the Arctic, and Asia, little concrete action is being taken globally to prepare for the inevitable changes to sea levels. One of the reasons is that the discussions about how much, where, and why sea levels are rising have often been so varied and couched in such cautious academic language that they have been easy to ignore. Some observers feel that since the scientists can't agree, why worry? However, in one fundamental respect, almost all the scientists do agree. Sea levels are already rising and will continue to rise.[4] Recent studies are forecasting a foot-and-a-half to three-foot average rise by the end of the century. Average levels increased around an inch between 1995 and 2005—twice as fast the rate of rise over the last 50 years.[5] As we've seen before, the sea level rise is only part of the problem, with much of the immediate damage being caused by the accompanying stronger sea swells and fiercer storms.[6] Even the lower end of the sea level rise estimates would mean that, globally, at least tens of millions would have to move.[7]

There are a few different factors that can cause sea levels to rise. One of the main ones at the moment is thermal expansion, which occurs when the air temperatures rise, heating the waters below. That causes the water to expand and sea levels to rise. The oceans have been relatively slow to warm because they can absorb a lot of heat. The top ten feet of ocean stores as much heat as the whole atmosphere above it. However, once warm, water is so good at keeping heat that even when air temperatures level off, the water retains the heat, possibly even for centuries.[8] It's the reason why we use water in radiators to heat houses, and not air. It's also why, even if air temperatures level off, the water will continue to rise for, at the very least, decades.[9]

Sea levels won't rise uniformly across the planet. The oceans aren't flat. Currents and the Earth's rotation create watery valleys and mountains. Climate change can rewrite that aquatic map.[10] Those regional variations can be intensified by a range of contributing factors, including local weather, topography, and currents. Man can also fiddle directly with results, usually for the worse. River deltas are particularly vulnerable. They typically sink about 0.4 inches a year on their own. In the Bangladesh delta, as with the U.S. Gulf Coast, that sinking can be accelerated by extracting groundwater, oil, and gas. Though the fast, strong rivers pouring into the delta bring so much sediment that, in areas, they might even see a build up of land, the UN projects that in a hundred years—even without a glacier collapse—Bangladesh could lose thousands of square miles of coastline, displacing millions of people.[11]

In Egypt's Nile Delta, a three-foot sea level rise could directly affect 1,737 square miles of cropland and more than six million people.[12] This is all possible before the end of the century.[13] In many major coastal cities, such as New Orleans, Shanghai, Tokyo, Osaka, and Bangkok, large areas are already below mean sea level. All of these cities already have pumps and protections in place, and yet, still face challenges.

There are also other factors that are poised to add to sea levels, such as the thawing of the permafrost, which causes the water previously trapped in frozen ground to stream off. The melting mountain glaciers in the Himalayas, Alps, Andes, and elsewhere can all contribute. And increased global precipitation could result in more runoff. Additionally, increasing floods, storms, and downpours might result in less water soaking into the ground, and transfer more sediment into the ocean, making the ocean floor itself higher in places.

The oft-repeated nightmare scenario for sea level rise is the collapse of one of the great ice sheets, the country-sized shrouds of ice covering huge sections of the Earth's land. The melt in the Arctic is already well advanced, but most of the ice is already in the ocean displacing water (and blocking sea lanes), so it won't have a pronounced effect on sea levels. The situation is different when it comes to the Antarctic and Greenland. There the ice is mostly on land, so if any of it melts or slides into the ocean it can cause water levels to rise fast and high, like dropping a boulder into a bathtub. About 10 percent of the Earth's land is covered by glaciers. During the last ice age, that coverage was up to 32 percent, and sea levels were up to 500 feet lower than they are now. If all the ice on land melted, it could raise global sea levels by around 230 feet.[14] If just 15 percent of Greenland's ice sheet melts, that would be enough to put much of Florida, Bangladesh, the Nile Delta, and the Netherlands (just to name a few low-lying regions) under water.

While the melting of the Antarctic and Greenland ice sheets are no longer outside the realm of possibility,[15] because of the timeframe and because even a conservative analysis provides us with enough problems, they are outside the scope of this book.

One of the geological formations at most obvious risk of being lost is tiny coral atolls, like the ones that make up the country of Tuvalu. Atolls are found mostly in the Pacific and Indian Oceans and are very low-lying and narrow. According to the Honourable Tom Roper, former Australian minister for planning and environment, "[A]toll-type islands are the most vulnerable, and we've already seen what is likely to happen because of the [2004] tsunami. The Maldives lost something like 15 percent of their land area. They had to rush in desalt plants in order for people to remain living there. Their gardens were damaged and still haven't come back to full productivity. Their fishing was affected by the destruction of reefs and so on. That's a good example of what's going to occur over a period of time in a number of countries." [16] For some atolls, that time is now.

Many atolls are only a few feet above sea level. Most have a natural protective barrier in the form of coral reefs. The reefs act like a wall around a medieval city—breaking the force of the onslaught of the destructive storm surges. There was hope that the reefs would grow to keep pace with rising sea levels but, all around the world, they are dying instead. Coral is made from colonies of tiny coral polyps, a distant cousin of jellyfish and anemones, living symbiotically with algae. The polyps shelter the algae, and the algae converts sunlight into energy for the polyp. It's a perfect marriage, but a fragile one. It can't survive for long outside a narrow temperature band that settles on 79 degrees Fahrenheit, but can temporarily fluctuate about 7.2 degrees to 10.8 degrees Fahrenheit either way. If it gets too hot, the polyps evict the algae, possibly because they turn toxic. Without the algae, they lose their color (or "bleach") and can soon starve. During 1997–98, a particularly strong El Niño year that gave a hot flash of things to come, almost all reef regions in the world experienced some bleaching and 16 percent died.[17] Since then, many have not been able to recolonize and have crumbled to the sea floor. As reefs also support more than 25 percent of all known marine species, it is not surprising that areas that were the worst hit have seen about a 50 percent drop in fish species diversity, and some species seem to have become locally extinct.[18]

Another problem is that as the atmosphere fills with carbon dioxide, more carbon dioxide is absorbed by seawater and is turned into carbonic acid. That makes the oceans more acidic, which can decimate marine life in general, and corals in particular, because it reduces the availability of the carbonate ions that corals use to harden their structure.[19] Research involving growing more resistant algae and possibly hardier coral provides some small hope, but so far is unproven on a large scale. Meanwhile, one study predicts that all the coral in the Indian Ocean could be dead in 20 years; another gives the Great Barrier Reef only until about 2050; and a third suggests that 60 percent of the world's coral reefs could be lost in the next 10 to 30 years.[20] There are many implications arising from a large-scale death of coral. Apart from loss of fish, the disruption of entire ecosystems, and massive coastal erosion once the reefs go, many island nations dangle their colorful reefs like bait to attract tourists. The Seychelles, Maldives, Fiji, Belize, and most countries in the Caribbean have economies that are largely dependent on tourism. And that tourism largely depends on being able to swim in calm, pretty, and protected waters.

For some countries, however, particularly the microstates of the Pacific, the loss of the coral is not just a matter of economic ruin; it's a matter of survival. The low-lying coral atolls depend on the reefs to break the relentless and increasingly aggressive assaults of the ocean. But the reefs are failing them. And the water is rising.[21] Meanwhile, in far-off capitals, assaults of a different kind are being planned. And the atolls of the Pacific are equally unprepared for those as well.

10

DRAWING LINES
IN THE WATER

What do you know about China's position on Taiwan?

—A Chinese representative in Tonga[1]

We are here, on one of those tiny, low-lying islands, lost in the vast Pacific Ocean. They are often described as once-upon-a-time idylls. However, others, such as some strategists in China and Taiwan, think of them as pawns on a vast geopolitical chessboard. The two economically powerful nations push and pull on the little independent countries, maneuvering for advantage. That was why, in 2003, you had to feel sorry for Anote Tong, the president of one of those little Pacific countries, the Republic of Kiribati. Tong had made a difficult decision, one that created a deep chasm in his family. He was sure that he had done what was right for the nation, but the Chinese ambassador wouldn't stop calling, trying to get him to change his mind. Occasionally, the calls would come in the middle of the night. Enough is enough, Tong decided. And he changed his phone number.[2]

Tong's country, Kiribati, is a scattering of postcard-perfect, white-sand and palm-fringed atolls in the central Pacific. It has a population of around 100,000, spread out over hundreds of tiny, narrow, crescent-shaped islands, most just a few feet above sea level. Many are only wide enough for a single path running through the center of the island. From the path, through the swampy beds of the taro plants and the thickets of banana, coconut, and breadfruit trees, you can see the turquoise glow of the sheltered lagoon on one side, and the steel-like glint of the slowly rising Pacific on the other. It is a slender slip of land and humanity in a very watery world. Every inch of land is valued. Every plant has an owner. Every plant has a purpose. But it is the uneasy relationship with the ocean that suffuses the culture. The ocean's waves take away refuse and give purity. They give fish and take lives. Here, the folklore is all about flying canoes, water witches, and holes in the sea that suck you down into a world of talking dolphins.

It is an unlikely place to be at the center of a major geopolitical battle, but for years China and Taiwan have been fighting it out for influence in this seeming political backwater. The most recent round was triggered by events in the late 1940s. After World War II, the Chinese Nationalist government, under Chiang Kai-shek, fought a losing battle against Mao and his Communists. In 1949, Chiang and his followers withdrew to the island of Taiwan, 124 miles southeast of mainland China. From his island fortress, Chiang declared that the entire Chinese mainland was rightfully his. Meanwhile, Mao declared Taiwan a breakaway province that must be "reunited" with the mainland at (almost) any cost.

Today, Taiwan, which has been self-governing since World War II (and a dependency of Japan for decades before that), has renounced its claim on the mainland, and largely considers itself independent. However, it is difficult for Taiwan to secure official recognition from other nations because China cuts ties to any country that acknowledges an independent Taiwan. With China in ascendance, and so many major nations hungrily eyeing China's cheap goods, relative access to capital, and vast markets, few are willing to risk being shut out. Without official recognition, economically mighty Taiwan is treated like the illegitimate child of geopolitics: Everyone knows it's there, but it's not invited to sit at the family table, having even been stripped of its seat at the UN.

The tiny nations of the Pacific, having little need for Chinese imports and even less to export to the Chinese market, are among the few countries in the world (along with some in Africa and the Caribbean) that are more or less free to do whatever they please when it comes to the China-Taiwan situation. Given enough inducements, the countries of the region happily, and sometimes not so happily, jump from one camp to the other.

The political machinations in the Pacific are interesting in that they show some of the dynamics at work in other places where big powers are in competition. China's foreign policy of nationalistic capitalism is also on display, and easier to analyze in such small countries where there are few other elements to factor in. All in all, the way China handled Kiribati and other microstates in the Pacific offers valuable insight into its general foreign policy approaches, objectives, techniques, and weaknesses. This is like looking at the conditions that created the 2005 tragedy in New Orleans in order to understand other potential vulnerabilities across the United States.

So, what exactly is happening in the Pacific? In Kiribati's case, the country was in the China camp, and in return, China gave the country around $2 million in "aid" a year and built a base near the capital, Tarawa. Officially the base, known as the China Space Tarawa Tracking and Control Station, was used for space exploration. It was key to China's successful manned space flight in October 2003. It was also likely being used for missile and space warfare programs, and possibly for keeping an eye on the relatively nearby U.S. base in the Marshall Islands.[3] Then, in November 2003, Anote Tong made his decision. He declared he was switching Kiribati's allegiances to Taiwan—for an alleged $8 million in aid. His brother, Dr. Harry Tong, also a politician, sided with China. China didn't go without a fight. Not only were there the midnight calls, there were bribes, threats, and declarations by the Chinese Foreign Ministry that Tong's decision was an "open betrayal."[4] The money and pressure suddenly injected in Kiribati by China and Taiwan threatened to overwhelm the small and close-knit political system and brought it to the brink of crisis—in spite of the fact that China often claims that it does not interfere with the politics of other nations.

Finally, after a month of heavy politicking, China suddenly packed up its base and left, saying it was taking the equipment away for "upgrading." Taiwan moved in and turned the site into an agricultural demonstration farm. But China hadn't completely disappeared. Three Chinese diplomats stayed behind, to the consternation of Tong, who was quoted as saying, "I think we have to keep an eye out on their real role, the role they are playing in staying back." But at least the calls stopped.[5]

The Kiribati tussle was not an isolated incident in the region, and China's willingness to destabilize perceived "anti-China" governments is often on show in the area. Conversely, China rewards loyalty. Samoa's prime minister was the first foreign leader to visit China after the Tiananmen Square crackdown in 1989. Not long after, China built Samoa a new $12 million government office block.[6] Some countries play China and Taiwan against each other in ways bigger countries can only dream of. Not long after Taiwan gave Nauru (total population around 13,700) $5 million to help it host the 2001 summit of Pacific Island leaders, Nauru promptly jumped ship to China, which provided a $2.5 million thank-you envelope. Then, in May 2005, perpetually cash-strapped Nauru found true geopolitical love again with Taiwan. It is not known for how much.[7]

Sometimes playing both sides doesn't work out so well. Not long after the Kiribati episode, the prime minister of Vanuatu went to Taiwan to try to strike a similar deal. While he was away, his parliament back home revolted. Perhaps coincidentally, it convened in a building built by China and donated as a monument to China-Vanuatu friendship. The pressure applied by China resulted in the prime minister eventually losing power, and Vanuatu staying firmly in China's camp.[8]

Usually these shenanigans are reported in the Western media in an amused, condescending tone as skirmishes on the periphery of geopolitics. But they give valuable insight into how China conducts its foreign policy, and how, in spite of assurances that it doesn't meddle in the affairs of partner nations, it can and will force changes of government if it doesn't get what it wants, a message that becomes more important as China extends its reach across Asia and into Africa and Latin America.

Due to pressure from China, all Pacific island countries have had to pick a side in the China/Taiwan debate. However, the methods and goals of China and Taiwan have been different and serve to show by comparison some of the unique qualities of China's foreign policy and its pervasive drive to secure resources and geopolitical advantage. Taiwan is largely concerned with bolstering claims to statehood, securing fishing rights, and creating a (mostly psychological) buffer zone around itself by developing friendly relations in its region. China, as in Panama, is fitting the Pacific into a larger long-term plan that involves aggressively enlisting a range of allies in a range of ways while trying to position itself as a geopolitical fulcrum. Outmaneuvering Taiwan is just one of its aims. China is moving toward its ultimate goal of reclaiming what it thinks of as its historic position in world affairs by becoming an undisputed superpower.

China is working toward that goal in stages, and is focusing first on becoming the acknowledged leader of the developing world. Already, if the United States wants to negotiate with North Korea it asks China for assistance, even though China helped create the situation in the first place through technical support to North Korea. Similarly, China is considered essential to resolving crises in Sudan at the same time as it fuels the tension through weapons transfers and military training. In another example, political maneuvering in Pakistan is now influenced as much (if not more) from Beijing as from Washington. In myriad ways across the world China is positioning itself to be a key actor in international affairs.

The Pacific is a critical component of China's global positioning. The countries of the Pacific, being so small, are relatively politically transparent and offer an unobstructed view of some common tactics used by China to gain and maintain geopolitical leverage. For example, in 2006, Chinese premier Wen Jiabao went to the region and pledged around $275 million in preferential loans to friendly Pacific nations—an amount that exceeds the annual GDP of some of the recipients. The premier said it was a "strategic decision," from one developing country to others, "without any strings attached."[9] However, there was one very big, thick, almost rope-like string. The country had to be 100 percent loyal to China, and if that meant altering domestic policies, so be it. As University of the South Pacific professor emeritus Ron Crocombe pointed out: "China peruses its self-interest more forcefully, interferes more in Pacific Islands' internal affairs, and has more strings on its aid than any other country."[10] That kind of a relationship is the sort China seeks to replicate all over the world, and it can be destabilizing, as some of the countries in the Pacific have learned.

While in Kiribati the pressure from China was largely economic and political, other Pacific nations, for example Tonga, have also been beset with serious social problems arising from their relations with China. The Kingdom of Tonga is one of the last places to expect riots. Normally, it is suffused with a charm that makes every walk down the street a delight. You never know what you are going to see, from a formal Chinese military delegation to the elegant transvestite contestants of the annual Miss Galaxy competition. It's also a tight-knit nation—deeply religious and quite traditional. In its own way.

Tonga is the last of the Polynesian kingdoms—the only country in the Pacific to escape colonization, if not conversion. Tonga officially entered the China camp in 1998.[11] Since then, China has given the royal family everything from military cloth to Land Rovers. Royals personally have done well from selling the country's satellite rights to China and one Tongan princess was the nation's ambassador to Beijing.[12] The sort of infrastructure development China does in Africa and elsewhere is also on display in Tonga. China has a band of construction workers that goes from Pacific country to Pacific country erecting public buildings to "show friendship." Apart from work in Tonga, they built government buildings in Vanuatu and Samoa, and the sports stadium in Fiji.[13] The last time I saw the Chinese construction workers, they were building the courthouse in the Cook Islands.

As in partner countries in Africa and elsewhere, China is popular with the leadership in Tonga. Part of the reason is that China gives loyal governments what they want rather than, as the West often does, what it thinks they should want (or what it wants them to have). For example, some of Canada's official priorities in Tonga are "to promote the participation of women in development [. . .] protect and promote human rights [. . .] protect the environment."[14] While laudable, to some in the Tongan government, it sounds like Canada is saying "you are doing a lousy job of running your country and we are going to show you how to do it." Compare that to what China offers: a high-end car, uniform cloth for the police, trips to China for officials, a few thousand dollars here and there for pet events like the National Music Festival, bilateral trade agreements, and equipment for the Tonga Defense Services with the goal of "improving military logistics and forging closer working links with the Chinese People's Liberation Army."[15]

Given the choice between lectures that might encourage dissent, and being given goodies and treated with apparent respect, it's not surprising which gets higher priority among certain governments. It's a model that China has been using with great success across the developing world, especially in more repressive regimes. Under the guise of "non-interference in internal matters," China establishes substantial relations with countries, like Robert Mugabe's Zimbabwe. It will also fund multiple sides in a conflict, to some degree or another, in order to have leverage with the eventual winner. As a result, China is accused of sustaining brutal governments and lengthening civil wars, but, in the meantime, it is extending its reach and gaining access to much-needed resources for its domestic market.

Another way China ensures that its long-term interests are protected is by encouraging the expansion of Chinese businesses and nationals into "partner" countries. This seems to be what happened with our case study, Tonga. Starting around the mid-1990s, Chinese nationals suddenly acquired the vast majority of small shops in the Tongan capital, Nuku'alofa. This was not a haphazard migration. It happened quickly and the influx was just from China. The same sort of politics by demographics has been seen repeatedly in some of China's other "interests." Authorities in Papua New Guinea estimate around 10,000 Chinese have been smuggled into the country; many come on Chinese fishing vessels and jump ship on arrival, with no complaints of desertion from their shipmates. In Fiji, the number was around 7,000 in three years.[16] Big numbers for small countries. As China's foreign policy is remarkably consistent, it is not surprising that the "influence through population" strategy also seems to be followed in places such as Africa and Siberia. Internally as well China has attempted to increase control over "ethnic" areas such as Tibet and Xinjiang by encouraging a massive influx of Han Chinese.

Not all Chinese migrants to the Pacific are illegal. In some Pacific island nations, at least, the aid given by China seems to have been reciprocated, at least in part, by the easing of visa restrictions for Chinese who want to emigrate legally.[17] The new residents are clear on their allegiances, at least as far as issues pertaining to China are concerned. Part of the reason is that, from China's point of view, there are no "hyphenated" populations, just Chinese people who happen to be living outside China at the moment. Therefore an ethnic Chinese shopkeeper in Tonga is not considered a Sino-Tongan, he is deemed "overseas Chinese." Loyalties to the fatherland often remain strong. For example, on January 18, 2004, the Tonga Council for the Promotion of Peaceful Reunification of China (aka "Take Back Taiwan") was founded in Nuku'alofa. There were around 150 delegates at the opening session, including Chinese engineers working in the country. They were sent telegrams of congratulations from similar organizations in Australia, New Zealand, and Fiji. The overseas Chinese political network is well organized and strong.[18]

However, overseas Chinese can also be the Achilles' heel in China's foreign policy planning. Domestically, Tibet and Xinjiang aside, the CCP is used to a population that is relatively compliant, assuming basic needs are met and there is the promise of growth. The CCP is not adept at understanding the dynamics of ground-level social discontent. It often discounts the importance of popular sentiment, believing instead that if it controls the government, and other key players, it controls the country. This fallacy has led to considerable pain on all sides in Tibet, and undermines China's position elsewhere. For example, in April 2008, South African longshoremen refused to unload a Chinese ship laden with weapons destined for Zimbabwe, even though the South African government declared the shipment legal. In that case, ground-level dissent effectively vetoed a component of South Africa's China policy.

The potential for friction with the local population was also demonstrated in the Pacific. In Tonga, the Chinese shopkeepers maddened the locals by refusing to give credit, undercutting prices, and staying open hours longer than Tongan-owned shops. One Tongan member of parliament was quoted as saying, "The Chinese here are virtually taking over a commercial sector. I say I don't want to see Tonga being dominated as far as the commercial sector by non-Tongans."[19] Tensions resulted in waves of violence, including scores of attacks on ethnic Chinese and their shops. Even the king of Tonga couldn't mitigate local anger against the recent immigrants. In 2001, after a Tongan-Chinese shooting, the Tongan government announced that all Chinese would have one year to leave the country (the year's grace period was said to be out of "Polynesian courtesy"). The edict was never enforced, but it gives an idea of the level of local resentment.[20] Following riots in Nuku'alofa in 2006 (triggered by domestic political issues), around 30 Chinese-run shops were destroyed. In a demonstration of the continuing ties between Chinese immigrants to Tonga and the Chinese government, Beijing sent a plane to evacuate more than 200 of its citizens.[21]

There is, of course, a long history of ethnic Chinese leaving China, usually for economic reasons, and peacefully integrating into Pacific society. Some families have been settled in the region for more than a hundred years and many are well established in business, politics, and their communities. Anote Tong, the Kiribati president who decided on the shift to Taiwan, is of part-Chinese descent. So is his brother who favored staying with China. As is Robert Wan, the "Black Pearl King" of French Polynesia. These families are part of their nations, yet even some of them have qualms about the newcomers.[22] There are concerns that, apart from disrupting local economies, the new settlers are bringing in organized crime, in particular drug trafficking, prostitution, and gambling.[23] In Fiji, authorities broke up one of the world's largest heroin smuggling rings, seizing 787 pounds of heroin. Then they found a $753 million crystal meth lab. Both had links to Chinese organized crime.[24] In Papua New Guinea, the police minister said: "Chinese mafia have bought off officials throughout the system."[25]

Popular discontent with China's role in the Pacific has turned violent in places other than Tonga. Solomon Islands saw major anti-Chinese episodes, mostly over concerns that local politicians were being corrupted. As John Lemani from the *Solomon Star* newspaper observed, "People were watching the Chinese arrive here, and within two weeks they would have buildings on prime sites. People started asking: 'What's going on here?'"[26] Then, in one huge convulsion of anger, in April 2006, riots broke out. Ninety percent of the capital's Chinatown was burnt down, and 400 ethnic Chinese had to take refuge at the police station. More than a thousand were officially registered as displaced by the Red Cross, having lost everything.[27] Again, the Chinese government chartered flights and repatriated hundreds of its nationals back to China.[28] Tensions between Chinese migrants and threatened locals are starting to flare up in other parts of the world as well. In August 2009, there were race-based street fights in Algeria.[29]

There are setbacks, but the expansion continues, even though concern over China's role in the Pacific is becoming embedded in regional political systems. In 2005, when China tried to buy a regional airline, the Fiji chief executive officer for the transport and aviation ministry called it a subtle attempt by China to impose its influence in the region. Another offer from China, a $30 million loan to help Fiji develop the country's information and technology sector, was also turned down.[30] That changed after a 2006 military coup in Fiji. The new self-appointed prime minister, Frank Bainimarama, was shunned by the West. In a typical example of the global trend of Western nations pushing potential allies so hard they end up in the other camp, Bainimarama came out in support of China following the March 2008 crackdown in Tibet. Suddenly, Chinese aid starting flowing liberally to Fiji, with announcements of plans for a new hospital, bridge, and mini-hydropower station.[31]

In spite of the difficulties with local populations and some governments, China continues in its efforts to gain sway over the Pacific. That is because China's strategic analysis of the region extends far beyond Taiwan—it knows that the Pacific is vastly undervalued and it could, in fact, be essential to China's global aspirations. What China realized years ago, many in the West are only starting to understand.

There are at least four reasons, well understood by China, why the Pacific region is much more significant than it might seem. It has: geostrategic importance; natural resources; critical trade routes; and disproportionate influence in international fora. As those reasons will only become more important as the environment changes, they bear further examination.

GEOSTRATEGIC IMPORTANCE

As a whole, the Pacific region is of great geostrategic importance. It is situated between the Americas and Asia and functions as a buffer zone, as the rusting wrecks of Japanese and American World War II planes and ships dotting the most remote atolls can attest.[32] In terms of modern conflicts, the area is strategically vital from under the seas (blue water navies) to up in the skies (satellites) and is an essential sector if there is ever any need to move U.S. or allied troops closer to, say, Taiwan. Yet, it is an area that is hard to chart and not well known. In January 2005, a U.S. nuclear submarine ran aground near the U.S. military base in Guam, in the western Pacific, an area that was thought to be relatively well explored.[33] As sea levels and currents change, and storms become stronger and more unpredictable, it will only become more difficult to navigate the region.

From China's point of view, this zone, which it considers its bailiwick, is now a potentially vulnerable vast backdoor, with a string of "stepping-stone" islands leading from the Americas right up to the China mainland. This isn't complete paranoia. While corporate America might be mesmerized by China at the moment, many in U.S. security circles have watched as China revives after nearly two centuries of anemia. In a June 2005 article in *The Atlantic Monthly*, titled "How We Would Fight China," Robert Kaplan writes that the "American military contest with China in the Pacific will define the twenty-first century."[34] Some military strategists think that the age of direct engagement is waning, and that with modern surveillance, U.S.-based missiles can be guided by satellites to hit targets, obviating the need to send a flotilla. While that may be true for large, static targets, such as cities or known military bases, it's more difficult to hit moving naval vessels, especially as China has developed weaponry that can blind U.S. satellites.[35] Barring an overwhelming unilateral attack, it means that in the case of a confrontation with China, there is likely to be some naval maneuvering first, and that maneuvering would likely be in the Pacific.

There are already suggestions that the United States set up more bases at sea. A 2003 U.S. Defense Science Board Task Force report on seabasing concluded that the United States is "an island power with the need to project military power across two great oceans."[36] (As an aside, that quote exemplifies the U.S. strategic analysis deficit when it comes to the Arctic. Note the assumption that Canada—and one assumes Mexico—are considered part of the North American "island," and yet the analysis doesn't mention the vulnerability of the third ocean, the Arctic.) The report continues, explaining that due to U.S. interests in many areas of actual and potential conflict, seabasing is going to become increasingly important for several reasons. Apart from concerns about the vulnerability of fixed bases, one of the main reasons for seabases is that many countries are now unwilling to host U.S. bases on their territory. The report states that

> recent events in Kosovo, Afghanistan, and Iraq have underlined, however, that the availability of [land] bases is, more often than not, uncertain due to physical or political factors that delay, limit or prevent their

use. [. . .] The assumption of readily available, secure land bases is now open to serious question. [. . .] The refusal of Turkey to grant access in return for $6 billion and loan guarantees a harbinger of the future. [. . .] Sea basing represents a *critical future join military capability* for the United States. It will help to assure access to areas where US military forces are denied access to support facilities. [. . .] Seabases are sovereign, not subject to alliance vagaries.[37]

In effect, the report acknowledges that the U.S. military is becoming unpopular and politically marginalized globally, yet still has international commitments to fulfill. Therefore one option is to base in international waters, where there are no politics. This is one reason for the tenacious support in some military circles in the United States for "freedom of the sea"—even though in some cases, such as the Northwest Passage, it compromises security rather than enhances it.

The report continues: "Likely future operations will be within range of the sea, including North Korea to the Middle East, South America and Africa."[38] Reaching those areas from the United States could mean passing through the Panama Canal and very possibly the Northwest Passage. It also assumes the Pacific will be a secure area for the United States.

China, in its quest for regional, if not global, hegemony, is countering that assumption by making military purchases of submarines, ships, and weapons systems that back up its navy's doctrine of "offshore active defense,"[39] with the goal of asserting "effective control of the seas within the first island chain," likely including Taiwan, the South China Sea, and beyond.[40] The official position of the People's Liberation Army Navy, seemingly taken right from the pages of *The Art of War*, is that "We cannot resolve problems with political or diplomatic measures until we have naval strength, and only then will it be possible to 'overcome our enemies without engaging in battles.' If intimidation fails to achieve any effects, we would then be able to actually deal an effective blow."[41] The program of achieving naval strength is well underway. In 2006 China showed it could get within torpedo range of U.S. warships without being detected when a Chinese sub audaciously surfaced within strike distance of the USS *Kitty Hawk* when it was between southern Japan and Taiwan.[42] And in a series of encounters in early 2009, small Chinese boats harried U.S. military ships off the Chinese coast. These not-so-subtle hints by China are making the Chinese position loud and clear: The CCP wants the United States off its (perceived) turf.

At the same time, China is creating its own network of potential physical bases that (along with the commercial ports previously mentioned) could act as forward staging points in any Pacific conflict, and could potentially isolate Taiwan, Japan, South Korea, and even, eventually, the Middle East from U.S. reinforcements. China could also potentially use the network to affect the outflow of oil supplies to the West. Theoretically, the debilitating effect could be compounded by Russia cutting off its pipelines to Europe at the same time. While not a sustainable long-term strategy, it could do damage over the short-term if that was expedient.

NATURAL RESOURCES AND CRITICAL TRADE ROUTES

As the largest ocean in the world, the Pacific is a vast store of essential and strategic commodities. Kiribati alone is nearly 2,500 miles from east to west and more than 1,250 miles from north to south in places, with an exclusive economic zone of about 1,158,000 square miles—or about the size of India.

The underwater seabed is a potential treasure trove—cadmium and titanium have already been found, and the region has barely been surveyed. Also, as the Atlantic is fished out, and acidifying oceans threaten global supplies, the surviving stocks in the Pacific will become even more valuable. China has realized this and has become a major fisheries nation for the first time. Taiwan is already there.[43]

Control over the Pacific also means control over trade routes—the civilian component of the geostrategic routes described above. Again, China is more than aware of this. Not only does it want more influence in the Pacific, it wants to secure the sea-lanes to its range of new allies, including the ones in South America. China is wooing South America the same way, and it approaches Africa for the same seasons. China sees the continent not only as a potential market for its goods, but as a major source of raw material needed to shore up its domestic supplies. China is also trying to make inroads into U.S. influence in the region. Historically, the United States has played a dominant role in the Americas, as with the development and control of the Panama Canal. But, also as with the Panama Canal, in some areas, that grip is loosening, leaving China ready and waiting to pick up the slack. To get there, however, China needs to cross the Pacific first.

DISPROPORTIONATE INFLUENCE
IN INTERNATIONAL FORA

The Pacific countries are considered a big bang for the buck when it comes to geopolitical influence. There are 14 small Pacific nations with a combined population of approximately 8 million. Some of the countries, such as Tuvalu and Nauru, have populations of less than 12,000. However, there are at least 40 global organizations that work on a one country, one vote principle. These include the Asian Development Bank, International Labor Organization, Food and Agriculture Organization, and UNESCO. This means that about 8 million people get around fourteen major international votes compared to China's billion-plus people and their one vote.

China isn't the only country courting those votes. According to University of the South Pacific professor emeritus Ron Crocombe,

The Northeast Asians are masters at massaging egos of politicians. And the politicians love their egos to be massaged. They look after them in ways most other countries don't. [For example] Japan and Korea were bidding strongly for [the position of head of the Asia Pacific division of the World Health Organization]. Japan sent a delegation of eight senior officials to every country in the Pacific Islands to try to persuade them to get Japan's man elected rather than Korea's man. Korea also came around with a big team. Both sides were saying, "Nobody would say we came to buy your vote. We just came to see if we can help with your health system because we are terribly interested in helping your people. And what are your needs in your hospital?" And so on and so forth. Sometimes they will say to a minister that they really need his advice because he is so wise and so important to them. "We will take you to our country in Asia and we need your advice." Why do they want his advice on something he knows nothing about? So they can pay him a consulting fee before he votes. But Japan, I suppose, broadly, is a more genuine aid donor. China is a more cunning aid donor. Small amounts of aid but much more strategically oriented for public viewing, for building up public relations, for buying of particular powerful individuals and solving political problems for leading politicians, and giving them trips, and treating them like they have never been treated before.[44]

Again China shows that it is planning long term, long past the tenure of the head of a specific UN agency.

China seems to be one of the few countries that is actively trying to secure its position at multiple levels over the long term. However, its ascendancy is not yet certain and it is worth looking at the roles of some of the other major powers in the region to see if China's growing dominance might be challenged.

Each of the powers vying for leverage in the Pacific Island nations comes with its own baggage. Taiwan, for example, has a relatively positive image, particularly as there is genetic evidence that the original Polynesians are descendants from the early Taiwanese.[45] The country plays up the link in order to reinforce social bonds (though the ethnic group related to the Polynesians are now a minority in Taiwan itself). For other nations, most of the baggage is negative. Japan's progress is hampered by the memories of its brutal occupation of many of the islands during World War II. After the war, the two main colonial powers in the region, the UK and France, along with the United States, conducted nuclear tests in the area, infuriating—and, in some tragic cases, irradiating—the local residents.[46]

In the 1960s, echoing the nationalist movements seen elsewhere, particularly after the Suez Crisis, some of the UK colonies became independent. Most recently the UK has seemed to largely abandon interest in the Pacific nations, shutting three embassies and high commissions in the region. This was part of the closure of nine of its embassies and high commissions that saved the UK around $12 million.[47] Comparatively, Taiwan thought Kiribati alone was worth an investment of around $8 million.

France, however, held onto its colonies outright and is reluctant to leave, but it may not have a choice. One of its main possessions in the region, French Polynesia, is a modern country with strong nationalist sentiment. Many are still furious about the nuclear tests and perceived general French condescension. In 2005 in French Polynesia, a pro-France government lost power after a long and dirty political battle and was replaced by a pro-independence administration.[48] There are certainly local people who would like to see France's influence limited in the Pacific for a range of valid reasons, however, there may be external factors at play as well. It would be interesting to know if the nationalists were being externally funded in any way, and if they plan to support China post-independence.

As we've seen, after the Cold War the U.S. focus shifted more toward the commercial rather than the strategic and it started losing interest in the Pacific. To a large extent the United States pulled out—although it held onto its military bases, especially in the central and northern Pacific. Now, with the Chinese dragon awakening, America is taking the area a bit more seriously again.

The main U.S. ally in the region, Australia, holds quite a bit of sway, but is often resented for perceived heavy-handed interference. Some regional governments think Australia is arrogant and a regional bully, though they will often look to Australia (and, to a lesser degree, New Zealand) in times of crisis.[49] It's a complicated, and not particularly healthy, post-colonial relationship. Australia also has close ties with China and sometimes tries to interfere on its behalf. When Papua New Guinea (PNG) looked to Taiwan for a possible relationship, PNG's top aid donor, Australia, used its weight to help scuttle the deal.

India, as elsewhere, has been trying to broaden ties, building on existing relationships born during the Cold War, when it was a leader of the Non-Aligned Movement. In 1976, long before China and Taiwan started their games in the Pacific, India conferred an honorary doctorate on the king of Tonga. Taiwan didn't get around to doing that until 1994. Japan quickly followed in 1995, and Korea in 1997.[50] In the Pacific, the same fishing, mining, and telecom rights and access to secure sea-lanes that are luring other countries are of interest to India as well.[51] And, as India increasingly follows its own path, those votes in international fora can certainly be of use. Generally, India is trying to gain access to the same commodities and leverage as China, but its style is different. It prefers a low profile, so there is little pressure for partner countries to make overt stands in India's defense, and it doesn't actively insert populations to advance a nationalist agenda. As a result, it is less potentially destabilizing for partners. Moreover, its assimilation into the English-speaking world makes it easier for the country to work with others in the region, including Australia and New Zealand.

India is well placed to go into the Pacific and benefit strategically, economically, and politically, especially if seen as a sort of less heavy-handed bridge to the West. As the Indian navy expands its reach, the Pacific becomes an interesting staging area, especially as India follows its "look East" policy. It has already has signed a security Memorandum of Understanding with Vietnam, is working closely with the Singapore military, and has offered to help patrol the Malacca Straits chokepoint.[52] It also needs to secure its own "back door" as well as control its access to allies in the Americas. There are indications that India is sniffing around, but it may not yet be ready (or able) to set up a base. It can't, however, be discounted. Due to its relatively non-invasive approach and cultural ties to the region, India has the potential to be a readily accepted all-around force in the Pacific.

The vast, strategic expanses of the Central and Southern Pacific Ocean are undergoing enormous political change. At stake is access to fisheries, sea-lanes in relatively calm waters, control over regional security, unknown underwater resources, geostrategic advantage, and geopolitical political leverage. European powers are increasingly being pulled out (Britain) or being pushed out (France). Russia seems primarily interested in resources, mostly fish. India is interesting, and interested, but it has catching up to do. New Zealand has strong cultural links to the Pacific but doesn't wield much practical power. Australia would like to think it has some control, and it does, but it is disliked for its perceived colonial attitudes and must balance its relationship with the region with its relationship with China. China is hobbled by a growing distrust, but it is still strong and, if problems on the home front don't cause it to retract from some foreign regions, it might even be in a position to dislodge Australia once it becomes a bit more entrenched; though China will probably still find it more practical to have Australia go in and get its hands dirty quelling riots, and so on.

This exceptionally rich area is undervalued by the United States, largely out of the control of the EU, and coveted, but not yet secured, by China. It is a rare opening in history, when the international political future of an entire region is being decided. And things will only become more critical once the waters start to rise.

11

FIGHTING OVER ATLANTIS

"It is our view," said Slant, turning his chair slightly so that he did not have to look at Vimes, "that the new land is ours by Eminent Domain, Extra-Territoriality and, most importantly, *Acquiris Quodcumque Rapis . . .*"

At the end of the table Vimes's lips were moving. "Let's see, '*Acquiris . . .*' You get what you grab?"

—Terry Pratchett, *Jingo*[1]

While strategists in Beijing and elsewhere make their plans, in the Pacific nation of Tuvalu the capital, Funafuti, has already been briefly completely inundated, with waters flooding the airport and leaving residents ankle-deep, surrounded by thousands of miles of ocean. As Hilia Vavae, Tuvalu's chief meteorologist, explains, "In the late 1990s, water started coming out of the ground—first puddles, then a whole sea. That has nothing to do with rain."[2] The country doesn't rise much more 6 feet above sea level and, at its widest, it is only 1,300 feet across. Some islets have already been

abandoned, and crops have been lost. The persistent fear is that one cyclone, its storm surge compounded by rising sea levels and its advance
barely dented by weakened coral reefs, could kill the country in a single blow. It's happened to a smaller degree before; in 1972 Cyclone Bebe
left Funafuti wrecked and 800 people homeless. The country's total population is slightly more than 11,000.[3]

I f Tuvalu and/or other countries have to be abandoned because they
become uninhabitable, it could have profound repercussions for the
global balance of power. The question would be, if Tuvalu and other
states physically disappear, do they cease to exist as a legal country? Do
they lose their seat at the UN? Does their territory become international
waters? Or do vast swaths of ocean end up being administered by a population that doesn't live there? If so, do their descendents have a right to
return if, eventually, the islands reappear?

These are legal questions with complex geopolitical implications,
and in many places they have yet to be asked, let alone answered. For
many Pacific leaders, the imminent threat of flooding or loss of resources
is so overwhelming that it seems impossible to plan much ahead.[4] However, the issue needs to be addressed, in part because, should relocation
become necessary, retaining some sort of sovereignty would give the
refugees badly needed revenue through access to resource rights (fishing,
undersea mining, offshore oil and gas, etc.), a voice in international fora,
and possibly the right to return if the seas eventually recede. It would
also turn the refuges from a burden on the host nation to a population
with something to offer in exchange for resettlement. This is uncharted
legal territory but it would seem that the first step would be to affirm
statehood. As a guideline on what might constitute legal requirements,
Article 1 of the Montevideo Convention on Rights and Duties of States
(1933) sets out the following four criteria for the existence of a state: (1)
a government; (2) a defined territory; (3) a permanent population; and (4)
a capacity to enter into relations with other states.[5]

When the elements are examined one by one, some of the far-reaching repercussions of the situation become clearer.

1. A GOVERNMENT

The first condition for statehood, a government, has a few possible solutions. Once a state becomes uninhabitable and the population has left its country, there would need to be a way to administer the assets of the nation. One option is that, once resettled, a system could be developed to manage the resources of the sunken country for the benefit of its citizens in exile. They could, for example, run the country like a company, with each citizen holding a voting share and distributing annual dividends on the proceeds from the lease of fishing and other rights.

Alternatively, the administrative system could be similar to models developed by North American First Nations to manage and distribute the proceeds of land claim settlements.

Or, perhaps something based on the Tibetan government in exile would work. Politics aside, it is an interesting structure. There is a parliament with representatives from Tibetan communities around the world, a taxation system, and an effective global communications network for keeping the community at least virtually linked.

An odder example of a crypto-nation with no fixed address is the Order of the Knights Hospitaller of St. John's of Jerusalem. The Order was born during the Crusades as a hospital order and relocated from country to country, retaining its influence for centuries. Today, one branch, the Sovereign Military Order of Malta, has permanent observer status at the UN, and some countries consider the Order an independent country, in spite of the fact that it has no territory. It issues its own passports and stamps, and has extra-territorial embassies. It is, in effect, a peculiar semi-country, with some, but not all, of the privileges of a full-fledged state.

None of these are ideal solutions, and each affected country would have to decide for themselves which elements would suit them and ease the pain of relocation. Whatever structure is developed, it is essential to start planning now. If plans are not put in place, it is possible that when the territory physically disappears, a sort of legal limbo will exist, with people holding passports from a non-existent country. There is a precedent for that as well. The Russian Revolution created at least a million refugees, mostly in Europe, with no legal papers. They were no longer under the legal protection of what had been Russia; nor were they legal residents in their new countries. They could not work, marry, travel, or legally immigrate. As a result, the League of Nations issued "Nansen Passports," named after Fridtjof Nansen, the first high commissioner for refugees. Hundreds of thousands of Nansen Passports were issued, allowing for an orderly integration and movement of refugees.[6] The current UN convention on refugees also covers "stateless persons"—and it would be difficult to be more stateless than if your country physically disappeared. Unless a country has not signed on to the convention, or has specifically excluded people affected by environmental change, it would be legally obliged to take in the refugees—something many countries, such as Australia in the Pacific and the United States with the Caribbean, are concerned about.[7] Given that, one way or another, the refugees will have to be settled somewhere, it seems desirable for the sake of global stability that some governance method and resources administration system be developed before the dislocation occurs.

2 AND 3. A DEFINED TERRITORY
AND A PERMANENT POPULATION

The definitions of a defined territory and a permanent population can be quite contentious, as can be seen by the maneuverings in the South China Sea.

The same sort of jockeying for position on display in the Pacific is even more extreme in the South China Sea. Prestige positions are completely secondary to the higher-stakes games of securing energy supplies. That takes a strong military and the willingness to use it. The sea, in the northwestern Pacific, is ringed by China, Taiwan, the Philippines, Malaysia, Brunei, Indonesia, Singapore, Thailand, Cambodia, and Vietnam, and is speckled with hundreds of rocks, islands, and reefs, most of them uninhabited and uninhabitable. Normally, these geographic features would primarily be considered shipping hazards, but the region also has proven oil fields, rich fishing grounds, strategic sea-lanes, and areas of military importance. Given that claiming one semi-submerged rock allows a country to try to make a claim for the 200-nautical-mile exclusive economic zone (EEZ) around it, it's not surprising that just one section of the area, the Spratly Islands, which might contain as much as six billion barrels of oil beneath its seas, is claimed in parts by six nations. Sovereignty over the tiniest islet could mean vast resources.[8]

China, in particular, has been focused about dominating the South China Sea. A 1988 Chinese article made the nationalist agenda clear and underscored the sort of Chinese maneuvering seen elsewhere: "In order to make sure that the descendants of the Chinese nation can survive, develop, prosper and flourish in the world in the future, we should vigorously develop and use the oceans. To protect and defend the rights and interests of the reefs and islands within Chinese waters is a sacred mission. [. . .] The [Spratly] Islands not only occupy an important strategic position, but every reef and island is connected to a large area of territorial water and an exclusive economic zone that is priceless."[9]

China's stand is not just rhetorical, it is considered self-preservation due to its need for resources to shore up its domestic deficits. In April 1987 Vietnam moved in on one of the Spratly reefs. China objected in no uncertain terms, blaming in part a Soviet-Vietnamese alliance, and demanded that Vietnam withdraw from the previously uninhabited islands. China declared, "Vietnam's purpose in illegally dispatching troops to [the area] is to occupy the continental shelf nearby and pave the way for its future exploration of oil,"[10] something which China itself intended to do. By late 1987, China had conducted several "scientific" expeditions to the Spratlys consisting of research ships accompanied by warships. "Scientists" and building materials were dropped off in strategic locations, and China suddenly decided to build a "sea-level weather research station" on a Spratly reef, thus satisfying the "permanent population" part of a territorial claim.

Vietnamese air and sea patrols tried to monitor Chinese progress and there were several tense encounters, with diplomatic sparks flying off from the chaffing, flinty proximity. Then, in March 1988, China sank a Vietnamese transport ship, killing dozens of soldiers. By April, China claimed six previously uninhabited reefs in the regions. By 1992, the Soviet Union was being eulogized and erstwhile partner Vietnam had to look locally to find friends to help it counter China and secure regional resources. The Vietnamese government reached an agreement with Malaysia to co-develop their overlapping offshore oil claims. By mid-1992, Vietnam's offshore oil production was greater than China's. Not coincidentally, in that same year, China passed a law stating that all the Spratlys (and another South China Sea area called the Paracels) belonged to China. It also gave itself the right to expel all other navies from the region.[11] Within a month, a clash between China and Vietnam broke out on one of the islands.[12] There has been an ongoing inch-by-inch tussle ever since, but slowly China is consolidating its position, in spite of regional neighbors trying to secure their own toeholds. In 2008, Vietnam signed a security Memorandum of Understanding with India.

In a familiar pattern, U.S. involvement in the South China Sea is primarily commercial, with American companies working with whoever happened to be in control of the patch of ocean being drilled. But, again, there are concerns about this approach within the U.S. security establishment and, again, the concerns have to do with sea-lanes and chokepoints. According to a study by the United States Institute of Peace, a bi-partisan Congress-funded think tank,

> The importance of the South China Sea as a strategic passageway is unquestioned. It contains critical sea-lanes through which oil and many other commercial resources flow from the Middle East and Southeast Asia to Japan, Korea, and China. Safety of navigation and overflight and the freedom of sea-lanes of communication are critical strategic interests of the United States, which uses the South China Sea as a transit point and operating area for the U.S. Navy and Air Force between military bases in Asia and the Indian Ocean and Persian Gulf areas. Any military conflict in the South China Sea that threatens the strategic interests of the United States or the security and economic interests of Japan might be seen as sufficiently destabilizing to invite U.S. involvement to preserve navigational freedom in these critical sea lanes.[13]

However, given some of the factors exposed in the context of the Panama Canal, such as political ties cemented by nationalistic capitalism and balance of trade issues, it would be difficult for the United States to wade into the South China Sea militarily. For now, it is China, not the United States, that is in the position to make unilateral statements about control and follow them up with action.

All in all, the situation in the South China Sea, with its rich resources, strategic sea-lanes, and long list of countries jostling for a position, is a microcosm of what the geopolitics of the Pacific can become. It shows how uncertainty around statehood and territory can be severely destabilizing. And it underlines the importance (and potential for inventive application) of key legal concepts from the Montevideo Convention, such as a "defined territory" and "permanent population." China and others have staked claims in the South China Sea by building what are essentially military outposts on reefs that are barely above water. They use "permanent presence" to claim the surrounding "defined," though contested, territory.[14]

Citing the South China Sea situation, if Tuvalu goes under, it could theoretically tether a ship to its old island (or dump enough sea breaks to form a new island on top of the old island), keep a few people resident there to maintain a permanent population, and then administer the territory—and its attendant exclusive economic zone—through a government in exile in another country. The problem (and it is a problem that could also wreak havoc in the South China Sea as sea levels rise and submerge those reefs and rocks) is that the law is clear about artificial islands. Artificial islands only get a 1,640-foot safety zone, not the bountiful 200-nautical-mile exclusive economic zone "real" coastlines get. However, at least the artificial island option might preserve the necessary territory and permanent population to claim sovereign state status. Even with a reduced EEZ, the sovereignty in itself could be a commodity, with many microstates, for example, using their sovereignty to financial advantage by becoming tax havens or ship registries, and selling passports, stamps, or even domain name suffixes, as is the case with Tuvalu (.tv).

If the Tuvaluan government decided to hold on to sovereignty through establishing artificial islands, it would have to be careful to ensure that it kept a loyal settlement on site, not only to satisfy the "permanent population" clause, but also because others might try to move in. In the South China Sea, the International Court of Justice ruled that one basis for a territorial claim was "effective occupation," potentially giving squatters rights in places where there is a vacuum.[15]

With planning, it might be possible for countries like Tuvalu to satisfy the sovereignty demands of a defined territory and a permanent population in an era of rising sea levels, but under the current letter of the law the territory might be vastly reduced and the population base tenuous. That leaves just one more box to be checked for sovereignty to survive under the Montevideo guidelines.

4. A CAPACITY TO ENTER INTO
RELATIONS WITH OTHER STATES

The final requirement for statehood shows that, when it comes right down to it, international law is largely a matter of international politics. This requirement is not so much a matter of having the capacity to talk to others; rather it's more about getting the others to talk to you. Officially. As Taiwan knows, given enough incentive, a country with a question mark over it can quickly find itself in political limbo. In the case of Pacific islands, the impetus for de-recognition might come from nations that don't have a relationship with the sinking country and want a legal way to get at their resources. If there is no advance planning and a country abruptly ceases to exist, either by inundation or a mass evacuation, and its waters revert to international waters, it's a whole new game. As with the EU's stand on the Northwest Passage, from a commercial point of view, if a nation cannot claim exclusive ownership over a distant tract of ocean that it seeks to use, it might seem preferable to lobby to get the area declared international waters. That means that countries with a strong naval presence might challenge the right of a Tuvalu consisting of a few people on a pile of concrete to exist, if it seems an expedient way to get at its resources unimpeded.

The problem with lobbying for open access in a geopolitically important area, especially at a time when geopolitics themselves are in flux, is that it might be good for business in the short term, but it sets a precedent that could be disastrous for security. For example, the United States and the UK both have geostrategic bases on low-lying coral atolls. Erasing Tuvalu's EEZ from the map could create the justification for others to try to go after the EEZs (and de facto safety zone) of those bases.

To understand how critical these installations are, it's useful to see how far nations will go to acquire them. Take, for example, the case of

Diego Garcia. Diego Garcia is in the Chagos Archipelago in the Indian Ocean, roughly equidistant from Africa, the Middle East, Northern India, and Indonesia. It is a UK possession leased to the U.S. military. The island is home to about 2,000 U.S. personnel, mostly military, and around 2,000 support workers from the Philippines.[16] Most live in the 30-acre Camp Justice housing complex on the island. They work at one of the most strategically located U.S. bases. The base monitors communications from the Middle East, East Africa, and southern Asia. Its airfield is big enough for nuclear bombers, and it has an advanced supply and maintenance system for other ships stationed in the theater. Bombers from Diego Garcia flew missions in both Iraq wars.[17] The island is at threat from rising seas.[18]

Exceptionally low-lying, it was only lucky coastal geography that prevented it from being washed out in the 2004 tsunami. The United States and the UK don't want to lose it. The base is a key negotiating pawn that Britain has to offer the United States. If it goes under and, as a result of a successful legal challenge, is "derecognized" as a territory with a 200-nautical-mile EEZ, the United States could lose a critical base, and the UK will lose exclusive access to that crucial bit of ocean. Many of the U.S. bases around the Pacific and elsewhere are also at similar legal risk.[19] So, just as it may be in the interest of China to support the Pacific Islanders' claims in order to bolster its own stand in the South China Sea, it may be in the strategic interest of the United States, UK, and others to do so as well in order to maintain clear legal jurisdiction over the area around their bases.

All in all, the Montevideo Convention on Rights and Duties of States might provide some guidelines, but because it isn't designed to address the changing parameters caused by environmental change, it risks becoming at best highly contested, and at worst a cause of more conflict than it solves. Unfortunately, it isn't the only agreement that could complicate matters as the world readjusts.

There is a relatively new legal mechanism that is supposed to guide nations safely through the troubled waters of international maritime law. The UN Convention on the Law of the Sea (UNCLOS) attempts to create global norms for determining boundaries, and the International Tribunal for the Law of the Sea (ITLOS) is designed to be a forum for resolving disputes.[20] They have a lot of work to do, even without climate change. Only 160 of the potential 365 maritime boundaries worldwide have been agreed upon.[21] UNCLOS and ITLOS have widespread support. As of this writing, the only major hold-out is the United States, with some senators saying that it impedes freedom of navigation. However, many in Congress have indicated a willingness to sign, in part to help resolve Arctic claims.

UNCLOS states that a country's maritime EEZ extends 200 nautical miles off its coastline, unless it has a continental shelf, in which case the seabed claim can be extended up to 350 miles from the coastline.[22] Unfortunately, UNCLOS has the same weakness as the Montevideo Convention. It takes for granted that physical territory won't change much, which is not the case in an era of environmental change. In Bangladesh, for example, a relatively small sea level rise might flood the coastline for hundreds of miles inland. Under UNCLOS, that might mean that Bangladesh's EEZ would also retreat dramatically, potentially putting its off-shore fossil fuel resources in international waters, or allowing them to be claimed by neighbors India or Myanmar. To get around this, a special one-off deal was made with Bangladesh to "fix" its coastline. However, as more and more coastlines inundate and change, hand-tailoring the law will become unfeasible.

In another example of the sort of geopolitical quagmire that could potentially be created, a country has a 200-nautical-mile EEZ from its coastline, unless it overlaps another country's EEZ. If that happens, the two countries normally split the difference. So, if two nations are 90 miles apart, each country gets 45 miles off their coastline.[23] This is the case with the regularly renewed bilateral maritime border agreement between the United States and Cuba. In a world of rising seas, this means that if low-lying southern Florida goes under, the new maritime zone of the United States could be measured from the new coastline, possibly north of Miami. Meanwhile, relatively mountainous Cuba wouldn't lose that much ground. In theory, Cuba's maritime zone could expand because the American one it was butting up against had retreated, and Cuba could be drilling for oil where Miami used to be. It could also put the entrance to the Gulf of Mexico in Cuban territorial waters and, while Florida would be submerged, it would still be an impediment to shipping, meaning traffic would have to loop down through Cuban waters.[24] Obviously this isn't going to happen. The United States won't allow it—even though it could get tricky as Russia is now drilling in Cuban waters, and might be inclined to back a Cuban challenge. The example serves to underline that when the law falls out of synch with realities and fails, politics take over, if you are lucky. If you are not, it's the military that does the heavy lifting.

The law was simply not designed for dramatically changing coastlines. The UNCLOS procedure freezes coastlines (and so borders) at a specific point in time—until challenged or revised. So, a Pacific nation like Tuvalu submits a map claiming its oceanic territory and, until it submits a new map, or another country challenges the accuracy of the claim, Tuvalu will legally exist, even if it's underwater. This leaves whole nations open to geopolitical blackmail. Offshore oilrigs could end up in another territory, or in international or disputed waters, and borders could be shifting faster than a marble in an earthquake. No one wants that. Even small border disagreements can lead to war. Parts of Asia, the Middle East, and Africa flare up in periodic, vicious conflicts over borders. The current calm (such as it is) is only maintained through a seemingly irrational belief that, unlike every other period of human history, the borders as they are now will not change. Environmental change is going to make that an assumption of the past.

Due to flooding coastlines, most coastal countries could suffer a net territorial loss as a result of UNCLOS as it is now formulated. However, there is one relatively easy option for mitigating some of the effects of this unhappy meeting between environmental change and international law. There should be an urgent global effort to legally freeze borders according to a time-linked baseline. For example, all the borders, and border negotiations, could be done on the basis of satellite imagery from 2000 (or whatever recent year provided reliable global assessments). Also other laws, treaties, subsidies, regulations, and other such conventions (such as the Montevideo Convention) should be reexamined to see if they resolve problems or exacerbate them in a time of environmental change.

From now on, not only should agreements, laws, treaties, and such be examined for legality, etc., they should also be assessed for their ability to adapt to changing environmental circumstances. This is the same problem the United States has with legislation, such as the National Flood Insurance Program, that doesn't take into account geophysical changes—and it is far from the only example. For instance, river water–sharing treaties that are based on volume, rather than percentages, could be be difficult to sustain as water levels fluctuate with environmental change. If one of five states sharing a given river is promised X million gallons a day—as opposed to being promised, for example, 15 percent of flow—and the whole river level drops to X–1 gallons, the treaties can actually become an impediment to a fair sharing of scarce resources. Similarly, international fishing quotas will need to take into account the movement of stocks and the change in species proportions. Unfortunately, there are myriad examples in international and domestic law and trade treaties where environmental change has yet to be factored in.

Hopefully, some of the most egregious laws will be amended soon, but, while waiting, it would only be prudent for those adversely affected to try to protect themselves, and that includes the small countries of the

Pacific. Nations in danger of submersion might want to sidestep the flawed legal system and start exploring arrangements with more powerful protector states in order to be in a better position to retain at least partial control over their resources and, potentially, their sovereignty. For example, the Republic of Maldives, a group of low-lying coral atolls in the Indian Ocean off the southwest coast of India with a population of around 330,000, could enter into an arrangement with India before inundation. India could agree to take in the environmental refugees; settle them, at least initially, and provide them with appropriate Dhivehi-language schools; grant settlers some sort of specific Indo-Maldivian citizenship (with a system in place for how that can pass from generation to generation); give the Indo-Maldivians the exclusive or major share in the exploitation of the resources in the ocean area that used to be their home; and possibly even allow them a right to return if the islands re-emerge.

In exchange, India would get a strategically useful, vastly increased maritime zone that it agrees to protect in international fora against challenges. In the case of the Maldives and India, this sort of arrangement would be building on a strong pre-existing relationship. In 1988, Indian paratroopers and navy forces helped put down a coup attempt at the request of the Maldivian government, and Maldivian forces have trained in India. India was also at the forefront of emergency aid to the Maldives after the 2004 tsunami. If the Maldives were to disappear, working with India to make the transition as painless as possible makes sense. It would also help to show India's commitment to friendly regional neighbors as well as give it strategic advantage and an expanded EEZ.

This state-within-a-state model may not last the millennia that climate cycles can take, but it would be mutually beneficial and at least soften the impact of relocation, allowing the refugees to come in voluntarily, with something on offer, and with an adaptation structure in place, rather than as downtrodden drifters who are dislocated and desperate—and potentially destabilizing.

Whether individual countries survive or not, and in what form, there will still be an increasingly complex situation in the Pacific leading to the question: Who will dominate in the next few decades? Much depends on how well the groundwork is laid in the next few years. For example, with environmental change, there will be an increased need for foreign intervention in the region, from emergency search-and-rescue operations to evacuations. Facilitating regional assistance gives outside countries a humanitarian excuse to base a navy in the region. Once the serious, persistent flooding begins, political capital can be gained by taking in refugees. The countries that host the most refugees from a given swamped territory will then be in the best position to claim a "special relationship" with the patch of ocean where that territory used to be, and potentially to develop the same sort of economic and political relationship proposed for the Maldives and India. As it stands now, the most likely home for many of the refugees is New Zealand and, to a lesser degree, Australia. However, there is no reason that China, for example, can't take in Tongans. In a reverse of its policy of exporting Chinese to Pacific nations to establish a beachhead, it could import Pacific Islanders to strengthen Chinese claims over areas of the Pacific.

Ultimately influence in the Pacific is likely to be a matter of power. There are four ways countries can try to reach an understanding with each other. In incremental order they are: friendly negotiations (i.e., a Maldivian merge with India), the courts (i.e., taking a claim to the International Tribunal for the Law of the Sea), raw politics (i.e., China and Taiwan outbidding, outbribing, and outblackmailing each other), and the military (i.e., China versus Vietnam in the South China Sea). The countries of the Pacific probably only have a small window of friendly negotiations and legal positioning left; after that it'll be raw politics. Hopefully it will stop short of military intervention.

Currently, barring a late start from India, China seems on course to increase its hegemony over large sections of the Pacific. The United

States is hindered by a lack of sustained interest in the Pacific. Additionally, the United States is over-stretched in too many theaters and is already having problems basing, strategizing, recruiting, training, and equipping against so many varied threats. The United States knows it is being left behind and is making some efforts to gain position. The U.S. government declared 2007 the "Year of the Pacific," and in May 2007, it sponsored a meeting of Pacific island leaders in Washington for the first time.[25] The State Department said it was "part of US efforts to expand engagement with the vast and important Pacific region through closer political, economic, and cultural ties."[26] However, rather than talk about issues of concern to Islanders, such as rising sea levels and illegal fishing, Secretary of State Condoleezza Rice condemned a coup in Fiji and lectured the assembled prime ministers and presidents, saying, "The Pacific cannot evolve into an area where strongmen unilaterally decide the fates of their countries and destabilize the democratic foundations of their neighbors."[27] It was unfortunately a lost chance to win the hearts and minds of Pacific leaders who have vivid memories of the United States unilaterally expropriating valuable land for military bases and detonating nuclear devices that contaminated entire islands.

Meanwhile, the Pacific has China's focused attention. China's diplomatic battle with Taiwan is only a short- to medium-term issue. If Taiwan remains outside Chinese mainland control, it is likely that the situation will eventually normalize as the two countries' economies become even more symbiotic. Under Taiwan's current China-friendly government, elected in 2008, policies have already softened. There has been a de facto ceasefire on trying to lure away countries from each other's sphere of influence and, in an apparent move to avoid annoying China, Taiwan canceled a summit with its six Pacific-friendly nations.[28]

Conversely, the more serious China is about invading Taiwan, the less important it is for China to secure official government-to-government relationships in the Pacific as, if there were a successful Chinese attack on Taiwan, the small Pacific countries recognizing Taiwan would quickly change allegiances in order not to be on the losing side of future aid packages. Either way, the China-Taiwan tug-of-war in the Pacific should be over within a generation or two. Meanwhile, China's long-term, nationalistic capitalist strategy is to get people on the ground, owning shops and businesses, and gaining local influence. Economic reasons alone make this sound policy for China. The strategic and political reasons make it an obvious course to follow. China is creating a firm buffer of its own design around Taiwan (and perhaps even Japan and South Korea), making it difficult for the United States to get in and protect its allies. The more entrenched China becomes in the Pacific, the farther afield it can base submarines and missiles, and the harder it is for the United States to defend Taiwan, except by remotely bombing the Chinese mainland. That in itself is unlikely, as China has made it clear that it is willing to retaliate (or even preempt) with a nuclear attack on the United States—something that few American presidents can risk.[29]

In keeping with China's foreign policy in the rest of the world, in the Pacific China is acting with focus and in the perceived best interest of its nation, giving it an advantage in the region. According to Professor Ron Crocombe, the United States:

> has the power in terms of directing what your policy shall be. Well, they are going to lose that in the Pacific to China. The difference is that the Americans are short-term thinkers and the Chinese are long-term thinkers. The Chinese are working for the future. I have spoken to the Ministry of Foreign Affairs in Beijing. No doubt about it, they were very clear. They are talking in thousand-year periods. Americans are thinking weeks ahead. That's why China does not want to take over from the United States today. They know they are going to take over—later. The Pacific has gone through 200 years of domination by Europe. The factors that led Europe to dominate are now such that they will lead Asia, particularly North Asia, to dominate for the next

long period. That process is already advanced. China is in no hurry—
it is just laying the groundwork to make certain that it works. And it
is laying it very effectively.[30]

China's strategy has been largely successful so far, though it is engen-
dering discontent among the locals that still leaves an opening for others who are willing to work with Pacific Islanders on their own terms.
However, as of now, no major power seems ready or able to take up the
challenge.

So far China has been very thoughtful (or lucky) about choosing its
allies in the Pacific. One of its strongest allies, Tonga, has mountainous
islands that are likely to survive climate change. Meanwhile, some of the
main allies of the United States in the Pacific, the Marshall Islands and
the Federated States of Micronesia, are mostly low-lying and might be
undermined by climate change. The traditional major regional partners
of the United States, such as Japan and South Korea, will become even
more important if the United States wants to keep a toehold. However,
unless the United States has something concrete to offer (such as an effective military balance to China), the United States risks losing influence
even with those regional allies as they try find their place within the new
equilibrium in Asia and consider other partners, such as India, who can
help with their security.

Human and ecological disasters aside, once sea levels start rising substantially, strategically speaking there will be two types of islands in the
Pacific: islands that sink and become potential shipping hazards; and islands that stay above water and become potential geostrategic commercial and military bases. In determining which bit of ocean belongs to
whom, international politics will likely play a more prominent role than
what is currently looking like flawed international law.

Not long ago, the norm for determining maritime boundaries in Europe was the "cannon shot" rule, in which a state was awarded the mar-

itime area that could be covered from a cannon shot from its shore (this is the origin of the "three-mile limit").[31] The clear implication was that, if you could defend it, you could have it.

It is possible that, in a chaotic future of environmental change, where laws are unclear and power is in flux, the same will be increasingly true again. Countries that want internal stability, influence over allies, control over sea-lanes, and access to critically important resources better start planning now. The storm is coming.

CONCLUSION

WEATHERING CHANGE

The English climate, so long considered a capital joke, is becoming a very serious matter. They were not Dog-Days last summer; they were Hyaena, Kangaroo, Elephant, Boa-Constrictor Days. If so unnatural a state of things is to be repeated, England will no longer occupy her present position in the world. She will be somewhere else. There will be no place like home. Home itself will not bear the slightest resemblance to it. We shall all be abroad—Every British child will be born a foreigner. Nationality will be at an end. With the loss of our climate, on which the British Constitution so closely depends, it is impossible that we should continue to be the same people.

—*The Comic Almanack* for 1853[1]

Remember that monsoon from the beginning of the book? And that ice storm? And that hurricane? They are all coming back. And, like it or not, each time they return, they change us. Meanwhile, tectonic geopolitical and geoeconomic shifts are also reshaping the world. The United States and the rest of the West face increasing difficulties in places as far apart as the Arctic and the Pacific. China seems to be making headway in building alliances; albeit some more brittle than they seem. India is slowly working its way up the inside track. And the Russian bear, swaggering with surplus energy, is taking a new look at old stomping grounds.

Yet so far none of these major powers has fully taken on board the problems that environmental change will cause. As a result, they are unknowingly racing each other through a minefield. They may seem to surge forward in turn, but without a proper examination of the ground ahead, they risk sudden and explosive disaster.

Environmental change is a sustained and pervasive attack on the status quo. Nothing can be taken for granted, and that includes global transportation, international law, borders, food supply, stability of infrastructure, access to resources, ability to project power, and economic stability. As it stands, *no* country is prepared. The United States has major vulnerabilities with water supplies and flooding along its coasts that will exacerbate existing social, political, and security problems. Europe's infrastructure is woefully inadequate, its foreign policy is fractured and often outdated, and its domestic bureaucracy is ill-equipped to handle the sort of complex renegotiations that will have to happen around water sharing, fisheries, and agriculture. China's water supply is dwindling and its mega-engineering solutions might only make things worse. India's central government has yet to show the sort of concerted political will necessary to protect against the undermining of national security through the erosion of environmental integrity. And the world community as a whole is still passing laws that don't factor in the inevitable, major change.

Ever since the days of the Sumerians there has been an assumption that great powers could buy their way out of problems by shoring up domestic deficiencies with imported supplies and political alliances. Again, we are seeing a scramble to secure resources and allies, with some countries, such as China, clearly considering commodities, such as grains, part of its national security essentials. However, the disruption caused by environmental change is likely to be so severe that simply importing will not be enough. Domestic fallibilities will need to be addressed as well. A key first step toward understanding those vulnerabilities is an accurate assessment of where exactly some of the problems lie, followed by a plan to counter them.

Broadly, there are two types of vulnerabilities: sudden, sharp shocks to the system and relentless erosion of stability.

SUDDEN SHOCKS

As seen with Katrina, when a major U.S. city was brought to its knees, one can't make general assumptions about who is best able to absorb sudden shocks. To understand real weaknesses, one has to break down the challenge into more manageable components to best gauge the vulnerabilities of a given country or region, and to formulate what must be done to enhance stability in a crisis. Using that approach, one can see that the human, economic, political, and security cost of a crisis can be mitigated at three stages, which we will call the "Three Rs"[2]:

- *Reinforce.* Shore up defenses by adapting to new conditions before the crisis comes. This can include sound assessment of the threats, appropriate city planning, good implementation of existing plans, the construction of communication links, and the enactment of suitable regulations, thereby ideally heading off the disruptive events before they can happen—or at least dampening the impact.
- *Rescue.* Marshall and effectively manage the whole range of emergency services if a crisis does occur to best mitigate the trauma and damage.
- *Recover.* Implement a long-term regional recovery plan to lessen the disruption, especially during a prolonged stress period such as a drought. This has the added benefit of restarting the process of reinforcing.

Each of these three categories operates at four levels: government, society (including non-profits), the private sector, and the media. The importance and role of each sector varies by local realities, national imperatives, and type of crisis. The result is 12 areas that can be enhanced to create better defenses against disaster—or, looked at another way, 12 areas of vulnerability. A breakdown of these 12 elements gives an idea of how ready a place is to survive a blow. A small sample of things to aim for:

By applying this table to specific cases, and regions, one can see that some of the most developed countries are also among the most wanting of protective measure. In the United States, for example, Katrina showed failures in all 12 boxes. By comparing what happened in New Orleans to what happened under similar conditions in other locations, we can see that the across-the-board failure wasn't necessary. And we can learn how to do it better next time.

The Montreal ice storm was fairly calm, and a lot of the credit for that goes to the people and emergency personnel of the region, but an ice storm is not a flood. There was comparatively little property damage, and cold weather tends to keep people inside rather than roaming the streets looking for provisions.

However, around the same time Katrina hit New Orleans, Mumbai received the most rain ever in a single day and flooded. Mumbai officials were largely unprepared, but locals stepped in, providing shelter and food for the stranded, actively policing their own neighborhoods, spreading information about evacuation routes, and even arranging for drinking water for those trekking out of the city. Indians are used to disruptions of services, and many have access to generators, water tanks, and other essentials. Around a thousand people died during the Mumbai flood, and there was an estimated $1 billion in damages, but crime dropped dramatically and the society didn't fragment. Mumbai failed with Reinforce (in the government, private sector, and media), Rescue (in the government and private sector), and Recovery (in government), but

	Reinforce	*Rescue*	*Recovery*
Government	• Climate proofing infrastructure (including decentralizing power grid) • Adequate training and equipping of emergency services • Disasters plans in place and regularly updated • Strong alliances with other nations • Assessment of laws, regulations, subsidies, etc., to ensure they are making things better, not worse	• Clear, viable command and control structure • Good communications between rescuers and those affected • Operationally flexible and easily implementable plans and measures	• Economic incentives to help rebuild economies in environmentally stable areas • Clear communication about progress of recovery • Honest lessons learned assessment of future vulnerabilities
Society (NGOs, Faith-Based Groups, etc.)	• Public awareness of disaster plan and citizen participation • Large, aware social networks • Adequate inter-citizen communications	• Strong social cohesion in crises situations • Adaptability to swift changes in conditions and needs • Ability to not rely exclusively on government or other external assistance	• Extensive non-governmental support networks to help rebuild socially and economically • (In partnership with government) effect a social services/NGO call-up to mitigate trauma of recovery and, if needed, resettlement
Private Sector	• Disaster plans in place that cover corporate as well as employee interests • Ensure investments are environmental/climate change-proofed, and generally plan for long-term • Lobby for regulations/policies that promote stability and sustainability in the market	• Work with government and society to mitigate disruptions • Resist crisis profiteering that will hamper rescue effort and create lingering resentment	• During rebuilding phase, focus on long-term stable growth rather than short-term gain that can contribute to future instability
Media	• Cover regional vulnerabilities and question plans that exacerbate them • Maintain up-to-date information on emergency procedures and contacts	• Ensure dissemination of accurate information • Calm panic	• Participate in lessons learned phase with a focus on how to move forward

the strength of local social networks and self-reliance helped with Rescue (social) and Recovery (social, private sector, and media).[3]

Also telling is what happened to coastal southeast China in the summer of 2006. By August 11, the area had been hit by eight typhoons, including the most powerful one in half a century. In all over 1,700 people died, more than 5 million homes and 125,000 square miles of farmland were destroyed, and there was at least $20 billion in damages. At the height of the biggest typhoon, the government used all means possible, including TV, the Internet, and text messages, to get the word out about escape routes. In all, more than 1.5 million people were evacuated, 40,000 ships were recalled to ports, and all business "not related to fighting the typhoon" was suspended. Society did not break down, and all levels of government, including the military, came together to effectively limit additional cost and suffering.[4]

Here, and almost every summer since, China failed in Reinforcing (in government), in part through replicating the United States in allowing development in flood-prone areas, but it came through very well in Rescue (in government and media). However, countries with a strong government response, such as China, need to be careful to include the population in all three phases, otherwise they will end up with a population that is incapable of self-reliance in an emergency. These countries need to provide reliable information to people and teach them adequate response patterns, so that the capping and rolling back of vulnerabilities becomes politically and logistically feasible. Adaptation can only come about if entire populations get involved, not just governments and the private sector. Involvement of the latter two is necessary for success, but not sufficient. This, of course, means that countries like China need to loosen up access to reliable information, especially about environmental vulnerabilities, for the sake of their own stability.

Another problem for China is that Recovery is largely left to local government and could contribute to large sections of society losing everything and becoming dangerously disenfranchised, and there don't seem to be lessons learned that are leading to better Reinforcement the next time around (again a problem with information flow).

Clearly, globally, there is a huge range of adaptive capabilities, and some of the richest countries can learn from some of the poorest. According to Saleemul Huq, the director of the climate change group at the International Institute for Environment and Development, "Bangladesh has a very effective notification and evacuation system against floods. In the big flood of 2004, 30 to 40 percent of the country was inundated and millions of people were displaced, but only 200 to 300 died. That's because people knew about the flood—from the government, the media, NGOs—and they moved. Compare that with Haiti, which was hit by a hurricane that same year. Haiti lost more than 2,000 people, from a much smaller population."[5]

What's worse is that sometimes the West is getting in the way of indigenous adaptive capacity elsewhere. Professor Anthony Nyong, from Nigeria, explained:

> Africa is really, really, really going to be very negatively impacted by climate change. There's going to be declining productivity for the crops, fisheries, and livestock. And we don't want situations where three quarters of the money that is supposed to go to adaptation is spent in doing workshops to show us how to adapt. We're tired of having workshops. Africans have been dealing with the issues of climate change for a long time. A lot have developed ingenious methods. What we need to do now is build on what we already know. How can we make it more effective? How can we make it more climate-proof? The Western world understands thermohaline circulation, and so on. But when it comes to adaptation, it's a developing country science. But unfortunately, the money for adaptation is in the West. So far, it's been promises and promises and promises.[6]

Globally, there simply needs to be a new way of looking at environmental change and vulnerabilities. All countries, even the seemingly strongest, are exceedingly exposed to the risks. Had the U.S. Gulf Coast been hit by eight major storms in a row, as China was, human tragedy aside, the U.S. and global economy could have been thrown into complete disarray. Western agriculture, infrastructure, and social cohesion are all exposed to great risk. Also, in the West, given higher property values and construction costs, it takes a smaller amount of damage to create large losses and the population has much higher expectations for safety, compensation, and governance. The advantage that countries like China and India have is that construction is relatively cheap and the population has relatively low expectations. And, as they are still developing, they are used to having long-term goals that take a national will to ensure. If they start now, they can incorporate policies into their plans that will mean that, in the coming decades, they have developed on a sound foundation.

Conversely, policy makers in the West tend to think that their "development" is already complete, and just needs a bit of fine-tuning from time to time. This "developed country complacency syndrome" gives a false sense of security. The West's foundations are at risk, and, to use military terminology, its future operating environment is going to be so different that it needs to start thinking about itself as developing toward being able to survive, and even thrive, under very different conditions. It needs a top-to-bottom reevaluation.

The lexicon of mitigation and adaptation should be supplemented by the concept of *integration*, in which planning is not simply "adapted" to environmental change, but change is "integrated" into the plans from the start, potentially altering the whole nature of the project. Otherwise, the shocks to the system and the increasingly regular strain on the military, social services, insurance industry, local councils, business community, and others could create a destabilizing effect and, at the very least, a loss in confidence in the government.

Developers can still get rich, politicians can still get payoffs, megaprojects can still be funded, but it needs to be in the context of strengthening defenses against environmental change, not weakening them—because once they get too weak, no one is going to be making money anymore. In a time of environmental change, limiting loss will be just as important as promoting growth.

RELENTLESS EROSION OF STABILITY

A critical component of creating resilience to relentless environmental change is integrating new conditions into existing systems. Many current policies and proposals seem to be focused on changing behavior by punishing "bad" deeds, primarily through taxation, rather than making resilience-enhancing options more attractive. In its most basic form this means higher taxes for vehicles with higher emissions. While these can be effective aversion tools, they risk adding to the already increasing pressures on the poor and middle classes unless alternatives, such as efficient and affordable public transport, are also made available.

The same is true in a range of sectors. For example, small-scale, local renewable energies and a decentralized power grid can be more efficient, and can help develop new industries, contribute to regional employment, and aid national security by building redundancy into the system, yet they tend to be more expensive for the consumer to purchase and are not supported or promoted by government to the same extent as other energy sectors.

Unless there is a marked shift in practices, due to environmental change and other factors, the cost of living in the West is likely to increase, and infrastructure is likely to degrade. For the sake of stability, the burden on citizens needs to be lifted, not increased. Positive schemes such as reduced tax on energy-saving materials and government cooperation with the insurance industry on flood defenses are a good beginning. That approach now needs to be expanded across the board to motivate civil society, academia, business, and government to find and implement viable, long-term solutions.

The times are a-changing, and if industry, local governments, consumers, and others are going to be nudged down a more resilient road quickly and relatively painlessly, it would be helpful to use more carrot and less stick. As it is, it will take enormous efforts to avoid being badly bruised by environmental change. It would be best to avoid adding unnecessary self-flagellation to the mix.

In terms of international action, to date much of the West's engagement has been focused on highlighting the importance of climate change mitigation through the cutting of carbon emissions. This is often an unpopular message. Many, especially in developing countries, feel that the West benefited from unbridled emissions during its development, and is now using climate change as an excuse to hamper global competition from those who are still trying to develop. Again, it does not matter if that is true or not; what matters is that many influential leaders in the developing world believe it. Perceived lecturing may be counterproductive.

What may be more effective is increased partnerships between the scientific communities, and between scientists and policy makers. The UK and United States, for instance, are global leaders in climate and environmental science. Flagship research institutions, such as the UK's Hadley Centre and the U.S. National Oceanic and Atmospheric Administration, should be better funded so that they can work more closely with international researchers. Once international partners have a better understanding of the potential impacts of environmental change on their nations, there will be more internal political momentum and they will be better equipped to try to counter the coming disruptions. Additionally, increased scientific engagement will help to gauge the true strengths and weaknesses in our highly interconnected world.

Scientific collaborations could also help to fill in some of the knowledge gaps necessary for building domestic resilience. We will need to better understand the implications of the complex interplay between climate change and other forms of environmental change. We will also need to assess how best to adapt to those changes—ideally through collaboration between expert sectors, such as climate scientists, engineers, insurers, and developers—and formulate methods to integrate them into planning and policy. And we will need to devise resilience techniques.

Through international partnerships we may find innovative international solutions to domestic challenges. Given that many developing nations are subject to regular natural disasters, some have developed pioneering, low-cost methods for dealing with crises. Bangladesh, for example, has been living with flooding for centuries and has refined several innovative evacuation and safety methods. In finding a way forward, everyone has something to learn from others.

Geopolitically we will all need more, and varied, friends.

Canada will need allies to protect its position in the Arctic.

China will need to sort out its domestic environmental mess if it is going to be on a strong enough footing to sustain its power projection abroad. It will also need India at least neutral, and a better working relationship with not just the elite, but also with ordinary citizens at home and abroad.

Russia will need to reassess the stability of its infrastructure, the nature of its relationship with China, and its position on the Arctic.

In order to compete with China, the UK is going to have to either start implementing policies that plan for the long run (and possibly practice more nationalist capitalism as Norway is doing with its fossil fuel supplies), and try to build global relationships based on equality, or else it may need to lower its standard of living expectations.

The EU is going to have to figure out what its bureaucracy can manage, and not try to overregulate areas that will need quick responses and flexibility for adaptation. Member states will also have to decide, clearly, on how to ensure an EU foreign policy that best serves their interests. They will have to make adjustments to retain current levels of influence in a world where they aren't the only ones writing the rules anymore.

And the United States is going to have rebuild domestically and shore up alliances abroad, or risk its ability to influence global affairs over the short term, and its internal stability in the medium term.

Pulling all the threads together, the world of tomorrow looks chaotic and violent. Even more so than usual. And even more than expected. We are living in the good old days. Just as India built and grew around its monsoon cycle, the rest of the world has also blithely built entire social, political, security, and economic structures on the assumption that there are certain geophysical and climatic constants to act as a foundation. There aren't. There never have been. And there never will be.

As pressure is put on food, water supplies, and national boundaries, famine and war may become more frequent. This instability may make populations more tolerant of autocratic governments, especially nationalistic capitalist ones where the political, economic, and military sectors combine to protect existing resources and aggressively try to secure new ones. China and Russia already have a head start on this model.

Although the West is exposed, everyone will be hit to some degree. The U.S.'s disorganized and shambolic reaction to the disaster caused by Hurricane Katrina shows how even predicted climate events can bring the mightiest to their knees, and potentially leave them less able to defend themselves at home and abroad. The West will have to devote much more money, energy, and thought to domestic crises. There needs to be a reevaluation of the role of the armed forces, and a retraining to cope with domestic natural catastrophes.

Unless the West is content to stagger from disaster to disaster, and risk severe national security issues, it also must undertake a major redesign of infrastructure and government policy. Highways near eroding coastlines will need to be moved. Low-lying cities like London, Washington D.C., and New York will need to be protected—or parts will have to be abandoned altogether. Crops will have to be rethought, water-saving techniques developed, and sewage systems redesigned. Transportation systems and the nature of, and adherence to, international law will have to be reexamined.

Preparing for environmental change will take political will, good basic engineering, public education, long-term planning, and sustained funding. Where it doesn't happen, economies will be bled dry by a thousand environment-related cuts. Meanwhile more environmentally adaptive countries will rise. As will countries with less expensive infrastructures that can take hits and still stay functional, like India. Environmental change is the wild card in the current high-stakes game of geopolitics.

That variable can be mitigated, but there is no one-size-fits-all solution. Each country has its own strengths, weaknesses, national character, and geopolitical direction. Honest assessments of vulnerabilities and adaptive potential using techniques such as the Three Rs need to be implemented through systems that will work locally. That could mean policies that come from the bottom up, as in India; from the top down, as in China; or are market friendly, as in the United States. We have the answers; we just have to be willing to ask the questions. We have adapted to environmental change before, and we can do it again.

It would just be nice if, this time around, there weren't quite so much human sacrifice involved.

ACKNOWLEDGMENTS

You'll have to bear with me. This is the closest I am likely to get to an Oscar acceptance speech, there are a lot of people who made this book (and me) possible, and there is no music to play me off. So settle in. Or go for a wander. It'll be over soon.

There is a reason people thank their agents first (or perhaps second, after their chosen deity). My agent, Rick Broadhead, is the godfather of this book. He persisted, negotiated, and encouraged long after any sane person would have given up. And, even more miraculous, he returns calls.

The only person who had more faith in this project than Rick was my husband, Jens Christian Svabo Justinussen. He patiently endured endless conversation (ok, monologues), while theories were worked out, all the while feeding me tea and cookies. What more could you want?

Once the book actually existed, the outstanding team at Palgrave toned and honed it and made it presentable. Thank you to the extremely talented and dedicated Jake Klisivitch (who has excellent taste in poutine joints), Colleen Lawrie, Jen Simington, Donna Cherry, Christine Catarino, and Sarah Thomas.

The people who taught me to think in the first place bear no responsibility for what I later actually ended up thinking. They did their best. And I am deeply grateful. They include Stan Paskal, Merrily Weisbord, Arnie Gelbart, Tom Paskal, Adam Gorwic, Ewa Gorwic, Professor Michael Maxwell, Professor W.M.S. Russell, Claire Russell, Professor M.D. Nalapat, and Professor Vladimir Keilis-Borok. I think therefore you are.

I have been very lucky over the years to work with excellent editors, and even luckier that many then became friends. These are the people who taught me how to write and report, and made sure my infinitives remained un-split. I owe them more than I can say. They include Shelley Ambrose, Dianne de Fenoyle, Joanne Sasvari, Deborah Stokes, Annarosa Sabbadini, Noah Richler, Larry Bleiberg, John Moore, Jim Byers, Rob Crew, Susan Pigg, Giles Gherson, David Wallis, Simon Calder, Charlotte Hindle, Margaret May, and the fine folks at Travelers' Tales. Thank you as well to Elizabeth Klinck, who not only anointed me the voice of Betty Koala, but who can get permissions from a stone, rolling or otherwise.

In London, I have had the pleasure and honor to work with brilliant people who have helped illuminate some of the most pressing and critical issues. Thank you, Beverley Darkin, Bernice Lee, Susan Ambler-Edwards, Jonathan Mirksy, Isabel Hilton, Adrian Moon (the best unofficial clipping service in existence), Reza Afshar, Jeffrey Mazo, Shiloh Fetzek, Brett Lovegrove, and Gemma Green, and the always insightful team at Chatham House.

In India, I have been blessed with some of the smartest and warmest friends and colleagues imaginable. Thank yous are more than due to the Nalapat and Das families, the Shah family, Pramod Thevannoor, Indu Nair, Princess Nikki, the S.C.M.S. family, Arvind Kumar and the dedicated team at Manipal University, the Guptas and to Lakshmi Bayi, who is a wonderful friend. Buy her book.

In Washington, hard-working people are doing fascinating work, and I've been privileged to get to know some of them and even call them friends, including Carol Dumaine, Chad Briggs, Larry Lanes, Anita Street, and the rest of the innovative and committed team at Global EESE, Geoff Dabelko the genial overlord of the Environmental Change and Security Program at the Wilson Center, and the incredibly accomplished Julia Watson and Martin Walker.

Researching this book was only possibly because I have a lot of friends, family, and colleagues who are extraordinarily kind, wise, uncomplaining, and sometimes even have spare bedrooms in far-flung corners of the world. Time with them over the years has kept me happy, sane, and, in many cases, out of the rain. Thank you Marinda van Dalen (and family), Jeannie Samuel (and family), Cathy Hennessy (and family), Harriet O'Brien (the only friend who will regularly visit me in Reading), Robin Bain (best Christmas card maker ever), Mark Achbar Inc., Stella Galea (who writes better than she realizes), Dave Apen, the Lavuts, Mari Sato, Keibo Oiwa, Fiuza Fathimath, Valerie Kaye, Jane Drabble, Bill Nemtin, Terry Moser, Mary Hughson, Jeremy Stevenson, Jane and Jonathan and family, the Plachowskis, the Bakers, the Masrys, the Sterns, Gina Roitman, Seamus Cassidy, Jennifer Barclay, and all the Justinussen and í Sandagerði family who have made me feel so welcome in the Faroe Islands.

And then there is Montreal, my home. And what is home without family. Thanks don't seem enough, but it'll have to do for now, topped up with some love for Kim Kachanoff, Sylvain Desjardins, Anna Paskal, Jim Thomas, Phyllis Amber, Lia, Eva, Asha, Cassidy, Noah, Josh, Emma, the Lavignes, the Schwartzbergs, and everyone at Weisbord Acres.

There are also those from Montreal who are just like family, but much better looking: Caroline Markos and her much nicer younger sister (and even nicer father, who is the only one on the planet who has remembered to call me on my birthday since I was thirteen); Judith and Rosa Kovalski, who mean more to me than they can imagine; Clayton Bailey (if you meet him, ask about the Icelanders); the Silverstones; the Samuels; the deVolpis; Gerty Birchwood and family; Ermin and family, Leihua and Ye; Justin "Graphic-Master" Estrela-Reis; Jessica Andrade; the rest of Jason's moveable feast of a posse; and the wonderful Nicholsons, who open their minds, hearts, house, and bar every Wednesday night.

This seems to have devolved from an Oscar speech to a high school yearbook entry so I'll end it here. Except for one more: a special thank you to my little brother, Jason J. F. Lavigne-Paskal, who always (mostly) uncomplainingly does what it takes to make it all work. Jason, sorry about the middle name. It seemed a good idea at the time.

NOTES

INTRODUCTION

1. Paul Simon, "The Only Living Boy in New York," *Bridge over Troubled Waters,* Columbia Records, 1970.
2. "Monsoon gloom strikes South Asia," *New Scientist,* May 24, 2006.
3. *WMO statement on the status of the global climate in 2008,* World Meteorological Organization, Geneva, 2009.
4. "Little Ice Age: Big Chill," History Channel, November 26, 2005. Much of the research around climate and geopolitics moves so quickly that often reliable TV documentaries get out up to date research before books can.
5. Ibid.
6. Nick Squires, "Swiss villagers pray for glacier," *The Telegraph,* August 7, 2009.
7. Katharine Anderson, "The weather prophets: science and reputation in Victorian meteorology," *History of Science* 37 (1999): 179–216.
8. Ross Couper-Johnston, *El Niño; the weather phenomenon that changed the world* (London: Coronet Books, 2000).
9. Anderson, "The weather prophets."
10. For more on the history of the Met Office, see www.metoffice.gov.uk/.
11. www.metoffice.gov.uk/climatechange/science/hadleycentre/
12. The Intergovernmental Panel of Climate Change, www.ipcc.ch.
13. "Billions face climate change risk," BBC News, April 6, 2007.
14. Sun Tzu and Shang Yang, *The Art of War* and *The book of Lord Shang* (London: Wordsworth Editions, 1998), p. 63.
15. W. M. S. Russell, *Man, Nature and History* (London: Aldus Books, 1967).
16. Jay Chapman, "England's wine renaissance," *Geotimes,* August 2004.
17. Private correspondence with Prof. W. M. S. Russell, June 2006.
18. Ibid.
19. "National security and the threat of climate change," The CNA Corporation, 2007, http://securityandclimate.cna.org/.
20. Ibid.
21. Ibid.
22. John Neander, *El Niño—its far-reaching environmental effects on Army tactical decision aids,* U.S. Army Topographic Engineering Center, Alexandria, Virginia, 1996.
23. "National security and the threat of climate change."
24. Ibid.
25. "The world at six billion," United Nations Secretariat, 1999.

26. Nick Joliat, "Delta region: subsidence," *Mission 2010*, Massachusetts Institute of Technology, http://web.mit.edu/12.000/www/m2010/finalwebsite/background/deltaregion.html.

27. "Katrina report blames levees; Army Corps of Engineers: 'We've had a catastrophic failure,'" CBS News, June 1, 2006. "Report: Criticism of FEMA's Katrina response deserved," CNN.com, April 14, 2006.

28. This, of course, has nothing to do with what the individual citizens of a country may be like.

29. M. L. Parry et al, *Climate Change 2007: Impacts, Adaptation and Vulnerability* (Cambridge: Cambridge University Press, 2007).

CHAPTER 1

1. North Atlantic Subregion, North America, Working Group II, *Climate Change 2001: Impacts, Adaptation Vulnerability*, Intergovernmental Panel on Climate Change (IPCC) (Cambridge: Cambridge University Press, 2001).

2. Sven Anemüller, Stephan Monreal, and Christoph Bals, *Global Climate Risks Index 2006: Weather-related loss events and their impact on countries in 2004 and in a long-term comparison*, Germanwatch, Bonn, 2006.

3. Interview with Dr. Virginia Burkett, of the U.S. Geological Survey and a co-author on the IPCC coastal study, UNFCCC, Montreal, December 2, 2005.

4. Joanne R. Potter, Michael J. Savonis, Virginia R. Burkett, *Impacts of Climate Change and Variability on Transportation Systems and Infrastructure: Gulf Coast Study*, Department of Transport, March 12, 2008, www.climatescience.gov/Library/sap/sap4-7/final-report/sap4-7-final-all.pdf.

5. Interview with Dr. Virginia Burkett.

6. "Hurricane Katrina—Most destructive hurricane ever to strike the U.S.," National Oceanic & Atmospheric Administration, U.S. Department of Commerce, February 12, 2007, www.katrina.noaa.gov.

7. Ceci Connolly, "Thousands of Katrina 911 calls went astray," *Washington Post*, November 8, 2005.

8. "Katrina Killings," *Anderson Cooper 360°*, CNN, August 27, 2006, transcript available at edition.cnn.com/TRANSCRIPTS/0608/27/acd.01.html.

9. Adam Nossiter, "Teens recall drinking Katrina's fetid waters while stuck in prison," *New York Times*, May 10, 2006. "Katrina jail 'horror' condemned," BBC News, August 11, 2006.

10. "Katrina Killings."

11. Ibid.

12. Ibid.

13. Griff Witte, "Private security contractors head to Gulf," *Washington Post*, September 8, 2005; "Hurricane Katrina: Why is the Red Cross not in New Orleans?," American Red Cross, September 2, 2005, www.redcross.org/faq/0,1096,0_682_4524,00.html.

14. Witte, "Private security contractors."

15. "FEMA fraud paid for football, vacations, erotica," Associated Press, June 14, 2006.

16. Monica Guzman, "Westbury High tension explodes into a brawl," *Houston Chronicle*, December 8, 2005.

17. Nick Miles, "Crime spike hits Katrina evacuees," BBC News, August 15, 2006.

18. Arian Campo-Flores, "Katrina's Latest Damage," *Newsweek*, March 13, 2006.

19. Ibid.

20. "Soldiers deployed in New Orleans," BBC News, June 20, 2006.

21. Sharon Schmickle, "Mental health problems abound a year after Katrina," *The Mercury News*, August 19, 2006.

22. For economic costs and damages caused by Katrina, see http://lwf.ncdc.noaa.gov/oa/climate/research/2005/katrina.html.

23. Jonathan Weisman, "Projected Iraq war costs soar," *Washington Post*, April 27, 2006.

24. Potter, Savonis, and Burkett, *Impacts of Climate Change.*

25. MMS Updates Hurricanes Katrina and Rita Damage, www.mms.gov/ooc/press/2006/press0501.htm.

26. Potter, Savonis, and Burkett, *Impacts of Climate Change.*

27. "Rita clips Mumbai choppers' wings," *Times of India*, December 2, 2005.

28. Potter, Savonis, and Burkett, *Impacts of Climate Change.*

29. Ibid.

30. "Ask the White House," The White House, May 5, 2006.

31. Martin Merzer, "Katrina-size hurricane would devastate South Florida, scientists say," Knight Ridder, May 6, 2006.

32. Christine Van Lenten, "Storm surge barriers for New York Harbor?" *Science & The City*, The New York Academy of Science, November 6, 2006.

33. *Climate Change and a global city: the potential consequences of climate variability and change*, Columbia Earth Institute for the U.S. Global Change Research Program, July 2001, http://metroeast_climate.ciesin.columbia.edu.

34. Ibid.

35. Ibid.

36. "Emergency in NY as city swelters," BBC News, August 3, 2006.

37. U.S. Army Corps of Engineers, www.usace.army.mil/about/Pages/Mission.aspx.

38. John Schwartz, "Army builders accept blame over flooding," *New York Times*, June 2, 2006.

39. Michael Grunwald, "Par for the Corps; a flood of bad projects," *Washington Post*, May 14, 2006.

40. Ibid.

41. Ibid.

42. Interview with Thomas Loster, UNFCCC, Montreal, December 3, 2005.

43. *Myths and Facts about the National Flood Insurance Program*, www.fema.gov/library/viewRecord.do?id=3002.

44. *NOW* transcript, show 227, July 7, 2006, www.pbs.org/now/transcript/227.html.

45. Gilbert M. Gaul, "Repeat claims strain federal flood insurance," *Washington Post*, October 11, 2005.

46. Ibid.

47. Elizabeth Williamson, "Taxpayers May Face Hurricane Tab," *Wall Street Journal*, May 31, 2008.

48. Ann Scott Tyson, "Many lessons in disaster drill," *Washington Post*, May 14, 2007.

49. Ibid.

50. Richard A. Clarke, *Against all enemies* (New York: Free Press, 2004), p. 271.

51. Liz Sidoto, "Guard stretched between Katrina, wars," Associated Press, September 10, 2005.

52. Laura Maggi, "City's population up 14 percent since July 2006," *The Times-Picayune*, May 3, 2007.

53. Cullen Murphy and Todd S. Purdum, "Farewell to All That: An Oral History of the Bush White House," *Vanity Fair*, February 2009.

54. "The rich, the poor and the growing gap between them," *The Economist*, June 15, 2006.

55. Ibid.

56. Carmen DeNavas-Walt, Bernadette D. Proctor, and Jessica C. Smith, *Income, Poverty, and Health Insurance Coverage in the United States: 2007*, U.S. Census Bureau, U.S. Department of Commerce (Washington, DC: U.S. Government Printing Office, August 2008).

57. Hunger in America 2006: a report on emergency food distribution in the United States in 2005, Executive Summary, America's Second Harvest, http://hungerinamerica.org.

58. "U.S. food stamp list tops 34 million for first time," Reuters, August 6, 2009.

59. "The rich, the poor."

60. Alan Wood, "The correlation of violence to socio-economic inequalities; an empirical analysis," World Organisation Against Torture, Geneva, October 2005.

61. Paige M. Harrison and Allen J. Beck, "Prisoners in 2004," *Bulletin*, Bureau of Justice Statistics, U.S. Department of Justice, October 2005.

62. Adam Liptak, "1 in 100 U.S. Adults Behind Bars, New Study Says," *New York Times*, February 28, 2008.

63. "Prison Town, USA," *POV*, PBS, July 24, 2007.

64. Richard L. Berke, "Cities Move to Curb Summer Crime Increase," *New York Times*, May 21, 1989. "Weather and Behaviour," BBC Weather, BBC Online, www.bbc.co.uk/weather/features/health_culture/behaviour.shtml.

65. "Prison Town, USA."

66. Alok Jha, "Boiled alive," *The Guardian*, July 26, 2006.

67. Juliet Eilperin, "More frequent heat waves linked to global warming," *Washington Post*, August 4, 2006.

68. "Climate study shows Europe risks," BBC News, October 27, 2005.

69. "Nuclear plant struck by jellyfish," BBC News, July 20, 2006.

70. *Climate change and London's transportation systems*, Summary Report, Greater London Authority, London, September 2005.

71. Ibid.

72. Ibid.

73. *The London climate change adaptation strategy*, Greater London Authority, August 2008.

74. An alternate rumor about why the Thames Barrier was built is that the government decided that if the Soviets exploded a major underwater device offshore, it could create a tidal wave that would flood many European cities, including London. It is one of the better conspiracy theories I've heard.

75. Polly Toynbee, "Forget drought: first we have to end this cowardice," *The Guardian*, May 23, 2006.

76. Paul Brown, "Outer barrier for Thames floated in river defence plan," *The Guardian*, January 11, 2005.

77. *London climate change adaptation strategy*.

78. Foresight, Flood and Coastal Defense, www.foresight.gov.uk/OurWork/Completed-Projects/Flood/KeyInformation/General_Reports.asp.

79. *Impacts of Europe's changing climate: an indicator-based assessment*, EEA Report No. 2/2004, European Environment Agency, Copenhagen, 2004, p. 67.

80. Nicholas Stern, *Stern Review: The economics of climate change*, Executive Summary, Cabinet Office-HM Treasury, London, 2006, www.hm-treasury.gov.uk/d/Executive_Summary.pdf. Cleo Paskal, "Nationalistic Capitalism and the Food Crisis," www.chinadialogue.net, 3 June 2008.

81. "Wheat prices jump to 10-year high," BBC News, October 11, 2006.

82. "Iberian misery as drought bites," BBC News, June 13, 2005.

83. Interview with Dr. Henry Venema, UNFCCC, Montreal, December 2, 2005.

84. Ibid.

85. Joseph Alcamo, Nikolai Dronin, Marcel Endejan, Genady Golubev, and Andrei Kirilenko, "A new assessment of climate change impacts on food production shortfalls and water availability in Russia," *Global Environmental Change* 17, no. 3–4 (August-October 2007): 429–444.

86. Interview with Dr. Henry Venema, UNFCCC, Montreal, December 2, 2005.

87. "Power generation growth plummets to 2.71% in FY'09," *Times of India*, April 9, 2009.
88. Cleo Paskal, *The Vulnerability of Energy Infrastructure to Environmental Change*, Chatham House and GlobalEESE, London, July 2009.
89. Michael J. Savonis et al., *Impacts of climate change and variability on transportation systems and infrastructure: Gulf Coast Study, phase 1*, U.S. Climate Change Science Program Synthesis and Assessment Product 4.7, U.S. Department of Transport, March 2008, pp. 4–38.
90. James Kanter, "Climate change puts nuclear energy into hot water," *New York Times*, May 20, 2007.
91. Vicky Pope, "What can climate scientists tell us about the future?" Met Office, www.metoffice.gov.uk/climatechange/science/explained/explained1.html.
92. David Shukman, "Flood risk fear over key UK sites," BBC News, May 7, 2008.
93. UNEP Risø Centre, http://cdmpipeline.org/cdm-projects-type.htm#6.

CHAPTER 2

1. Canadian Rangers, www.army.forces.gc.ca/land-terre/cr-rc/index-eng.asp.
2. "Climate change and the greenhouse effect: a briefing from the Hadley Centre," www.metoffice.com/research/hadleycentre/pubs/brochures/2005/clim_green/slide 34.pdf, accessed August 13, 2006.
3. "Impacts of a warming Arctic (Highlights)," Arctic Climate Impact Assessment, 2004, http://amap.no/acia/Highlights.pdf.
4. Steve Connor, "Global warming 'past the point of no return,'" *The Independent on Sunday*, September 16, 2005.
5. "Arctic Sea Ice Shatters All Previous Record Lows," National Snow and Ice Data Center, University of Colorado, October 1, 2007.
6. "Sea ice decline intensifies," National Snow and Ice Data Center, University of Colorado, September 28, 2005.
7. Connor, "Global warming"
8. Jonathan Amos, "Arctic summers ice-free 'by 2013,'" BBC News, December 12, 2007.
9. Clifford Krauss, Steven Lee Myers, Andrew C. Revkin, and Simon Romero, "As polar ice turns to water, dreams of treasure abound," *New York Times*, October 10, 2005.
10. Steven Lee Myers, Andrew C. Revkin, Simon Romero, and Clifford Krauss, "When is the Arctic no longer the Arctic?," *International Herald Tribune*, October 20, 2005.
11. J. J. Kelley, A. S. Naidu, and W. Splain, "Climate change effects on the Alaska coastal environment of the Beaufort Sea," EGS-AGU-EUG Joint Assembly, abstracts from the meeting held in Nice, France, April 6–11, 2003.
12. "Arctic Ocean ice crashes on Alaska shores," Associated Press, January 28, 2006.
13. "Naval operations in an iceless Arctic," Oceanographer of the Navy, Office of Naval Research, Naval Ice Center, United States Arctic Research Commission, 2001, www.natice.noaa.gov/icefree/Arcticscenario.pdf. Matt Crenson, "Report: Proof of global warming," Associated Press, November 15, 2004. "Global warming causing record Arctic ice melt," CTV News, September 28, 2005. Steve Connor, "Global warming 'past the point of no return,'" *The Independent*, September 16, 2005. Seth Borenstein, "Arctic ice melting rapidly, study says," Associated Press, September 13, 2006.
14. Vladimir E. Romanovsky, "How rapidly is permafrost changing and what are the impacts of these changes?," National Oceanic and Atmosphere Administration, www.arctic.noaa.gov/essay_romanovsky.html, accessed September 2, 2006. Molly Bentley, "Earth's permafrost starts to squelch," BBC News, December 29, 2004.
15. Usha Lee McFarling, "Ice mummies and artefacts emerge after dung age remnants surface," *Sydney Morning Herald*, January 18, 2003.
16. Cleo Paskal, "If you think daylight saving time is weird . . . ," *National Post*, October 24, 2000.

17. Interview with Rune Fjellheim, UNFCCC, Montreal, December 2, 2005.
18. "Impacts of a warming Arctic."
19. Robert Lee Hotz, "Warming reshapes Arctic ecosystem; Bering Strait changes 'profound'; Impact may be irreversible as animals struggle," *The Toronto Star*, March 11, 2006.
20. Interview with Rune Fjellheim, UNFCCC, Montreal, December 2, 2005.
21. Bethan V. Purse, Phillip S. Mellor, David J. Rogers, Alan R. Samuel, Peter P.C. Mertens, and Matthew Baylis, "Climate change and the recent emergence of bluetongue in Europe," *Nature Reviews Microbiology* 3 (February 2005): 171–181.
22. The capacity of the earth's surface to reflect light is known as "albedo." The lower the albedo of a particular surface, the more solar radiation is absorbed. The polar ice sheets reflect incoming short-wave radiation so effectively that there is little heat available for a rise in temperature. For further information see www.metoffice.com/education/secondary/teachers/atmosphere.html.
23. "Melting lakes in Siberia emit greenhouse gas," *Nature*, September 2006.
24. S. Perkins, "On the rise; Siberian lakes: Major source of methane," *Science News*, September 9, 2006.
25. Richard Black, "Global warming risk 'much higher,'" BBC News, May 23, 2006. While their research is interesting, I use the much more conservative *IPCC Fourth Assessment Report* estimates www.ipcc.ch/publications_and_data/publications_ipcc_fourth_assessment_report_wg2_report_impacts_adaptation_and_vulnerability.htm.
26. Rebecca Morelle, "Arctic's tropical past uncovered," BBC News, May 31, 2006.
27. Ibid. If the warming continues, this might happen again, eventually ushering in yet another ice age. But those timescales are outside the scope of this book.
28. R. C. L. Wilson, S. A. Drury, and J. L. Chapman, *The Great Ice Age: Climate change and life* (London: Routledge, 2001), p. 228.

CHAPTER 3

1. "A belated confession," *New York Times*, March 25, 1911, p. 10.
2. Based on the actual travel of a jacket as followed in *A Coat of Many Countries*, Josh Freed (dir.), Galafilm and CBC, 1999.
3. The shipping facts, unless otherwise noted, come from "International shipping and world trade; Fact and figures," International Maritime Organization, November 2008.
4. Shipping still tends to work on imperial measurement units, with the 20-foot and 40-foot containers being the standard size. Ship capacity is usually measured in 20-foot equivalent units (TEU) or 40-foot equivalent units (FEU). So, a ship that can hold 2,000 20-foot containers or 1,000 40-foot containers has a capacity of 2,000 TEU or 1,000 FEU. As of 2005, the largest container ships in regular operations are over 8,000 TEU and can carry hundreds of millions of dollars worth of cargo at a time.
5. "International shipping and world trade," November 2008.
6. Ibid.
7. Rockford Weitz, "Strategic Oceanic choke points; are they still important," working paper, Fletcher School of Oceanic Studies, Tufts University, December 12, 2000, http://fletcher.tufts.edu/maritime/documents/Oceanic_Chokepoints.pdf.
8. "International shipping and world trade," November 2008.
9. "International shipping and world trade; Fact and figures," International Maritime Organization, September 2006.
10. "International shipping and world trade," November 2008.

CHAPTER 4

1. *Suez: A very British crisis; Episode Two: Conspiracy*, BBC TV One, October 23, 2006.

2. "Suez Canal," *Encyclopædia Britannica 2007 Ultimate Reference Suite* (Chicago: Encyclopædia Britannica, 2006).

3. Rockford Weitz, "Strategic Oceanic choke points; are they still important," working paper, Fletcher School of Oceanic Studies, Tufts University, December 12, 2000, http://fletcher.tufts.edu/maritime/documents/Oceanic_Chokepoints.pdf.

4. "Case study 4 background: Living in the British Empire: India," National Archives, UK, www.learningcurve.gov.uk/empire/g2/cs4/background.htm.

5. "Strategic Oceanic choke points" and "Suez Canal."

6. Paul Reynolds, "Suez: End of empire," BBC News, July 24, 2006.

7. Dwight D. Eisenhower, "Top secret to Robert Anthony Eden, 31 July 1956," *The Papers of Dwight David Eisenhower*, ed. L. Galambos and D. van Ee, (Baltimore: The Johns Hopkins University Press, 1996), doc. 1935, http://eisenhowermemorial.org/presidential-papers/first-term/documents/1935.cfm.

8. *Suez: A very British crisis; Episode Two.*

9. 10. "U.K. pondered China nuclear attack," BBC News, June 30, 2006.

11. Reynolds, "Suez: End of empire."

12. Charles Levinson, "$50 billion later, taking stock of US aid to Egypt," *Christian Science Monitor*, April 12, 2004.

13. "Panama," "Panama Canal," and "Panama Canal Zone," *The New Columbia Encyclopedia* (London: Columbia University Press, 1975), p. 2055–6.

14. Eric Jackson, "As befits the occasion," *The Panama News*, January 12–25, 2003.

15. Transcript, Dean Rusk Oral History Interview III, January 2, 1979, by Paige E. Mulhollan, Lyndon Baines Johnson Library and Museum, www.lbjlib.utexas.edu/johnson/archives.hom/oralhistory.hom/rusk/rusk03.pdf.

16. "Terms of the Treaties," Panama Canal Treaties, Jimmy Carter Library & Museum, http://jimmycarterlibrary.org/education/panama/terms.phtml.

17. Ibid.

18. Andrew Cockburn, "Because we could," *The Nation*, November 8, 2004.

19. "1989: US forces oust General Noriega," BBC News, http: news.bbc.co.uk/onthis-day/hi/dates/stories/december/20/newsid_4054000/4054951.stm. James T. Alexander, "American Foreign Policy in the Third World: New World Order, Rhetoric or Reality?," ACDIS Occasional Paper, University of Illinois, April 1992.

20. Factors that have contributed to rising food prices include: global population increases; changes in consumption patterns; speculation in the marketplace; currently productive soils degrading, flooding, or drying out; crop pests and diseases moving into new areas or becoming more virulent in old areas; the large-scale switch to fuel crops; the spread of urban and industrial development into farmlands; the rising cost of fuel, transport, and fertilizers; and increasing extreme events.

21. Alaa Shahine, "China, Russia breach Darfur arms embargo: Amnesty," Reuters, May 9, 2007.

22. Hutchison Port Holdings, http://hph.com, accessed October 2, 2006.

23. Ibid.

24. Ronald H. Cole, *Operation JUST CAUSE: The planning and execution of joint operations in Panama, February 1988-January 1990*, Joint History Office, Office of the Chairman of the Joint Chiefs of Staff, Washington, D.C., 1995, p. 7.

25. "Hutchison Port ruled out of Indian ports bidding for security concerns," *People's Daily Online*, August 30, 2006, http://english.people.com.cn/200608/30/eng20060830_298178.html.

26. Lucian Kim and Torrey Clark, "Shell Cedes Sakhalin Stake, Strengthening Putin Grip (Update 5)," December 21, 2006, Bloomberg News, www.bloomberg.com/apps/news?pid=20670001&sid=aFF1FYXdrOqo.

27. Arshad Mohammed, "Rice confronts assertive Russia with less leverage," Reuters, May 13, 2007.

28. Jim Barnett and Kim Christensen, "Memo details Arcostrategy on gas prices," *The Oregonian*, April 25, 2001.

29. "Wyden fights to talk exports of oil drilled in Arctic Refuge," October 19, 2005, www.wyden.senate.gov/media/2005/10192005_fight_to_ban_oil_exports.htm, accessed October 23, 2006.

30. Mike Blanchfield, "Harper: Canada an 'energy superpower'," CanWest News Service, July 15, 2066.

31. Matthew Lee, "Rice decries Putin's power grab," *Associated Press*, May 10, 2007. Note that Rice's definition of "everybody in the world" seems to consist almost exclusively of countries in the West.

32. Indrani Bagchi, "Going after Rumsfeld is not a good idea: Cohen," *Times of India*, November 11, 2006. In a rapidly shifting world, certainty itself is a commodity. In those films where the aliens come down to negotiate with earthlings, they arrive saying "take me to your leader," not "take me to your lobbyists, committee hearings, and team of lawyers." Which, ironically, is probably one of the reasons why in the past the United States used to back military dictators like Saddam Hussein, Manuel Noriega, and Augusto Pinochet. It seemed to give it a stable, uncomplicated point of contact who was indebted to it. Of course, not all worked out as planned, and there is no question that democracy can be complicated to deal with. That said, apart from being better for its own citizens and region, democracy is much more stable in the long run. While democracies may go through phases, they function within certain boundaries and the rule of law is a constant. With dictatorships, over the very short term there may seem like there is control, but once the change comes, it is likely to be cataclysmic.

33. "Trade Goods (Imports, Exports and Trade Balance) With China," Foreign Trade Statistics, U.S. Census Bureau, Washington, DC, 2008.

34. "Major foreign holders of treasury securities," United States Department of the Treasury, August 17, 2009, www.treas.gov/tic/mfh.txt, accessed August 18, 2009.

35. "From T-shirts to T-bonds," *The Economist*, July 28, 2005.

36. Ian Williams. "China-US: Double bubbles in danger of colliding," *Asia Times*, January 23, 2004.

CHAPTER 5

1. Thomas Jefferson, *The Jeffersonian Cyclopedia*, Thomas Jefferson Collection, Electronic Text Center, University of Virginia Library, http://etext.virginia.edu/etcbin/foley-page ?id=JCE1094.

2. *The Colbert Report*, Comedy Central, March 28, 2007.

3. "Northwest Passage," *Encyclopædia Britannica 2007 Ultimate Reference Suite* (Chicago: Encyclopædia Britannica, 2007).

4. "Arctic ice cap melting 30 years ahead of forecast," Reuters, May 2, 2007.

5. "1st commercial ship sails through Northwest Passage," CBCNews.ca, November 28, 2008, www.cbc.ca/canada/north/story/2008/11/28/nwest-vessel.html.

6. "The Arctic Grail," CBCNews.ca, August 8, 2006, www.cbc.ca/news/background/northwest-passage.

7. The terminology underlines the Eurocentric origins of the issue. The Northwest and Northeast Passages are primarily west and east of Europe. The renaming of the Northeast Passage to the Northern Sea Route shows a Russian reappropriation of the geography, and an increasing ability to project the Russian view globally. These are small points, but important for understanding the shifting framing of the topic. I will use the terms Northeast and Northwest Passage simply because they are easier to visualize.

8. Climate Change and Borders Workshop, Chatham House, London, June 30, 2006.

9. Constantine Pleshakov, *The Tsar's last armada: The epic voyage to the battle of Tsushima* (New York: Basic Books, 2003), p. 69.

10. Clifford Krauss, Steven Lee Myers, Andrew C. Revkin, and Simon Romero, "Arctic riches coming out of the cold," *International Herald Tribune*, October 10, 2005.

11. Elizabeth L. Chalecki, "Climate change in the Arctic and its implications for US national security," IDEAS, April 2007, http://fletcher.tufts.edu/ierp/ideas/pdfs/issue2/Chalecki_Arctic.pdf.

12. Alex Duval-Smith, "Arctic booms as climate change melts polar ice cap," *Observer*, November 27, 2005. Ben Macintyre, "As the Arctic ice retreats, the old Great Game begins to boil over," *The Times* (London), February 11, 2006.

13. "Nordic storm sinks Swedish ship," BBC News, November 1, 2006. Krauss, Myers, Revkin, and Romero, "Arctic riches coming out of the cold."

14. Private conversation, November, 2008.

15. "Nordic storm sinks Swedish ship." Krauss, Myers, Revkin, and Romero, "Arctic riches coming out of the cold."

16. "Naval operations in an iceless Arctic," Oceanographer of the Navy, Office of Naval Research, Naval Ice Center, US Arctic Research Commission, 2001, www.natice.noaa.gov/icefree/Arcticscenario.pdf.

17. Margaret Munro, "'Sleeping giant' of the North," *Montreal Gazette*, October 2006.

18. David Wolman, "Train to the Roof of the World," *Wired*, July 2006.

19. Pankaj Mishra, "The train to Tibet," *The New Yorker*, April 16, 2007.

20. Mary Pemberton, "BP: Oil production may be closed months," Associated Press, August 7, 2006.

21. A. Kent MacDougall, "Empire—American as Apple Pie," *Monthly Review*, May 2005.

22. Ibid.

23. Ibid.

24. Paul Cellucci, Annual conference, Canadian Defence and Foreign Affairs Institute, October 30, 2006. Audio accessed online: www.cdfai.org/MP3/2006CanadaUSRelations.MP3.

25. Erastus Wiman, "Can we coerce Canada?," *The North American Review* (January 1891): 91–103.

26. "Creating a North American Community," Chairmen's Statement, Council on Foreign Relations, 2005. The board of the Council on Foreign Relations included Madeleine Albright, Colin Powell, Brian Mulroney, and David Rockefeller. The Canadian Council of Chief Executives describes itself: "Composed of the chief executives of 150 leading Canadian enterprises, the CCCE was the Canadian private sector leader in the development and promotion of the Canadian-U.S. Free Trade Agreement during the 1980s and of the subsequent trilateral North American Free Trade Agreement." www.cfr.org/content/publications/attachments/NorthAmerica_TF_final.pdf.

27. Wiman, "Can we coerce Canada?"

28. Ann Douglas, *The Complete Idiot's Guide to Canadian History* (Scarborough: Prentice Hall, 1997), p. 95.

29. Jonah Goldberg, "Bomb Canada," *National Review*, November 25, 2002.

30. United States Northern Command, www.northcom.mil/About/index.html.

31. "Northern Command to Assume Defense Duties Oct. 1," USNORTHCOM News, September 25, 2002, www.northcom.mil/News/2002/092502.html.

32. www.northcom.mil. Note that the website address is the more politically neutral contraction of "Northern Command." However, if you go to the site, it calls itself U.S. Northern Command.

33. "Fighter jets scrambled over U.S., Canadian cities after plane crash," Associated Press, October 11, 2006.

34. "Naval operations in an iceless Arctic."

35. "The Arctic Grail."
36. Chris Wattie, "US sub may have toured Canadian Arctic zone," *National Post*, December 19, 2005.
37. Carla Marinucci, "Chevron redubs ship named for Bush aide; Condoleezza Rice drew too much attention," *San Francisco Chronicle*, May 5, 2001.
38. Lee Berthiaume, "Canada should control Northwest Passage," *Embassy*, November 1, 2006. Doug Struck, "Dispute over NW Passage revived," *Washington Post*, November 6, 2006. For more on some U.S. policy makers putting narrow economic interests above national security, see Robert Baer's *See no evil: The true story of a ground soldier in the CIA's war on* terror (New York: Three Rivers Press, 2003).
39. *Polar icebreakers in a changing world: An Assessment of U.S. needs*, Committee on the Assessment of U.S. Coast Guard Polar Icebreaker Roles and Future Needs, National Research Council, 2006.
40. Ibid.
41. Ibid.
42. Colum Lynch, "U.S. pushed allies on Iraq, diplomat writes," *Washington Post*, March 23, 2008.
43. "Information memorandum for Mr. Kissinger The White House Subject: Imminent Canadian Legislation on the Arctic," Department of State, March 12, 1970, www.state .gov/documents/organization/52576.pdf.
44. "The Northern Dimension of Canada's Foreign Policy," Foreign Affairs and International Trade Canada, June 13, 2008, www.international.gc.ca/polar-polaire/ndfp-vnpe2 .aspx.
45. Scott Borgerson, "Breaking the ice up north," *International Herald Tribune*, October 20, 2005.
46. "Gazprom, Petro-Canada near gas agreement, Putin says," Bloomberg, July 15, 2006. The gas would be shipped to Quebec, perhaps one day via the Northwest Passage, and from there it would go to the U.S. market. The reason it can't go directly into the United States is because of tighter regulations in the heavily populated U.S. East Coast.
47. Ron Annandale, "Clear sailing in the North?," *Maclean's*, October 3, 2005.
48. Krauss, Myers, Revkin, and Romero, "Arctic riches coming out of the cold."
49. "Pandas and Snow Dragons: Chinese Polar Research During the IPY and Beyond," International Polar Foundation, July 20, 2007.
50. Geoffrey York, "Saskatchewan says China itching to acquire oil, uranium assets," *Globe and Mail*, October 26, 2006.
51. Ibid.
52. Rhéal Seguin, "Native group forging China link," *Globe and Mail*, November 13, 2008.
53. "Aboriginal chiefs pitch business deals to China," Canwest News Service, November 4, 2008.
54. Ibid.
55. Ibid.
56. "Canadian pipeline bomber renews threats to EnCana," Forbes.com, July 16, 2009.
57. "Canada to strengthen Arctic claim," BBC News, August 10, 2007.

CHAPTER 6

1. W. M. S. Russell and Claire Russell, *Violence, Monkeys and Man* (London: Macmillan, 1968), p. 10–11.
2. *The Concise Oxford dictionary* (Oxford: Oxford University Press, 1964), p. 1079.
3. This repeating cycle is exceptionally well examined in W. M. S. Russell and Claire Russell, *Population cycles and crises* (London: Galton Institute, 1999).

4. Russell and Russell, *Population cycles and crises*, p. 11–19. The region's population cycle was already well understood when described in 1377 A.D. by the great Arab sociologist Ibn Khaldun of Tunis.
5. For a detailed study see Russell and Russell, *Population cycles and crises*.
6. Andrew Lawlor, "Climate spurred later Indus decline," *Science*, May 18, 2007.
7. Robert Henson, *The Rough Guide to Climate Change* (London: Rough Guides, 2006), pp. 55–6.
8. "WMO statement on the status of the global climate in 2008," World Meteorological Organization, Geneva, 2009.
9. Africa is a tremendously varied continent, with some of the most corrupt regimes and some of the biggest political heroes on the planet. This is not meant as a comprehensive overview, just a general summary.
10. "Climate change a 'deadly threat,'" BBC News, May 15, 2006.
11. "WMO statement on the status of the global climate in 2008."
12. Anita Lichtarowicz, "'Millions more starving' by 2015," BBC News, February 17, 2006.
13. Interview with Joshua Wairoto, UNFCCC, Montreal, December 8, 2005.
14. Interview with Anthony Nyong, UNFCCC, Montreal, December 8, 2005.
15. Hereward Holland, "Africa Could Triple Food Output Quickly—UN," Reuters, June 17, 2008.
16. "National security and the threat of climate change," The CNA Corporation, 2007, http://securityandclimate.cna.org/.
17. Martin Walker, "Indian Ocean Nexus," *Wilson Quarterly* (spring 2008).
18. *National Action Plan on Climate Change*, Prime Minister's Council on Climate Change, Government of India, 2008, p 17.
19. "CIA Factbook: India," *CIA Factbook*, Central Intelligence Agency, updated May 15, 2008.
20. Nicholas Stern, *Stern Review*, Cabinet Office-HM Treasury, London, 2006, pp 94–95, www.hm-treasury.gov.uk/stern_review_report.htm.
21. Cleo Paskal, "Dire Warnings," *Hard News*, June 2006.
22. "India to import wheat," *The Economic Times*, New Delhi, February 3, 2006.
23. Unless otherwise mentioned, the climate forecasts referred to are from reports done by the Indian Ministry of Environment and Forests and the UK's Department for Environment Food and Rural Affairs in conjunction with scientists from all over India, including: the Indian Institute of Tropical Meteorology, Pune; the National Institute of Oceanography, Goa; the Indian Agricultural Research Institute, Delhi; the Indian Institute of Science, Bangalore; the Indian Institute of Management, Ahmedabad; the National Physical Laboratory, New Delhi; and The Energy and Resources Institute, Delhi. The reports can be found on: www.defra.gov.uk/environment/climatechange/index.htm. Another good source of information is *Environmental threats, vulnerability, and adaptation: Case studies from India*, The Energy and Resources Institute, New Delhi, 2004.
24. "India dam project grows higher—and hotter," CNN.com, October 19, 2000.
25. Dinesh Kumar Mishra, "The unbearable lightness of big dams," *Hard News*, October 2006. Himanshu Upadhyaya, "Cry me a river," *Hard News*, October 2006. Himnshu Thakkar, "Damn it, this was designed!," *Hard News*, October 2006. Monika Nautiyal, "Desert into sea," *Hard News*, October 2006. Ashok Patel, "Modidom's watery grave," *Hard News*, October 2006.
26. Mishra, "The unbearable lightness of big dams."
27. Stern, *Stern Review*, p. 33.
28. Ibid., p. 32.
29. "PM promises 'robust' disaster mgt system," *Times of India*, November 29, 2006.

30. Shardul Agrawala, Tomoko Ota, Ahsan Uddin Ahmed, Joel Smith, and Maarten van Aalst, "Development and climate change in Bangladesh: Focus on coastal flooding and the Sundarbans," Working Party on Global Structural Policies, Working Party on Development Co-operation and Environment, OECD, 2003.

31. Sonja Butzengeiger and Britta Horstmann, "Sea-level rise in Bangladesh and the Netherlands: One phenomenon, many consequences," 2004, p. 4, www.germanwatch.org/klak/fb-ms-e.htm.

32. Ramesh Vinayak, "The big meltdown," *India Today*, November 6, 2006.

33. Marq De Villiers, *Water: The Fate of Our Most Precious Resource* (Toronto: McClelland & Stewart, 2003), pp. 318–320.

34. Stern, *Stern Review*, p. 78.

35. *The fall of water*, UNEP, 2005, http://unep.org/PDF/himalreport.pdf.

36. Ibid.

37. Ibid.

38. Patrick Alleyn, "The Chinese Dust Bowl," *The Walrus*, October 2007.

39. *China, episode 3: Shifting nature*, BBC Two, June 27, 2006.

40. Henry Sanderson, "Canadian firm knocks Beijing water-diversion plan," *Globe and Mail*, June 26, 2008.

41. *China, episode 3: Shifting nature*.

42. Alleyn, "Chinese Dust Bowl."

43. *China, episode 3: Shifting nature*.

44. Ibid.

45. Ibid.

46. Jon Leyne, "'Water factory' aims to filter tensions," BBC News, September 7, 2004.

47. Jung Chang and Jon Halliday, *Mao; the unknown story* (London: Jonathan Cape, 2005), p. 449. John D. Spengler, "Global environmental thinking," Harvard School of Public Health, http://greencampus.harvard.edu/course/documents/Lecture3GlobalThinking-part2–6perpage.pdf, accessed November 10, 2006.

48. *China, episode 3: Shifting nature*.

49. The system is actually more complex than simply one child per couple. Minorities, some people in the countryside, and now two single children who marry, as well as some others, can all have more than one child without penalty. Regardless, it has achieved the desired result of creating sub-replacement fertility, though the population will only start to shrink mid-century. The policy has been extremely controversial due to reports of forced sterilizations, abortions, child abandonment, and even infanticide.

50. Claire Russell and W. M. S. Russell, "Population crises and population cycles," *Medicine, Conflict and Survival* 16, Issue 4 (October 2008): 383–410.

51. Edward Cody, "In fact of rural unrest, China rolls out reforms," *Washington Post*, January 28, 2006.

CHAPTER 7

1. Sun Tzu, *The Art of War* (Hertfordshire: Wordsworth Editions Ware, 1998), p. 222. In 2006, the Chinese military made study of *The Art of War* a compulsory part of training in order to "promote the strategic and command qualities of the PLA officers." "Chinese military includes 'Sun Tzu's Art of war' in curriculum," Press Trust of India, May 5, 2006.

2. Kautilya, *The Arthashastra* (New Delhi: Penguin Books India, 1992), p. 159.

3. Sudha Ramachandran, "'Youth Brigade' stirs up Indian politics," *Asia Times*, April 18, 2008.

4. Cleo Paskal, "Tempest in a tea bag; what the bag is hiding," *National Post*, June 6, 2000. "Opium Wars," *Encyclopædia Britannica 2007 Ultimate Reference Suite* (Chicago: Encyclopædia Britannica, 2006).

5. John Keay, *A History of India* (London: Harper Collins, 2000), pp. 437–439. "Indian Mutiny," *Encyclopædia Britannica 2007 Ultimate Reference Suite* (Chicago: Encyclopædia Britannica, 2006).

6. Jehangir S. Pocha, "Familiar tension before trip kills hope," *The Telegraph*, Calcutta, November 18, 2006.

7. J. N. Dixit, *India's Foreign Policy 1947–2003* (New Delhi: Picus Books, 2003), pp. 353–354.

8. Jung Chang and Jon Halliday, *Mao: The Unknown Story* (London: Jonathan Cape, 2005), p. 486.

9. Ibid.

10. Narendra Singh Sarila, *Untold Story of India's Partition: The Shadow of the Great Game* (New Delhi: HarperCollins, 2005). "Pakistan was created as part of the great game," *Daily Times* (Pakistan), March 26, 2006.

11. Philip Webster and Jeremy Page, "David Miliband comes under fire over Kashmir," *The Times*, January 22, 2009.

12. Tim Reid, "The Nixon Tapes II: Gandhi 'the witch,'" *The Times* (London), June 30, 2005. When the transcripts were declassified and released in 2005, Dr. Kissinger went on Indian TV to express regret. He said: "This was somebody letting off steam at the end of a meeting in which both President Nixon and I were emphasizing that we had gone out of our way to treat Mrs Gandhi very cordially. [. . .] There was disappointment at the results of the meeting. The language was Nixon language." "Kissinger regrets India comments," BBC News, July 1, 2005.

13. Jaswant Singh and Major General S. P. Bhatia, *Conflict & Democracy: US and The Birth Of Bangladesh, Pakistan Divides* (New Delhi: Rupa & Co, 2008), p. xxi.

14. "Memorandum of conversation 48123," Foreign Relations, 1969–1972, volume E–7, Documents on South Asia, 1969–1972, released by the Office of the Historian, www.state.gov/documents/organization/48123.pdf.

15. Keay, *History of India*, p. 526–527.

16. "Conversation between President Nixon and his assistant for National Security Affairs (Kissinger), Washington, December 10, 1971, 10:51–11:12 A.M," Foreign Relations, 1969–1972, volume E–7, Documents on South Asia, 1969–1972, released by the Office of the Historian, www.state.gov/r/pa/ho/frus/nixon/e13/72603.htm. The transcript also includes an interesting exchange about the role of France.

    Nixon: How about getting the French to sell some planes to the Paks?
    Kissinger: Yeah. They're already doing it.
    Nixon: All right, why not? I mean, if they need some supplies, why not the French?
    Kissinger: Yeah.
    Nixon: Now the French are just—they'll sell to anybody.

17. Singh and Bhatia, *Conflict & Democracy*, p. xxi.

18. "India's postwar foreign policy," Memorandum for Dr. Kissinger, National Security Council, April 24, 1972.

CHAPTER 8

1. Jon Lajoie, "Life Lessons with Jon Lajoie," www.youtube.com/watch?v=G4PgaX3cNpU.

2. "Medvedev says Russia-China force to be reckoned with," Agence France-Presse, May 24, 2008.

3. *Defense Science Board Task Force on Seabasing,* Department of Defense, Washington, DC, August 2003.
4. Ibid.
5. Ibid.
6. Ibid.
7. "MPs warn over US fighter jet deal," BBC News. December 8, 2006.
8. "Blair's Trident statement in full," BBC News, December 4, 2006.
9. The Shanghai Cooperation Organisation, www.sectsco.org.
10. Sergei Blagov, "Russia sees SCO as potential energy cartel," *Eurasia Daily Monitor,* December 5, 2006.
11. Chris Xia, "Asia to pool financial reserves," BBC News, May 5, 2007.
12. "Venezuela to pull our of World Bank, IMF," *The Washington Times,* May 1, 2007.
13. "Chavez: Bush 'devil'; U.S. 'on the way down,'" CNN.com, September 21, 2006.
14. Qatar Foundation, http://qf.edu.qa.
15. Martin Walker, "Walkers world: India's brain food," United Press International, March 19, 2007.
16. Tinku Ray, "India IT exodux from US 'to rise,'" BBC News, May 15, 2007.
17. James A. Baker III and Lee H. Hamilton, *The Iraq Study Group Report,* p. 28, http://media.usip.org/reports/iraq_study_group_report.pdf.
18. Maggie Michael, "Arabs say report shows Bush's failure," Associated Press, December 7, 2006.
19. Paul Richter, "Mideast allies near a state of panic," *Los Angeles Times,* December 3, 2006.
20. For more, see the *Final Report of the National Commission on Terrorist Attacks Upon the United States, Official Government Edition,* aka the 9–11 Commission Report, www.gpoaccess.gov/911/Index.html.
21. Baker and Hamilton, *Iraq Study Group Report,* p. 61.
22. Ibid., p. 60.
23. "Background Note: Qatar," Bureau of Near Eastern Affairs, U.S. Department of State, October 2006, www.state.gov/r/pa/ei/bgn/5437.htm.
24. Philip Shishkin, "In Putin's backyard, democracy stirs—with U.S. help," *The Wall Street Journal,* February 25, 2005.
25. Nick Paton Walsh, "India flexes its muscles with first foreign military base," *The Guardian,* April 26, 2006. "Defence Ties with Mongolia Expanded," *The Tribune* (India), August 9, 2007.
26. "PPP GDP 2005," World Bank, http://siteresources.worldbank.org/DATASTATISTICS/Resources/GDP_PPP.pdf, accessed November 17, 2006. An "international dollar" has the same purchasing power over GDP as a U.S. dollar has in the United States.
27. R. Swaminathan, "India-China relations in the emerging era," paper no. 2019, South Asian Analysis Group, Noida, India, November 9, 2006. Sawraj Singh, "India and China continue their march to Asia's century," www.indolink.com/printArticleS.php?id=1125 06050319.
28. Park Song-wu, "China stirs history furor," *Korea Times,* September 12, 2006.
29. Thomas Fuller, "'Sweatshop snoops' take on China factories," *International Herald Tribune,* September 15, 2006.
30. Zhu Zhe, "Plagarism, fake research plaque academia," *China Daily,* March 15, 2006.
31. "Google limits China searches," *Seattle Times,* January 26, 2006. "Cyber-dissident convicted on Yahoo! information is freed after four years," Reporters Without Borders, November 9, 2006.
32. Robert Spencer, Peter Foster, "Chinese ordered cover-up of tainted milk scandal" *The Daily Telegraph,* September 24, 2008.
33. Robert Marquand, "Research fraud rampant in China," *The Christian Science Monitor,* May 16, 2006.

34. China: Annual report 2006, Reporters without borders, www.rsf.org/IMG/pdf/Chinese _Report_2006–2.pdf.

35. "Cyber-dissident convicted on Yahoo! information is freed after four years," Reporters Without Borders, November 9, 2006.

36. "Xinhua: the world's biggest propaganda agency," Reporters Without Borders, September 30, 2005.

37. "China province said to close more mines," *Washington Post*, November 7, 2006.

38. M. D. Nalapat, "Authoritarianism and growth," *Far Eastern Economic Review*, January 16, 2003.

39. Susan Jakes, "Beijing hoodwinks WHO inspectors," *Time*, April 18, 2003.

40. "Thousands flee as storm hits China," CNN.com, July 20, 2005.

41. Bao Daozu, "Typhoon pounds Fujian, forcing evacuation," *China Daily*, September 2, 2005.

42. "630,000 evacuated from S. China provinces as Typhoon Chanchu approaches," *Xinhua*, May 17, 2006.

43. "Mighty storm buffets China," BBC News Online, September 19, 2007. "Shanghai: Evacuated residents return home," cctv.com, September 21, 2007.

44. Howard W. French, "China's Muslims awake to nexus of needles and AIDS," *New York Times*, November 12, 2006. "Drug trafficking: China arrests Pakistanis," *Times of India*, November 13, 2006.

45. *China, episode 3: Shifting nature*, BBC Two, June 27, 2006.

46. Pan Yue, "Tipping point," *Times of India*, December 2, 2006.

47. "Visions of ecopolis," *The Economist*, September 23, 2006. Frank Kane, "British to help China build 'eco-cities,'" *The Observer* (London), November 6, 2005.

48. "China wins quake lake "victory,"" BBC News Online, June 10, 2008.

49. M. D. Nalapat, "North Korea: a 'proxy' nuclear state?," *China Brief*, The Jamestown Foundation, March 25, 2003.

50. "Bush Says Trip Will Strengthen U.S.-India Strategic Partnership," Office of the Press Secretary, the White House, February 24, 2006.

51. Private conversation.

52. Ibid.

53. Interview with M. D. Nalapat, November 20, 2006.

54. "India, China among top arms buyers: Study," *Times of India*, June 10, 2008.

55. "China has 'endorsed' Indo-US nuke deal: Pranab," *Times of India*, November 27, 2006.

56. Singh, "India and China continue their march."

57. "Energy-needs bring India, China closer," *Times of India*, November 26, 2006.

58. "Chinese PM's visit to Bangladesh successful: report," *People's Daily* (China), April 11, 2005.

59. "Joshi claims Maoists got arms from China; demands clarification from Situala," *People's Review* (Kathmandu), July 6–12, 2006.

60. "Check madrassa growth along UP-Nepal border," Rediff.com, June 30, 2006.

61. "Pakistan printing fake Indian currency—Times of India," Forbes.com, September 18, 2006. The same sort of game can be seen in North Korea, a nation not usually known for its indigenous technical aptitude (apart from its China-sponsored nuclear program). Regardless, it is tagged as the source of nearly undetectable counterfeit "super notes" in U.S. dollars. Bill Gertz, "U.S. accuses North Korea of $100 bill counterfeiting," *The Washington Times*, October 12, 2005.

62. Subodh Ghildiyal, "Chinese firms may be barred from port race," *Times of India*, July 20, 2006.

63. Sudha Ramachandran, "Good deals, but no nukes for Pakistan," *Asia Times*, November 28, 2006.

64. A. B. Mahapatra, "China: base strategy—China acquires a base in Maldives against India with some help from Pakistan," *News Insight* (New Delhi), May 8, 2005, www .dhivehiobserver.com/speicalreports/China-base-in-Maldives0705051.htm.

65. Jehangir S. Pocha, "Indo-US partnership and China," *Businessworld Magazine*, March 13, 2006.
66. Kathleen Hwang, "Pacific island nations eye China's rise," United Press International, March 27, 2006.
67. M. D. Nalapat, "Capitulation!," *Organiser*, October 1, 2006.
68. Private conversation, 2008.
69. M. D. Nalapat, "Hu can have it better," *Organiser*, November 26, 2006.

CHAPTER 9

1. Randeep Ramesh, "Paradise almost lost: Maldives seek to buy a new homeland," *The Guardian*, November 10, 2008.
2. "Rising seas force Islanders to move inland, says UN," ABC news online, December 6, 2005, www.abc.net.au/news/newsitems/200512/s1524422.htm. Personally, I would have added "in modern times" as, undoubtedly over the millennia with the waxing and waning environmental change events, other communities have had to relocate as well. But I quibble.
3. John Vidal, "Pacific Atlantis: First climate change refugees," *The Guardian*, November 25, 2005. Alister Doyle, "Pacific Islanders move to escape global warming," Reuters, December 6, 2005. For an updated list of disappearing islands, see: www.globalislands.net.
4. M. L. Parry et al, *Climate Change 2007: Impacts, Adaptation and Vulnerability*, (Cambridge: Cambridge University Press, 2007), www.ipcc.ch/publications_and_data/publications _ipcc_fourth_assessment_report_wg2_report_impacts_adaptation_and_vulnerability.htm.
5. Ian Sample, "Scientists forecast metre rise in sea levels this century," *The Guardian*, March 24, 2006. Robert S. Boyd, "Sea levels rising at faster rate," *Charlotte Observer* (North Carolina), July 10, 2005.
6. Parry et al, *Climate Change 2007*.
7. Ibid.
8. Bob Holmes, "Ocean heat store makes climate change inevitable," Newscientist.com, March 17, 2005.
9. Parry et al, *Climate Change 2007*.
10. "Climate Change 2001: Working Group I: The scientific basis: Executive summary," Intergovernmental Panel on Climate Change, United Nations Environmental Programme and World Meteorological Office, 2001.
11. "Potential impact of sea-level rise on Bangladesh," UNEP, http://grida.no/publications/vg/climate/page/3086.aspx.
12. Ibid.
13. Ibid.
14. "All about glaciers," National Snow and Ice Data Center, University of Colorado, 2007.
15. Stefan Lovgren, "Warming to cause catastrophic rise in sea level?," *National Geographic News*, April 26, 2004. "Greenland melt 'speeding up,'" BBC News, August 11, 2006. Robert Roy Britt, "Runaway glacier may portend rising seas," *LiveScience*, December 9, 2004. Jonathan Amos, "Greenland glaciers race to the ocean," BBC News, December 8, 2005. Martin Mittelstaedt, *Globe and Mail*, February 17, 2006. Robert Lee Hotz, "Greenland's chilling mystery," *Montreal Gazette*, July 9, 2006. Paul Rincon, "Greenland ice swells ocean rise," BBC News, February 16, 2006.
16. Interview with Hon. Tom Roper, UNFCCC, Montreal, December 5, 2005. It's worth noting that the waves that hit the Maldives were only 9 feet high. C. Gramling, "Still standing," *Science News*, March 25, 2006.
17. Richard Black, "'Hope for coral' as oceans warm," BBC News, June 7, 2006.
18. Paul Rincon, "Warming set to 'devastate' coral," BBC News, May 15, 2006.

19. Carolyn Fry, "Acid oceans spell doom for coral," BBC News, August 29, 2004.
20. Black, "Hope for coral."
21. Rincon, "Warming set to 'devastate' coral." Black, "Hope for coral." "Tiny polyps gorge themselves to survive coral bleaching," Research Communications, Ohio State University, April 26, 2006. Roger Harrabin, "A people dependent on coral," BBC News, July 8, 2006.

CHAPTER 10

1. Interview with Jens Christian Justinussen, Montreal, November 10, 2006.
2. Graham Norris, "Pawns in the game," *Pacific Magazine*, May 2004.
3. Michael Field, "Tackling China: Kiribati," *Islands Business*, 2007, www.islandsbusiness .com/islands_business/index_dynamic/containerNameToReplace=MiddleMiddle/focus ModuleID=4981/overideSkinName=issueArticle-full.tpl
4. Mac William Bishop, "Kiribati plays the game," *Pacific Magazine*, September 2004.
5. Bishop, "Kiribati plays the game." Rowan Callick, 'Chinese storm in a Pacific teacup,' *Far Eastern Economic Review*, December 4, 2003. Norris, "Pawns in the game."
6. Callick, "Chinese storm in a Pacific teacup."
7. Ibid.
8. Callick, "Chinese storm in a Pacific teacup." "China, Vanuatu pledge to boost bilateral ties," *Xinhua English*, January 18, 2005.
9. Nicholas Zamiska and Jason Dean, "China and Taiwan spar over friends in small places," *Wall Street Journal*, May 9, 2006.
10. Michael Field, "China's intriguing move." *Islands Business*, 2007.
11. "Tonga," Bilateral Relations, Ministry of Foreign Affairs of the People's Republic of China, December 9, 2003.
12. Robert Keith-Reid, "Oceania outlook 2002," *Pacific Magazine*, January 2002.
13. Norris, "Pawns in the Game."
14. "The annual report of the Minister of Foreign Affairs and Defence for the year 2000," Ministry of Foreign Affairs, Government of Tonga, 2001.
15. "Tonga."
16. Field, "China's intriguing move."
17. "MP calls for government to regulate number of Chinese workers in Tonga," BBC Monitoring Asia—Pacific—Political, text of report by Radio New Zealand International, July 19, 2002.
18. "Tonga council for promotion of peaceful reunification of China founded," *People's Daily* (China), January 19, 2004.
19. "MP calls for government to regulate number of Chinese workers in Tonga."
20. "Tonga to expel race-hate victims," *The New Zealand Herald*, November 22, 2001.
21. Qin Jize, "Chinese citizens evacuated in Tonga," *China Daily*, November 23, 2006.
22. "Fiji: Chinese businessman wants action against Chinese triad gangs," *Pacific Magazine*, May 11, 2005.
23. Nick Squires, "British sun sets on Pacific as China waits in shadows," *The Telegraph*, April 1, 2006.
24. Field, "China's intriguing moves."
25. Ibid.
26. Penny Spiller, "Riots highlight Chinese tensions," BBC News, April 21, 2006.
27. Ibid.
28. "Chinese nationals back home safe and sound," *Xinhua*, April 25, 2006.
29. "Chinese migrants in Algiers clash," BBC News, August 4, 2009.
30. "China eyes Pacific island airline startup," *Tok Blong Pasifik*, spring 2005.

31. "Nothing sinister in China support: Fiji," *The Age*, March 28, 2008. "China funds $16m for Fiji projects," Fijilive, April 18, 2008.

32. Tom Bailey, *Tarawa* (Derby, CT: Monarch Americana, 1962).

33. "US nuclear submarine runs aground," BBC News, January 8, 2005.

34. Robert D. Kaplan, "How we would fight China," *The Atlantic Monthly*, June 2005.

35. Francis Harris, "Beijing secretly fires lasers to disable US satellites," *The Telegraph*, September 26, 2006.

36. *Defense Science Board Task Force on Seabasing*, Office of the Under Secretary of Defense for Acquisition, Technology, and Logistics, Department of Defense, Washington, DC, August 2003.

37. Ibid.

38. Ibid.

39. Scott Snyder, "The South China Sea dispute: prospects for preventative diplomacy," Special Report No. 18, United States Institute of Peace, August 1996.

40. Ibid.

41. Michael W. Studeman, "Dragon in the Shadows: Calculating China's advances in the South China Sea," Masters Thesis, Naval Postgraduate School, Monterey, California, March 1996, www.dtic.mil/cgi-bin/GetTRDoc?AD=ADA313771&Location=U2&doc =GetTRDoc.pdf.

42. Bill Gertz, "China sub stalked US fleet," *Washington Times*, November 13, 2006.

43. Interview with Professor Ron Crocombe, conducted by Jens Christian Justinussen, Cook Islands, April 8, 2004. Graham Norris, "Fishing and Diplomacy," *Pacific Magazine*, May 2004.

44. Interview with Professor Crocombe.

45. T. Melton, R. Peterson, A. J. Redd, N. Saha, A. S. Sofro, J. Martinson, and M. Stoneking, "Polynesian genetic affinities with Southeast Asian populations as identified by mtDNA analysis," *American Journal of Human Genetics* (August 1995): 403–414.

46. "Blowing up paradise," BBC Four, March 16, 2005.

47. "UK set to cut back on embassies," BBC News, December 15, 2004.

48. "Veteran Polynesia leader ousted," BBC News, February 19, 2005.

49. "Six found dead after Tonga riots," BBC News, November 17, 2006.

50. Nelson Eustis, *The King of Tonga* (Adelaide: Hyde Park Press, 1997), p. 289.

51. "Convergence of interest brings India, Brazil together," *Hindustan Times*, June 30, 2005.

52. "India, Vietnam sign MoU for bilateral cooperation on security," *The Economic Times*, March 24, 2008. "India offers help to S'pore in Malacca Straights," *Indo-Asian News Service*, June 3, 2006.

CHAPTER 11

1. Terry Pratchett, *Jingo* (London: Victor Gollancz, 1998).

2. Leslie Allen, "Will Tuvalu disappear beneath the sea?," *Smithsonian* 35, no. 5 (August 2004).

3. Holley Ralston, Britta Horstmann, and Carina Holl, "Climate change challenges Tuvalu," Germanwatch, Berlin, 2004.

4. Interview with Masao Nakayama, UNFCCC, Montreal, November 28, 2005.

5. For the text of the Montevideo Convention, see http://avalon.law.yale.edu/20th_century/intam03.asp.

6. Roland Huntford, *Nansen* (London: Abacus, 2001), p. 634–635.

7. "Convention relating to the status of refugees," Office of the High Commissioner for Human Rights, United Nations, www.unhcr.org/refworld/pdfid/3be01b964.pdf.

8. Scott Snyder, "The South China Sea dispute: prospects for preventative diplomacy," Special Report No 18, United States Institute of Peace, August 1996.

9. Lieutenant Michael Studeman, "Calculating China's advances in the South China Sea," *Naval War College Review*, Spring 1998.

10. Ibid.

11. China has a habit of making rather grand declarations about what it owns. In November 2006, it claimed the entire Indian state of Arunachal Pradesh—a position that was so outrageous, there was a very unusual mild climb down. The strategy often works because, even if China knows it can't win, it has pushed the bounds of the debate so far into the opposing camp that any subsequent "compromise" would otherwise be considered a rather big win for China. "China calls for 'compromises' on Arunachal Pradesh," *The Hindu*, November 16, 2006.

12. Studeman, "Calculating China's advances."

13. "South China Sea dispute."

14. Climate Change and Borders Workshop, Chatham House, London, June 30, 2006.

15. "South China Sea dispute."

16. Paul Reynolds, "Paradise regained—for a few days," BBC News, April 3, 2006.

17. Scott Foster and Robert Windrem, "Tsunami spares US base in Diego Garcia," NBC News, January 4, 2005.

18. The Maldives-Lakshadweep-Chagos archipelago is composed entirely of low atolls, associated coralline structures, and sandy islands. Many islands compose each ring-shaped atoll, and the highest islands reach only 15 feet above sea level. The low level of these islands makes them very sensitive to sea level rise. See www.worldwildlife.org/wildworld/profiles/terrestrial/im/im0125_full.html

19. Interview with Hon. Tom Roper, UNFCCC, Montreal, 5 December 2005.

20. See www.un.org/Depts/los/index.htm. See www.itlos.org.

21. "Climate change and borders."

22. This is the basis of many of the Arctic claims.

23. Art. 15 of UNCLOS states that where the coasts of two states are opposite or adjacent to each other, neither of the two states is entitled, failing agreement between them to the contrary, to extend its territorial sea beyond the median line every point of which is equidistant from the nearest points on the baselines from which the breadth of the territorial seas of each of the two states is measured. See www.un.org/Depts/los/convention_agreements/texts/unclos/closindx.htm.

24. Under Art. 62.1(b) of the Vienna Convention on the Law of Treaties, changes to treaties can take place only if there is a fundamental change of circumstances that radically transforms the extent of the obligations to be performed under the treaty. But boundary agreements are expressly excluded, so that once they are fixed, they are fixed for all time. However, in the case of Cuba, there is scope for renegotiation because the bilateral agreement is renewed every two years. See www.walter.gehr.net/wvkengl.html, accessed August 14, 2006.

25. "Rice warns Pacific leaders over threat of 'strongmen,'" Channel NewsAsia, May 8, 2007.

26. "U.S. Engagement in the Pacific Islands Region: 2007 Pacific Islands Conference of Leaders and Core Partners Meeting," U.S. State Department, Washington, DC, May 7, 2007.

27. "Rice warns Pacific leaders."

28. "Taiwan cancels Pacific islands summit," Radio Australia, Australian Broadcasting Corporation, October 6, 2008.

29. Alexandra Harney, Demetri Sevastopulo, and Edward Alden, "Top Chinese general warns U.S. over attack," *Financial Times*, July 14, 2005.

30. Interview with Professor Ron Crocombe, conducted by Jens Christian Justinussen, Cook Islands, April 8, 2004.

31. Lawrence Schafer, "The cannon shot rule," in *Legal aspects of contemporary marine fisheries*, Rhodes University, 1997.

CONCLUSION

1. *The Comic Almanack with illustrations by George Cruikshank* (London: Chatto and Windus, 1881), p. 410. In the 1850s, the UK was coming out of the Little Ice Age and so, by comparison, the climate seemed exceptionally hot.
2. This section is adapted from: C. Paskal, "Three R's for surviving environmental change," Chinadialogue.net, January 18, 2008, www.chinadialogue.net/homepage/show/single/en/1634-Three-R-s-for-surviving-environmental-change.
3. "India counts the costs of floods," BBC News, August 2, 2005.
4. Jonathan Watts, "China hit by strongest typhoon for half a century," *The Guardian*, August 11, 2006.
5. Mark Hertsgaard, "Adapt or die," *The Nation*, May 7, 2007.
6. Interview with Anthony Nyong, UNFCCC, Montreal, December 8, 2005.

INDEX